BEING ENGLISH

This book critically examines the cultural desire for anglicisation of the Indian middle class in the context of postcolonial India.

It looks at the history of anglicised self-fashioning as one of the major responses of the Indian middle class to British colonialism. The book explores the rich variety of nineteenth- and twentieth-century writings that document the attempts by the Indian middle class to innovatively interpret their personal histories, their putative racial histories, and the history of India to appropriate the English language and lay claim to an "English" identity. It discusses this unique quest for "Englishness" by reading the works of authors like Michael Madhusudan Dutt, Rabindranath Tagore, Cornelia Sorabji, Nirad C. Chaudhuri, Dom Moraes, and Salman Rushdie.

An important intervention, this book will be of interest to scholars and researchers of postcolonial studies, Indian English literature, South Asian studies, cultural studies, and English literature in general.

Sayan Chattopadhyay is Associate Professor of English in the Department of Humanities and Social Sciences at Indian Institute of Technology, Kanpur. He received his doctorate degree from the University of Cambridge in 2014. He was the recipient of the 2010–2013 Smuts Cambridge International Scholarship and was the Baden Württemberg visiting fellow at the South Asia Institute of the University of Heidelberg in 2017. His research has been primarily in the area of Indian middle-class self-fashioning and its literary manifestations.

'I feel privileged to have been an early reader of Sayan Chattopadhyay's *Being English*. This monograph looks set to change the way we think about Indian writing in English. I recommend this groundbreaking, meticulously-researched book in the strongest possible terms.'
—Claire Chambers, *Professor of Global Literature, University of York, UK*

'Sayan Chattopadhyay provides fine-tuned, sensitive interpretations of Indian intellectuals in a colonial set-up and circumspect analyses of their writings. Smart and well-written, *Being English* will be a very welcome contribution to the study of Indian English literature.'
—Hans Harder, *Professor of Modern South Asian Languages and Literatures, University of Heidelberg, Germany*

'Sayan Chattopadhyay's book will be regarded as an important addition to Indian colonial and postcolonial studies as the critically informed chapters open up new vistas of perception by foregrounding anglicization as a conscious choice of empowerment, through a process of self-fashioning, appropriation and abrogation. The book significantly debunks the overwhelming postcolonial discourse about cultural colonization and mimicry.'
—Sanjukta Dasgupta, *Professor of English (Retd), University of Calcutta, India*

BEING ENGLISH

Indian Middle Class and the Desire for Anglicisation

Sayan Chattopadhyay

LONDON AND NEW YORK

First published 2022
by Routledge
2 Park Square, Milton Park, Abingdon, Oxon OX14 4RN

and by Routledge
605 Third Avenue, New York, NY 10158

Routledge is an imprint of the Taylor & Francis Group, an informa business

© 2022 Sayan Chattopadhyay

The right of Sayan Chattopadhyay to be identified as authors of this work has been asserted in accordance with sections 77 and 78 of the Copyright, Designs and Patents Act 1988.

All rights reserved. No part of this book may be reprinted or reproduced or utilised in any form or by any electronic, mechanical, or other means, now known or hereafter invented, including photocopying and recording, or in any information storage or retrieval system, without permission in writing from the publishers.

Trademark notice: Product or corporate names may be trademarks or registered trademarks, and are used only for identification and explanation without intent to infringe.

British Library Cataloguing-in-Publication Data
A catalogue record for this book is available from the British Library

Library of Congress Cataloging-in-Publication Data
A catalog record has been requested for this book

ISBN: 978-0-367-40858-9 (hbk)
ISBN: 978-1-032-15882-2 (pbk)
ISBN: 978-0-367-80949-2 (ebk)

DOI: 10.4324/9780367809492

Typeset in Sabon
by Deanta Global Publishing Services, Chennai, India

*TO
BABA AND MA*

CONTENTS

Acknowledgements viii
Introduction: Contours of Englishness in colonial India ix

1 Nineteenth-century Bengal and the emergence of Indian middle-class anglicisation 1

2 Images of Indian womanhood and the "English" self of Cornelia Sorabji 27

3 The tradition of national autobiographies and Nirad Chaudhuri's homeward journey to England 51

4 Anglicisation, citizenship, and Nirad Chaudhuri's critique of the colonial metropolis 76

5 Dom Moraes's anglicisation and the ambiguity of return 103

Coda: Anglicisation and aporia 130

Bibliography 147
Index 158

ACKNOWLEDGEMENTS

This book grew out of my PhD thesis and therefore my intellectual debts are primarily owed to my thesis supervisor at the University of Cambridge, Dr Priyamvada Gopal. Her exacting standards and critical wisdom have shaped this book in more ways than I can record. I am grateful to Mr Tim Cribb of the University of Cambridge for the kindness and insightful suggestions that I received from him during the early days of this project. I am also grateful to my colleague, Dr Munmun Jha of IIT Kanpur, for his constant support and encouragement. Finally, thanks are due to my mother, Dipa Chattopadhyay, for her faith in me, to my wife, Ishita Basu, for keeping things on an even keel, and my brother, Sharanya Chattopadhyay, for good cheer.

Some of the chapters in this book are reworked versions of articles that I have previously published in different journals. I list these articles below and I record here my gratitude to the publishers for their permission to use the material:

- Chapter 2 was earlier published as "Disowning "Indianness": Images of Indian Womanhood and the "English" Self of Cornelia Sorabji". *Prose Studies: History, Theory, Criticism* (Routledge). 37 (1): 2–20, 2015.
- Chapter 3 was earlier published as "Homeward Journey Abroad: Nirad C. Chaudhuri and the Tradition of Twentieth Century Indian National Autobiographies". *The Journal of Commonwealth Literature* (Sage). 49 (2): 157–172, 2014.
- Chapter 5 was earlier published as "Reconstructing the History of Exile and Return: A Reading of Dom Moraes's The Long Strider". *Journal of Postcolonial Writing* (Routledge). 48 (1): 79–91, 2012.
- The conclusion of this book, titled "Coda: Anglicisation and Aporia", was earlier published as "From Indianness to Englishness: The Foreign Selves of Michael Madhusudan Dutt, Nirad C. Chaudhuri, and Salahuddin Chamchawala". *The Journal of Commonwealth Literature* (Sage). 53 (2): 412–429, 2018.

Note on translation: All translations from Bengali sources in this book are my own unless indicated otherwise.

INTRODUCTION: CONTOURS OF ENGLISHNESS IN COLONIAL INDIA

Jawaharlal Nehru, the first prime minister of independent India, apparently told the celebrated American economist, John Kenneth Galbraith, "You realize, Galbraith, that I am the last Englishman to rule in India" (Nehru quoted in Galbraith 132). Coming from one of the most prominent figures of India's anticolonial struggle against the British empire, this statement sounds baffling and perhaps even scandalous if we read it as Nehru's claim to be the last of the colonisers to rule over India. However, I suggest that Nehru in claiming himself to be an Englishman was not confessing his political affiliation to the colonial rule. Rather, he was foregrounding his cultural affiliation to "Englishness". Indeed, trying to be "English" was one of the most important ways in which a significant number of middle-class Indians, born and brought up under the colonial rule, sought to fashion their self-identities. Though such self-fashioning was inspired by a desire to culturally emulate the British colonisers who governed India, it was by no means an uncritical endorsement of their rule. Among the anglicised Indians there were, of course, many who supported the British Raj. But as the example of Nehru shows, there were also Indians who were staunchly against the British colonial rule and yet considered themselves to be English. Even more importantly, there were anglicised Indians who supported the idea of the colonial rule as a civilising mission but were extremely critical of how the British rulers treated the colonised Indians in practice. This book traces the history of such diverse middle-class Indians whose unique efforts to anglicise themselves remain one of the least explored chapters of India's cultural response to the colonial rule.

Indian middle class and the contours of the modern self

Before discussing why and how a section of the Indian middle class sought to anglicise themselves, it is important to clarify my use of the term "middle class". Here I take my cue from Sumit Sarkar who defines the Indian middle class as a distinct social group that emerged during the nineteenth century with the spread of Western-style education in colonial India (*Modern India*

65–70). For the first half of the nineteenth century, Bengal was the main seat of this new kind of education system and, consequently, it was here that the middle class first made its appearance. Writing about the socio-economic roots of this new Bengali class, Sarkar states:

> It searched for its model in the European "middle class", which, as it learnt through Western education, had brought about the great transformation from medieval to modern times through movements like the Renaissance, the Reformation, the Enlightenment, and democratic revolution or reform. Yet its own social roots lay not in industry or trade, increasingly controlled by British managing agency firms and their Marwari subordinates, but in government service or the professions of law, education, journalism or medicine—with which was very often combined some connection with land in the shape of the intermediate tenures which were rapidly proliferating in Permanent Settlement Bengal.[1]
>
> (67–68)

As the middle class emerged in other parts of India, one could notice minor variations from the economic profile that Sarkar describes above.[2] But, in spite of these differences, the three features that remained uniformly constant for the colonial middle class[3] throughout India were an exposure to Western education, engagement in government service or professions, and desire to model oneself after the "Europeans" or the "English" (I would later explain my interchangeable use of these two terms).

Apart from these above-mentioned commonalities, what the colonial middle class also shared was the notion of a "modern self" that could be shaped or fashioned at will. I borrow the term "modern self" from Dipesh Chakrabarty's *Provincializing Europe* where he uses it to refer to the birth of a new kind of subjectivity among the section of Indians exposed to "Europe", which he in turn defines as "an imaginary figure that remains deeply embedded in *clichéd* and shorthand forms in some everyday habits of thought that invariably subtend attempts in the social sciences to address questions of political modernity in South Asia" (4). Chakrabarty argues that one of the main features that distinguish this modern self, embedded within the matrix of a European modernity, is its generalisability. He writes, "This self has to be generalizable in principle; in other words, it should be such that it signifies a position available for occupation by any body with proper training" (119). Such an ability of the modern self to offer its subject position to be occupied by another and in turn itself occupy the subject position of someone else assumes at least two things. Firstly, it assumes that human nature is something that is shared in general and therefore can be accessed equally by all through the exercise of the universal human faculty of reason. As Chakrabarty writes, "Reason, that is, education in rational

INTRODUCTION: CONTOURS OF ENGLISHNESS IN COLONIAL INDIA

argumentation, was seen as a critical factor in helping to realize in the modern person this capacity for seeing the general" (120). The second assumption is that an individual's self has a certain degree of malleability which allows it to be fashioned through conscious training to be like another's so that it doesn't merely comprehend through reason someone else's subject position but can also occupy it. Within the Indian context, none of these assumptions can be made about the self that was embedded within the conventions of a strictly caste-based society which had not been exposed to the transformative influence of European modernity. In a rigidly caste-based society, the trajectory of one's identity is predetermined by the laws of one's occupational or ritual status within the society. Hence, there is neither a concept of general human nature nor a concept of a mouldable self that can be fashioned differently through conscious training. This is not to say that one absolutely cannot find any historical instance of transformative self-fashioning within India's precolonial society that was not familiar with European modernity. However, my contention is that within a strictly caste-based society where "Europe" had not intervened, such self-fashioning would have been rare transgressions of the general rule. On the other hand, for the Indian middle class that developed under the influence of European modernity, such self-fashioning became the norm. Thus, as Sanjay Joshi states in his study of the colonial Indian middle class, "Being middle class ... was primarily a project of self fashioning" (2).

Dipesh Chakrabarty notes in *Provincializing Europe* that the rational capacity to access the idea of a general human nature and the concomitant ability to fashion one's self to occupy the subject position of another together form the public aspect of the modern self. He states that there is another aspect of the modern self which gives it its private character and makes it a site of individual uniqueness. Chakrabarty traces the emergence of this private aspect of the modern self to the rise in seventeenth-century Europe of the idea of private ownership which was vested on a self that was considered to be disembodied and occupying an interior space within one's being. As Chakrabarty writes, "The subject who enjoyed this right [of ownership], however, could only be a disembodied, private subject—for the object over which his right extended was his own body" (130). Chakrabarty further argues that by the nineteenth century, this private and interior aspect of the modern self came to be recognised as the site of an individual's private desires, passions, and sentiments which gave that person his or her peculiar human subjectivity. It was also simultaneously recognised that the modern self was situated in a relationship of conflict with the outside social and material reality that imposed limits and restrictions on the desires of individuals. Thus, a modern individual's attempt at self-expression was typically characterised by a struggle to manifest the desire of their inner self by combatting the hostility of an outside world which constituted not only of inimical social norms and regulations but indeed also of their own bodies.[4]

INTRODUCTION: CONTOURS OF ENGLISHNESS IN COLONIAL INDIA

As we shall see in this book, both these aspects of the modern self—its ability to fashion itself so as to occupy the subject position of another and its conflictual relationship with the outside world including the body—played a significant role in shaping the efforts of the colonial Indian middle class to be English. Whereas the first aspect allowed one to embark on a project of cultural emulation that would help him or her to be the equivalent of the English coloniser, the latter gave rise to anxieties about being trapped in an outside world and a brown body whose un-Englishness did not synchronise with the anglicised self that was inside a person.

English or British or European or Western?

We now return to the original question about what it meant for a colonial Indian middle class to be "English". One easy answer would be that it meant imitating the cultural mores of the coloniser. Within the context of British India, the colonisers acted as the "reference group"[5] for several Western-educated Indians who sought to emulate their values and standards so as to share the prestige that was otherwise reserved for the political elites. The problem with this answer is, of course, that the colonisers who formed the reference group for the Indian middle class were not all English. In fact, a middle-class Indian was as likely to encounter in the role of a coloniser a Scot or an Irish or a Welsh as he was to encounter an English. After all, the colonial project was a British enterprise rather than an exclusively English one. However, I would argue that for the purpose of this book, there is more merit in using the terms English and British interchangeably rather than trying to dwell upon their distinction. In fact, the terms English and British have a long history of being blended together. This is evident from Robert Colls's analysis of English identity where he associates Englishness primarily with a specific set of legal structures and state institutions that can be dated back to "the great Saxon codifications of customary law, written in English, beginning with Aethelbert in the early seventh century and reaching high points under Alfred (871–99) and Cnut (1016–35)" (13). Colls's writes:

> England is the authority and durability of the state. For over a thousand years state institutions have been absolutely critical to the identity of England. Kings and their agents built a central state which not only taxed and coined, made war, and left records, but also claimed to be based on laws common to the kingdom. If the English nation was made anywhere, it was made here, at the centre, in London, and across the axes of law and law-enforcement that ran out across the country right up to the military-juridical edge.
>
> (3)

Understanding English identity in terms of the territory over which the monarch in London exercises his or her legal and political authority allows

INTRODUCTION: CONTOURS OF ENGLISHNESS IN COLONIAL INDIA

very little distinction to be made between England and Britain and indeed between an English and a British empire. The history of Britain becomes the history of the ever-expanding English state which initially subsumes Wales, part of Ireland, and Scotland within its sphere of military-juridical influence and then goes on to conquer and rule over an enormous overseas empire. Consequently, the terms English and British become almost coterminous if not the same.

When viewed from the periphery of Britain's overseas empire, the distinction between English and British appeared to be even more blurred. Indeed, in a place like India, not only were these two terms used synonymously, they both were also merged with the more general term "European". Thus, Nirad Chaudhuri writes in *Autobiography of an Unknown Indian* that while growing up in the early twentieth-century India, he could conceptually make no distinction between the English, the Scots, the Irish, and the Welsh. England for him automatically included the territories and the inhabitants of Scotland, Ireland, and Wales and had as its "corona" the whole of Europe (109). This is, however, not an example of someone's childish inability to understand the basics of political geography. As historian Tapan Raychaudhuri points out, such a tendency to conflate English, British, and European was widespread throughout colonial India. He writes:

> The English continued to represent Europe even to those Indians who acquired a sophisticated understanding of the west. The terms "British" and "English" remained for the most part surrogates for "European", except where a more specific meaning was stated clearly.[6]
>
> (158)

Such a casual notion about the political geography of the metropolis in particular and of Europe in general meant that for most Indians the coloniser was a generic figure who could be referred to interchangeably as English, British, European, or even simply Western. This generic figure was characterised by certain easily noticeable physical markers that identified him as belonging to a distinct class of people. According to Raychaudhuri, the most obvious of these differentiating markers were the white skin, the trappings of his Christian faith, and the peculiarities of his clothing which was distinguished by the practice of wearing hats ("Europe in" 158). These physical features were the most rudimentary form in which "Englishness" was identified within the context of colonial India. However, for the Indian middle class, this understanding of the English identity was also very strongly supplemented by an identification of Englishness with a whole new Weltanschauung that was again variously referred to as English, British, European, or Western.

According to Ashis Nandy, this novel worldview started emerging in colonial India from around the early nineteenth century "when two sides

INTRODUCTION: CONTOURS OF ENGLISHNESS IN COLONIAL INDIA

in the British–Indian culture of politics ... began to ascribe cultural meanings to the British domination" (1983: 6). As Nandy writes, the new Weltanschauung came to be characterised by a belief "in the absolute superiority of the human over the non-human and the subhuman, the masculine over the feminine, the adult over the child, the historical over the ahistorical, and the modern or the progressive over the traditional or the savage" (1983: x). Hence, from the nineteenth century onwards, Indian self-fashioning as English meant not just the adoption of the colonisers' dress and physical habits, but also an internalisation of this English/British/European/Western world view so as to become more and more like the ruling class. Thus, as Nandy argues, by the nineteenth century, the "West" (and by implication all such cognate terms like "England", "Britain", and "Europe") was translated "from a geographical and temporal entity to psychological category" (xi) which was eagerly subscribed to by "[m]any Indians ... [who] saw their salvation in becoming more like the British, in friendship or in enmity" (7).

Anglicised self-fashioning and literature

At this stage, I would like to clarify the methodological bias of this book. My approach to the phenomenon of anglicised self-fashioning among the Indian middle class is guided by the interpretative conventions prevalent within the field of literary studies. One reason for this is, of course, my training as a student of literature, but there is also another more important reason. Writing about the self-fashioning that happened within the context of European Renaissance, Stephen Greenblatt states: "Literature functions within this system in three interlocking ways: as a manifestation of the concrete behaviour of its particular author, as itself the expression of the codes by which behavior is shaped, and as a reflection upon these codes" (4). The same also holds true for the Indian middle class self-fashioning as English. To begin with, it was the literature they encountered during the course of their Western education that provided the Indian middle class with a set of cultural code which guided their English self-fashioning. The most well-known document establishing this connection between literature and the anglicisation of the Indian middle class is perhaps T.B. Macaulay's minute on Indian education dated February 1835. The document records Macaulay's efforts to reinterpret an 1813 Act of the British Parliament that had set apart a substantial amount of money for the revival and promotion of literature for the benefit of the "learned natives" inhabiting the British-ruled territories of India ("Minute"). Macaulay argues that this directive was subsequently misconstrued to mean the promotion of Arabic and Sanskrit literature in India which, according to him, did not significantly contribute to the intellectual improvement of the colonised Indians. In contrast, Macaulay advocated the use of government funds to promote the study of the English language and European literature among the natives of India. As he provocatively

INTRODUCTION: CONTOURS OF ENGLISHNESS IN COLONIAL INDIA

suggests in his minute, "a single shelf of a good European library was worth the whole native literature of India and Arabia". Macaulay believed that such an exposure to "European" or "Western"[7] literature would encourage the process of anglicisation among the colonised Indians and result in the creation of "a class of persons Indian in blood and colour, but English in tastes, in opinions, in morals and in intellect" ("Minute") who could then be used by the colonial authorities to act as "interpreters" ("Minute") between themselves and the Indian masses.[8]

However, to interpret the phenomenon of Indian middle-class anglicisation merely as the outcome of a British conspiracy to strengthen their colonial rule by spreading Western literature is to grossly misunderstand it. In fact, the beginning of Western education in India which initiates the process of middle-class anglicisation predates Macaulay's 1835 Minute by at least two decades. Hindu College, the first major institute of Western education in India, was established in 1816 in Kolkata by orthodox Bengali Hindus like Radhakanta Deb and Ramkamal Sen so that "modern Western learning ... [could be] offered under orthodox supervision"[9] (Dalmia 46). This was during a period when the colonial government was spending all its education budget on the promotion of Arabic and Sanskrit studies. Indeed, by 1835, the Bengali middle class was so enamoured with Western learning that Macaulay could argue that while the colonial government was spending lakhs of rupees in printing Arabic and Sanskrit texts which remained unsold and unread, the "School Book Society [wa]s selling seven or eight thousand English volumes every year, and not only pa[id] the expenses of printing but realize[d] a profit of twenty per cent on its outlay" ("Minute"). Moreover, it must also be remembered that even after the colonial government took its cue from Macaulay and changed course after 1835 to encourage the promotion of Western learning, the process of anglicisation of the Indian middle class did not follow the expected pattern envisaged in the Minute. As the example of Nehru suggests, an English-educated anglicised Indian did not automatically become an "interpreter" who served the purpose of the colonial administration by spreading their message to the masses. As I show in this book, even the most ardent of Indian anglophiles who regarded the British Raj as ultimately a source of positive influence on the Indian society could be amply critical of the colonial rule and the ways in which it maltreated Indians in general. Thus, as Gauri Viswanathan notes, the intention with which the colonial government promoted Western education was often fundamentally at odds with the ways in which Indians chose to make use of it. Consequently, the Indian engagement with Western education and the resulting anglicisation of a section of the Indian middle class took on "a separate existence of its own, empirically distinct and historically independent of its generating principle" (Viswanathan 16). Therefore, even while acknowledging that the anglicisation of the Indian middle class was framed by the realities of the British colonial rule in India, one must be wary of linking colonial policies and the Indian middle-class desire to be English in a simple cause and effect chain.

Literature not only provided the behavioural code that shaped the anglicisation of the Indian middle class but also acted as, to borrow Stephen Greenblatt's phrase, "an extraordinarily sensitive register" (5) that recorded the complex strategies of their English self-fashioning. The transformation of the private self, located within the interior space of one's being, through following the behavioural codes or practices of a different community, constitutes what Sudipta Kaviraj has identified as a twofold process: "Firstly, the incorporation of these practices requires experimentation with their lives by adventurous individuals. But, secondly, these experiments cannot affect social practice without a discursive accompaniment" (*The Invention* 302). Thus, we have a rich array of literature that were produced by anglicised Indians as a discursive complement to their highly experimental lives. These discourses, which are mostly autobiographies or memoirs written in English, narrate the journey of their authors to discover and manifest the Englishness of their private selves and locate themselves within the metropolis which they saw as the most natural setting for their English identity. My primary concern in this book is with such life writings produced by three "adventurous individuals", namely Cornelia Sorabji (1866–1954), Nirad C. Chaudhuri (1897–1999), and Dom Moraes (1938–2004).

It is important to note here that by the late twentieth century, such autobiographical texts started giving way to an equally rich tradition of Indian English novels portraying the life trajectories of fictional characters engaged in a quest to anglicise themselves. This shift from autobiographical narratives to novels dealing with fictional individuals bear testimony to the fact that by the late twentieth century, the phenomenon of Indian self-fashioning like many other cultural legacies of the British colonial rule had started waning off. Thus, whereas the autobiographical writings of Sorabji, Chaudhuri, and Moraes present anglicisation as a lived reality, the Indian novelists of the late twentieth-century approach anglicisation mostly as a phenomenon of the bygone era which has lost its connection with the present. Whereas the former narratives put forward the anglicised lives of their authors as "a vindication that such a new kind of life for the individual is not merely desirable, but actually possible" (Kaviraj, *The Invention* 302), the later narratives evaluate these lives from a critical distance. The concluding chapter of the book focuses on this novelistic tradition of representing anglicisation by reading Salman Rushdie's *The Satanic Verses* which is one of the finest late twentieth-century fictions exploring the desire of the colonial Indian middle class to be English.

Addressing a lacuna

In spite of the existence of a large body of literary texts documenting and evaluating the Indian desire to be English, there exists no single

INTRODUCTION: CONTOURS OF ENGLISHNESS IN COLONIAL INDIA

comprehensive study that interrogates the complexities of the phenomenon of Indian anglicisation. The reason for this absence of critical commentary is perhaps best understood if we look at some of the main theoretical frameworks through which Indian writing in English has been studied for the past seven decades. Indian English writing, which is the main textual archive associated with the anglicisation of the Indian middle class, was already more than a century old by the time India became independent in 1947. Nevertheless, it was in the decades following the independence that initial efforts were made to construct a critical framework through which Indian writing in English could be discussed and analysed as an independent branch of literary studies. K.R.S. Iyengar's history of Indian writing in English was one of the first significant efforts in this direction. In the introduction to his study, Iyengar claims that since nationalist leaders like Sri Aurobindo, B.G. Tilak, G.K. Gokhale, and M.K. Gandhi widely used English as their means of self-expression, English can be rightfully regarded as "one of our national language, and Indo-Anglian literature … [a]s one of our national literatures" (15). To underline the fact that Indian writing in English is essentially Indian and therefore distinct from all other forms of English literature, Iyengar quotes the academician and political activist C.R. Reddy who asserts:

> Indo-Anglian literature is not essentially different in kind from Indian literature. It is a part of it, a modern facet of that glory which, commencing from the Vedas, has continued to spread its mellow light, now with greater and now with lesser brilliance under the inexorable vicissitudes of time and history.
>
> (3)

This notion of an essential Indianness, somewhat vaguely referred to in the above passage as "that glory", which apparently informs Indian writing in English and connects it with all other forms of Indian literature including the Vedas, was a recurring idea in the works of almost all major commentators on Indian English literature between the independence and the 1980s. Thus, we find the echo of the same sentiments expressed by Reddy and Iyengar in the following passage written by C.D. Narasimhaiah:

> Indian writing in English is to me primarily part of the literature of India, in the same way as the literatures written in various regional languages are or ought to be. It can present the life of a village like Bulashah or Kanthapura, a small town like Malgudi or Kedaram, or sweep through continents and eternity itself; and so long as the operative sensibility of the writer is essentially Indian it will be Indian Literature.
>
> (ix)

INTRODUCTION: CONTOURS OF ENGLISHNESS IN COLONIAL INDIA

We again hear the echo of an essential Indianness informing Indian writing in English in the form of a characteristic "sensibility" in M.K. Naik's *A History of Indian English Literature*: "The crux of the matter is [that] the distinctive literary phenomenon [i.e. Indian English literature] ... emerges when an Indian sensibility tries to express itself originally in a medium of expression which is not primarily Indian" (3).

Such assertions of essential Indianness or a typically Indian sensibility, which framed the study of Indian English literature for at least the first four decades following Indian independence, are problematic on various counts. First, the prioritisation of Indianness necessarily results in the exclusion from the field of critical vision the phenomenon of Indian self-fashioning as English. This is evident from the fact that the works of authors like Cornelia Sorabji, Nirad Chaudhuri, and Dom Moraes, who tried to articulate through their writings the Englishness of their identity, were relegated during the second half of the twentieth century to the periphery of Indian English literature. Cornelia Sorabji, for instance, was almost entirely forgotten as a litterateur after her death in 1954 and has been only very recently resurrected as an author worth exploring. Dom Moraes in his turn, though not exactly forgotten, has been persistently marginalised within the field of Indian English literature. Moraes, who became famous as a poet early in his life by winning the prestigious Hawthornden Prize in 1958 for his very first book of poetry *A Beginning*, remained active as an English poet throughout the second half of the twentieth century. Yet, none of the major anthologies of Indian English poetry published in the second half of the twentieth century, including V.K. Gokak's *The Golden Treasury of Indo-Anglian Poetry*, R. Parthasarathy's *Ten Twentieth-Century Indian Poets*, Pritish Nandy's *Strangertime*, and Keki Daruwalla's *Two Decades of Indian Poetry 1960–1980*, include his writings.[10] Along with poetry, Moraes also produced a substantial amount of prose literature. But given the way his poetry has been neglected, it is hardly surprising that his prose writings have never been extensively discussed by any scholar nor included in any anthology of Indian writing in English. Nirad Chaudhuri is perhaps the only one among the three authors whose presence in the field of Indian English literature has not been neglected and who has continuously attracted criticism right from the time he published *The Autobiography of an Unknown Indian* in 1951. Yet, in spite of this critical attention, Chaudhuri has been regularly viewed as an anomaly whose writings are not an integral part of Indian English literature. Rather, they are considered to be marked by what novelist Amit Chaudhuri has described as a "lonely and perverse intent" (50).

The problem with a theoretical framework that reads Indian English literature through the lens of essentialist Indianness is not merely that it marginalises the works of such individual authors like Sorabji, Chaudhuri, and Moraes but that it fails to take into account the broader phenomenon of Indian self-fashioning as English that these authors represent. Even more

INTRODUCTION: CONTOURS OF ENGLISHNESS IN COLONIAL INDIA

importantly, it fails to take into account the complex interrelation that exists between the notion of Indianness and the Indian desire for anglicisation. As I would argue below, the phenomenon of Indian self-fashioning as English was integrally related to the nationalist quest for Indianness that emerged among the Indian middle class during the late nineteenth century. Thus, any historically situated attempt to explore notions like "Indian sensibility" or "Indian glory" must also necessarily involve an exploration of the desire and anxiety that underlines the phenomenon of Indian self-fashioning as English.

One must acknowledge here that during the last decade or so, attempts have been made to supersede such literary histories like the ones produced by Iyengar and Naik. The most comprehensive effort in this direction has been the history of Indian English literature edited by Arvind Krishna Mehrotra, which consciously seeks to go beyond the idea of an essentialist Indianness that had informed the earlier studies.[11] Mehrotra in his editor's preface argues that Indian English literature has drawn from varied sources and thus has had a development that is "piecemeal and ragged, or like a fresh start each time" (xx), rather than being an expression of some unified sensibility of India. But the book being an anthology of essays written by several different authors, this nuanced editorial perspective is not found equally reflected in all its chapters. For instance, the chapter that Rosinka Chaudhuri writes on nineteenth-century Indian English poetry produced in Bengal still remains pivoted on concepts like "indigenous culture and tradition" (54) that echo Naik's "Indian sensibility". As I show below, such a perspective continues to resist a full appreciation of the phenomenon of Indian self-fashioning as English and makes the chapter impervious to the link between the Indian desire for anglicisation and the quest for indigeneity and tradition.

More recently, the process of reading Indian writing in English as well as the process of its canon formation has been profoundly influenced by the emergence of postcolonial literary studies. However, the criteria of selection and hierarchisation that operate within this comparatively new field of literary studies have done little to bring to critical focus the literature which acts as the register of the phenomenon of Indian middle-class anglicisation. The field of postcolonial literary studies from its very inception has been underlined by the ethical imperative to "unthink Eurocentrism" (Lazarus 10). This has resulted in a critical discourse that approaches the writers from the colonial periphery as Caliban-like figures who, having appropriated the coloniser's language, use what Homi Bhabha calls the "*menace* of mimicry" (88, emphasis in original) to "disclos[e] the ambivalence of colonial discourse ... [and] disrupt[ ] its authority" (Bhabha 88). Hence, within the field of postcolonial studies, the focus has been on texts which bolster the idea of an Empire writing/striking back with vengeance.[12] The figure of Caliban, however, proves to be a problematic model through which to approach

INTRODUCTION: CONTOURS OF ENGLISHNESS IN COLONIAL INDIA

such individuals like Cornelia Sorabji, Nirad Chaudhuri, or Dom Moraes who cannot be readily categorised as anticolonial authors in spite of their occasional criticism of the colonial rule. This lack of a more overt sense of anticolonial politics has meant that none of their writings has ever featured prominently in works of postcolonial studies. However, here again, what is significant is not that these particular authors have remained beyond the pale of critical inquiry. Rather, what is important is that the phenomenon of Indian self-fashioning as English, which they represent and which in turn represents a significant aspect of how Indians have sought to mould their cultural identity following the colonial impact, has remained unexplored.

Normative pattern of Indian middle-class anglicisation

In the absence of any readymade critical framework to explore the anglicised self-fashioning of the Indian middle class through its literary manifestations, I would like to begin by investigating a particular instance of such a self-fashioning so as to make visible some of the threads that weave together this phenomenon. The celebrated Bengali poet, Michael Madhusudan Dutt (1824–1873), who was one of the earliest Indians to try and anglicise himself, provides an interesting starting point. Dutt was an early student of the Hindu College and came from a family of professionals and landholders. He was thus in many ways a typical representative of the new Bengali middle class that came into being during the first half of the nineteenth century. During his college education, Dutt was introduced to the canons of Western literature and most importantly to the charms of the English language, and it is to this exposure that we can trace back the roots of his desire to anglicise himself. An essay that Dutt wrote while he entered his 30s makes evident the intense admiration that he had developed for the English language during his college days:

> I acknowledge to you, and I need not blush to do so—that I love the language of the Anglo-Saxon. Yes—I *love* the language—the glorious language of the Anglo-Saxon. My imagination visions forth before me the language of the Anglo-Saxon in all its radiant beauty; and I feel silenced and abashed.
> ("The Anglo-Saxon" 533, emphasis in original)

Accompanying this reverential admiration for the English language was an equally strong admiration for a dream England that Dutt had conjured up through his reading of English literature. In a letter to his friend and fellow student of Hindu College, Gourdas Basak, Dutt wrote:

> You know my desire for leaving this country is too firmly rooted to be removed. The sun may forget to rise, but I cannot remove

INTRODUCTION: CONTOURS OF ENGLISHNESS IN COLONIAL INDIA

it from my heart. Depend upon it—in the course of a year or two more—I must either be in England or cease "to be" at all;—*one of these must be done.*

(quoted in Murshid, *Heart* 33, emphasis in original)

For most of his career, Dutt was to remain engaged in this effort to be in England. It was, however, not until he reached his middle age that Dutt was finally able to arrive in London where he stayed for a couple of years before moving on to live in Versailles, France. As Michael Fisher has pointed out, Indians have been regularly travelling to Britain in various capacities from the seventeenth century onwards. However, what made Dutt's attempt to locate himself in the metropolis unique was its close interconnection with his attempt to become English. In this Dutt was a trendsetter and, as the following chapters reveal, the trajectory of Dutt's life that began with a starry-eyed devotion to English language and literature and culminated in a burning desire to be recognised as English and travel to England was to be retraced again and again by a number of Indian authors well into the twentieth century.

Dutt's endeavour to fashion himself as English, which made his journey to England such a novelty, included an effort to break away from the traditions of the orthodox upper-caste Hindu Bengali family to which he was born. It also included a simultaneous attempt to create for himself a new social and cultural identity by adopting Western clothes,[13] by converting to Christianity, and by marrying successively, within the span of a few years, two "English" ladies.[14] However, his most important effort to forge a new identity for himself was expressed through his writing of English poetry, which he believed would earn him a place among the canonical English poets whom he so ardently admired since his college days. His best creative achievement in the English language was the long poem titled *The Captive Ladie*, which was published in 1849. But soon after its publication, Dutt ceased writing in English and chose Bengali as his creative medium. Indeed, it was in Bengali that Dutt went on to compose the renowned epic *Meghnad-badh-kabya* (1861) on which his fame as a poet primarily rests today.[15]

Scholars commenting on Dutt have generally regarded his adoption of the Bengali language to be of momentous significance not only with reference to his own career but also with reference to the cultural and intellectual history of colonial India. They read Dutt's decision to write in Bengali as a moving away from an earlier derivative phase of English self-fashioning and a return to his indigenous cultural roots. Using such concepts like "shifting", "turning back", "return", and "recovery", these critics have woven around Dutt's adoption of the Bengali language a narrative of a radical change of course, which tells the story of a prodigal son initially wasting his creative energy in fruitless imitations and then finally coming back to his true native identity. In this narrative, Dutt's "English phase" becomes something of a false start, which then gives way to a more glorious and authentic "Indian phase" in which he achieves literary success and secures an everlasting place in the history of his country's national literature by choosing to write in Bengali. Interestingly, this narrative of a glorious return to indigeneity through the adoption of the Bengali language is as much subscribed to by scholars of Indian English literature as by scholars of Bengali literature. Thus, M.K. Naik in his *A History of Indian English Literature* includes a discussion on Dutt with what appears to be the sole purpose of berating his English works and telling the reader how "he was really able to spread his wings only when he turned to Bengali for artistic expression" (25). In the more recent survey of the history of Indian writing in English edited by Arvind Mehrotra, Rosinka Chaudhuri similarly emphasises Dutt's turn from English to Bengali and interprets it as presaging a wider nationalistic pattern among the Bengali middle class of returning to their indigenous cultural roots:

> The ... historic shift which Madhusudan made from English to Bengali was symbolic of the changes taking place in Bengal. The latter half of the century witnessed the birth of nationalism—in so much as nationalism signified a pride in and awareness of indigenous culture and tradition. The intellectual and well-to-do middle class in Calcutta, which had spoken English in preference to Bengali, and had found its cultural standards and mode of behaviour in the literature and manners of the West, now turned, with Bankimchandra Chattopadhyay and Ishwarchandra Vidyasagar, towards Bengali language and a Bengali identity instead.
>
> (54)

The connection between Dutt and the nationalism which gained prominence in Bengal during the latter half of the nineteenth century is important and I will have to come back to it later. For the moment, however, I would like to emphasise the particular way in which this nationalism is defined in the above passage as a disavowal of the cultural standards of the West and a turning towards "indigenous culture and tradition". By reading Dutt as the figure who symbolised this turning away, the passage reinforces the idea of a clear break, or as Rosinka Chaudhuri calls it, a "historic shift" in Dutt's career—a shift that ended Dutt's emulation of the West and began his quest to recover an indigenous cultural identity.

Amit Chaudhuri in his essay "Poles of Recovery" echoes this pattern of disavowal and recovery that Rosinka Chaudhuri locates in Dutt's career. He finds Dutt's adoption of Bengali suggestive of an even larger pattern that was not only indicative of the behavioural pattern of the Bengali middle class but also of the Indian middle class in general:

INTRODUCTION: CONTOURS OF ENGLISHNESS IN COLONIAL INDIA

> Inscribed into his life is ... [the] narrative ... [of] middle-class Indian self's struggle between disowning and recovering its—for want of a better word—"Indianness", a struggle that ... I found was a paradigm around which a substantial part of "modern" Indian literature and culture was structured.
>
> (40)

Amit Chaudhuri's hesitation to use the word "Indianness" is understandable given the difficulty, if not impossibility, to define such an essentialist category from within. But in the essay the term gains meaning from the way it is opposed to Dutt's efforts to fashion himself as an "English" poet by breaking the religious and social taboos of his family. These efforts are understood in Amit Chaudhuri's essay as part of a phase of disavowal or disowning which makes it distinct from the phase of recovery that began when Dutt started writing in Bengali: "Around the late 1850s, after the long process of disowning, began the process of recovery, the reappropriation, by Dutt of the Bengali language and culture, culminating in his epic poem, *Meghnadbadhkabya*" (41). Thus, here again, we come across the narrative of a prodigal son's return, and Amit Chaudhuri emphasises this narrative by foregrounding one of Dutt's sonnets to show how Dutt's turn to Bengali language and culture was the effect of an admonishment that made him repent his earlier attempt to become an English poet.

The sonnet that Amit Chaudhuri refers to in his essay is *Bangabhasha* (literally "Bengali language") in which Dutt speaks of being chastised by "the goddess of my lineage" (Amit Chaudhuri's translation quoted in "Poles" 43) for wandering in a "foreign country" (43), neglecting the riches contained in his "mother's womb" (43). The poem ends with Dutt being instructed by the mother goddess to "go back to your home" (43). The specific interpretation of this poem provided by Amit Chaudhuri is significant in understanding the discourse of disavowal and recovery of Indianness that has crystallised around Dutt's career and the way in which it interweaves an intellectual with a physical journey. I therefore quote it extensively:

> [Through this poem,] Dutt ... dramatize[s] the colonial, and postcolonial, movement from spiritual and geographical exile to cultural recovery. The general questions regarding exile and identity are posed in the first eight lines. Exile, distancing, or cultural disowning are represented implicitly by the probable location of the sonnet's revision, Versailles (Dutt was to write most of his sonnets in France).... At the ninth line, the 'turn', ... occurs as an interjection from the goddess, and the process of cultural recovery begins in the midst of exile; the turn of the sonnet becomes a cultural and almost physical turning towards the mother-tongue and one's

indigenous antecedents. ... As if taking the goddess's imperative by heart, Dutt returned to India not long after.

(44)

This passage when read along with the other sections quoted above from the essays of Amit Chaudhuri and Rosinka Chaudhuri suggests that Dutt was a threshold figure whose return to the Bengali language, accompanied by a physical homecoming to India, represents a definitive shift in the course of the history of Indian middle-class's engagement with Englishness. It assumes that self-fashioning as English—speaking "the glorious language of the Anglo-Saxon" in preference to Bengali or finding cultural standards and modes of behaviour in the literature and manner of the Western world—characterised an initial period of infatuation of the Indian middle class with the culture of the colonisers. Dutt himself apparently suffered from such infatuation, but, as the argument goes, he was also the harbinger of a later period when attempts by middle-class Indians to transform themselves into English got connected to a circuitous journey of disowning and recovery where anglicised self-fashioning was invariably followed by a return to the "indigenous antecedents" or, in other words, to "Indianness". Hence, the suggestion is that Dutt is to be regarded as a pioneer who both initiated the phenomenon of Indian middle-class self-fashioning as English and at the same time made it *passé*.

In this book, I show that rather than becoming redundant, the phenomenon of Indian self-fashioning as English and the process of emulating the cultural standards of the coloniser would actually become even more prominent during the period that followed Dutt. But for now, I would like to point out how a closer scrutiny of Dutt's own career problematises the simple trajectory of his rejecting the West and returning to Indianness. To understand the complicated connection that existed between Dutt's attempt to become English and his recovery of indigeneity, let us start by re-examining the pattern of Dutt's physical journeys which Amit Chaudhuri so neatly dovetails with Dutt's "turning towards the mother-tongue and ... indigenous antecedents". As mentioned earlier, *The Captive Ladie* was the most notable poem that Dutt wrote in English and he composed and published it while he was in Madras between 1848 and 1855. This was the first significant stretch of time that Dutt spent outside his native Bengal on a self-imposed exile, having broken away from his family by converting to Christianity. The Bengali epic poem *Meghnad-badh-kabya*, which Amit Chaudhuri considers to be the culminating point of the process of Dutt's recovery of Indianness, was begun in 1860 when Dutt came back from Madras to Bengal. This was also the year when in one of his letters Dutt told Gourdas Basak that he was planning to adapt the structure of the Petrarchan sonnet to Bengali. To show how well the metrical form of the sonnet might work in Bengali, Dutt provided in this letter a poem titled "Kabi-matribhasha" (literally "The

Poet's Mother-tongue"). It was this poem that was later slightly revised and republished as the more famous sonnet, "Bangabhasha", to which I have referred above. So far, the literary career and the choice of language of the peripatetic poet seem to conform to his geographical movements to and from his native Bengal. But it starts getting complicated from this point onwards because it was *after* the publication of his Bengali epic and *after* his writing in "Kabi-matribhasha" about his discovery of the riches of his mother-tongue that Dutt ultimately fulfils his life's ambition to locate himself in the metropolis. *Meghnad-badh-kabya* was published on 4 January 1861 and on 9 June 1862, Dutt was aboard a ship headed to England. Thus, we are faced here with a paradox where a cultural homecoming to Indianness gets translated into a physical journey that takes Dutt from India to England.

This paradox becomes even more problematic if we try to historically locate the admonishing voice of the "goddess of the Bengali race" that we hear in "Kabi-matribhasha"/"Bangabhasha" instructing the poet to return. The closest correlate of this dream-voice that Dutt could have heard in actual reality was, ironically, that of an Englishman by the name of John Drinkwater Bethune. Bethune was a law member in the Governor General's council who was sent to India in 1848 and who earned his reputation there as a champion of women's education. When *The Captive Ladie* was published, Dutt sent out copies to various British colonial officers in India, and Bethune was one of its recipients. It seems that Dutt set a very high value on the feedback that he received from these colonial officials irrespective of their capacity as literary critics. Thus, in spite of receiving unfavourable reviews on the poem, Dutt wrote to his friend Basak stating that he did not consider *The Captive Ladie* to be a failure because it had "opened the most splendid prospects for me" (quoted in Murshid, *Lured* 88). These "splendid prospects" chiefly consisted of his being received by the British Advocate-General of Madras, John Norton, "as kindly as I could expect" (88) and being allowed to converse with him "like friends" (88). This shows that one of the real driving forces in Dutt's literary career was to be accepted as an equal by the English colonisers who he could then claim as "friends". This also explains why Dutt, when he received a strong dose of negative criticism from the aforementioned Bethune, felt unsettled enough to altogether abandon writing in English and adopt Bengali as his mode of creative expression.[16]

Bethune's advice to Dutt, as passed on to him via Basak, was this:

[H]e [Dutt] could render far greater service to his country and have better chance of achieving a lasting reputation for himself, if he will employ the taste and talents, which he has cultivated by the study of English, in improving the standard and adding to the stock of the poems of his own language, if poetry, at all events, he must write.

(quoted in Murshid, *Lured* 89)

As is evident here, Bethune's criticism was not directed at any inherent literary merits or demerits of *The Captive Ladie*. In fact, he doesn't even directly engage with the poem. Rather, what Bethune criticises is Dutt's pretentious use of the colonisers' language. Thus, in effect, what Bethune's criticism amounts to is a refusal to accept Dutt as a fellow Englishman—a refusal to correspond with him on equal terms, "like friends". Indeed, Bethune's advice to Dutt is not that of a literary critic to a budding poet. Rather, it is the advice of a patronising colonial officer, engaged in a civilising mission, to a colonised subject whom he expects to learn from the English and then use that knowledge to improve the "native standards". From this perspective, Dutt's effort to turn himself into an English poet was not only unhelpful but ultimately futile because it was an attempt to bridge the unbridgeable gap separating the coloniser and the colonised.

Bethune's criticism presented Dutt with a unique dilemma whereby he could only become acceptable to the English by becoming an "authentic" Indian who was dedicated to "improving the standards" of his native language and poetry. Hence, Dutt's turn to Bengali cannot be interpreted as a simplistic return of an exile who had been called back by the goddess of his race. Rather, his quest for Indianness was fundamentally guided by the response of other Englishmen to his attempt to fashion himself as a fellow English. Consequently, the selective appropriation of indigenous culture that characterised Dutt's career after the publication of *The Captive Ladie* can be interpreted as being guided not by a wish to return but by a desire to create for himself an "authentic" identity that would make his authorial voice more acceptable to the English colonisers. Looked from this perspective, Dutt's recovery of Indianness becomes not a shift away from his desire for anglicisation but rather a part of his ongoing effort to integrate himself within the English/European community. Such an assessment of Dutt's motives finds confirmation in the letter that he writes to Basak from Versailles on 26 January 1865. In it Dutt states that he was not only writing his Bengali sonnets but also translating some of them, and these were "very much liked by several European friends" (67). Hence, it was not only *The Captive Ladie* that was valued by Dutt for earning him the friendship of Englishmen like John Norton, but also his Bengali sonnets that speak of an apparent homesickness. Such Englishmen, be it in the form of intimately known acquaintances or in the form of the more abstract metropolitan audience, would continue to remain a strong influence on all the later Indian authors whom I discuss in this book. They would mould in peculiar ways the desire of the colonised subjects to anglicise themselves by refusing to accept them within the metropolitan community unless as representatives of an exoticised version of their indigenous culture. Thus, for all the middle-class Indians, any attempt to try and be English and be recognised as a part of the English community invariably involved an engagement with images of Indianness.

INTRODUCTION: CONTOURS OF ENGLISHNESS IN COLONIAL INDIA

A closer look at Dutt's career gives us some clue about the kind of complexity involved in a middle-class Indian's engagement with such images of Indianness as part of his or her anglicisation process. In *Meghnad-badh-kabya*, which apparently marks the pinnacle of Dutt's "Indian phase", his putative return to Indianness is achieved through his adoption of the popular Hindu epic *The Ramayana*. However, though Dutt draws his themes and characters from this epic, he turns the whole orientation of the original narrative upside down. In his version of the epic, the Hindu god Rama is reduced to the status of an unjust and wily aggressor who is bravely challenged by Meghnad, the heroic son of the demon king Ravana who is the primary antagonist in *The Ramayana*. *Meghnad-badh-kabya* is thus imbued with a deeply contradictory gesture because it is as much a disowning of the author's indigenous antecedents as it is a return to it. This contradictory gesture is also perceived in Dutt's desire to remove himself from the sociocultural matrix of his fellow Indians, or at least fellow Hindus, even while appropriating their religious epic for his poetic purpose. Dutt explicitly articulates this desire in a letter that he wrote to Rajnarayan Basu on 15 May 1860 while composing the poem:

> [T]hough, as a jolly Christian youth, I don't care a pin's head for Hinduism, I love the grand mythology of our ancestors. It is full of poetry. A fellow with an inventive head can manufacture the most beautiful things out of it.
> (quoted in Murshid, *Lured* 129)

This oscillation between "loving" and "not caring a pin's head" speaks of Dutt's profound uneasiness about relating himself to the Indian material with which he was working, and ultimately to the Indian or Bengali identity that he apparently embraced.

As Dutt's career trajectory and the self-fashioning underlying it reveal, within the colonial context, the quest for Indianness did not necessarily mean a turning away from the attempt to fashion oneself as English. His life history bears testimony to the fact that the recovery of indigenous antecedents could be thoroughly implicated within the very attempt to be recognised as English. What is important to stress here, however, is that Dutt's career does not represent an isolated instance where these interconnections between self-fashioning as English and quest for Indianness are visible. In the following section, I show how these interconnections in fact informed the whole of late nineteenth- and early twentieth-century discourse of Indian middle-class nationalism.

Anglicisation and the Bengali Hindu nationalist discourse

At the root of the Indian middle-class nationalist discourse which first emerged in Bengal during the last decades of the nineteenth century was a notion of inadequacy. This was the product of the ambiguity that marked the British colonial project of privileging a certain section of the colonised society to create an indigenous elite that would collaborate with the Raj and bolster its imperial dominance. As discussed above, a crucial milestone in this project of creating a class of anglicised Indian collaborators was the 1835 Minute of Lord Macaulay. But the process of creating a privileged section of loyalist Indians can be traced even further back to the late eighteenth century when the colonial government headed by Lord Cornwallis tried to create a new class of Indian landlords with permanent rights to land. As historian Ranajit Guha points out, all such measures like the permanent settlement of land rights and the introduction of Western-style education were informed by the key notion of "improvement" through which the Raj sought to "persuade the indigenous elite to 'attach' themselves to the colonial regime" (Guha 33). However, for the colonised subject, to internalise this discourse of "improvement" was to be shunted from the present into what Dipesh Chakrabarty has called "an imaginary waiting room of history" (8). Though it was assumed to be possible for the colonised subject to ultimately acquire equality with the English colonisers after a necessary period of colonial tutelage, this promise was eternally deferred by the interdiction, "not yet" (Chakrabarty 8). Hence, to be caught within this waiting room of improvement was to be caught within a perpetual state of inadequacy, which was exacerbated by a colonial experience that offered Indians, including the middle class, meagre prospects of material prosperity, and political participation.

Importantly, this perception of inadequacy was set against a notion of a glorious Indian past, which was developed during the late eighteenth and early nineteenth centuries by British Orientalists like William Jones and H.T. Colebrooke. Through their reading of Sanskrit texts, these Orientalists had constructed an image of an ancient Indian "golden age", the knowledge of whose civilisational attainments was expected to usher in another Renaissance in Europe similar to the one that was achieved through being exposed to Greek and Roman literature and art.[17] As exemplified by the proto-nationalist poems of Henry Derozio, one of which I discuss later in this book, these notions of inadequacy and a glorious Indian past were woven by the Indian middle class as early as the first half of the nineteenth century into a redemptive teleological pattern in which the present state of inadequacy was understood as an intermediate phase in a circular journey which began in the past in a golden age and would ultimately move to a similarly glorious future. However, the most vivid representation of this circular journey occurs in Bankimchandra Chattopadhyay's (1838–1894) late nineteenth-century Bengali novel *Anandamath* where the protagonist Mahendra is shown three different images of the mother goddess—"Mother-as-she-was", "Mother-as-she-is", and "Mother-as-she-will-be"—each representing different states of the country in past, present, and future. The first

INTRODUCTION: CONTOURS OF ENGLISHNESS IN COLONIAL INDIA

image which depicts the goddess as the resplendent Jagatdhatri, "perfectly formed and decorated with every ornament" (149), represents the glorious past. The second image depicting her as Kali, who "has been robbed of everything" (150), represents the state of misery which the country has fallen into at present. And the third image depicting the mother goddess as Durga, "glistening and smiling in the early morning rays" (150), holds out the promise of a future regeneration of the ancient glories. Chattopadhyay uses this image cluster in his novel to argue that though the promise of a glorious future is there for the nation, it would require superhuman efforts on the part of the "*santans*" or the children of the motherland to rescue her from the present miseries. Yet, what had caused the fall from glory in the first place so as to require such superhuman efforts? For Chattopadhyay, the answer lies in India's loss of independence, which according to him began not with British colonialism but with the series of Muslim invasions of the subcontinent that took place between the eleventh and the sixteenth centuries.[18]

In this construction of Indian history, British rule occupies a uniquely ambiguous position. On the one hand, it marks the culmination of the series of conquests through which India was subjugated by foreigners; on the other hand, it sets the stage for the recovery of India's ancient glory. Hence, near the very end of *Anandamath*, Chattopadhyay introduces a long monologue to argue that English rule is necessary before the Hindus or Indians or Bengalis[19] can regain their competence to rule their own country and bring back its lost glory:

> Unless the English rule, it will not be possible for the Eternal Code [*sanatan dharma*] to be reinstated. ... To worship three hundred and thirty million gods is not the Eternal Code. That's a worldly, inferior code. Through its influence the real Eternal Code—what the foreigners call the Hindu rule of life—has been lost. The true Hindu rule of life is based on knowledge, not on action. And this knowledge is of two kinds—outward and inward. The inward knowledge is the chief part of the Eternal Code, but unless the outward knowledge arises first, the inward cannot arise. ... For a long time now the outward knowledge has been lost in this land, and so the true Eternal Code has been lost too. ... The English are very good in the outward knowledge, and they are very good at instructing people. Therefore we will make the English king.
>
> (229)

In the passage, Chattopadhyay hangs his argument on the distinction between "inward" and "outward" knowledge which might be roughly translated as a distinction between scientific knowledge of the physical world and the spiritual knowledge of God. Since the passage links outward knowledge with the English, it is possible to interpret the underlying cultural argument as an argument for synthesis—trying to assimilate elements of outward knowledge from the foreign colonisers within the indigenous Hindu spiritual framework.[20] Yet this interpretation would be fallacious because, for Chattopadhyay, both outward and inward knowledge are part of that one Eternal Code or *sanatan dharma* which "foreigners call the Hindu rule of life". Thus, the argument is that the outward knowledge was already known by the ancient Hindus but had been lost in more recent times. Hence, learning this outward knowledge from the English colonisers does not mean assimilating something new, but rather retrieving a knowledge that was already possessed and formed the basis on which the inward knowledge and ultimately the Eternal code rested. The English and the Hindus therefore do not present a binary in terms of knowledge, nor do they represent complementary halves that should be brought together in a synthesis to form a perfect whole. Rather, for Chattopadhyay, they represent cultural distances from the ideal Eternal Code. Ironically, the modern-day Hindus are considered by Chattopadhyay to be located at a greater distance from this ideal than the English because having lost the outward knowledge, they have also become dissociated from the true inward knowledge, confusing it with "a worldly, inferior code". The English, on the other hand, is closer to the Eternal Code because they excel in the outward knowledge, which is its fundamental prerequisite. This gives rise to a strangely paradoxical argument which suggests that the first step to reinstate the lost Eternal Code and to regain the true essence of Hindu or Indian glory of the past is, on the one hand, to distance oneself from the false dogmas and fallacious codes of living as practised by the Hindus of the present day and, on the other hand, to embrace the British rule and to try and become like the English colonisers. In other words, transforming oneself into a true Hindu or an authentic Indian involves becoming less and less like the people inhabiting the subcontinent in the present and becoming more and more like the English foreigners. Therefore, in the immediate present, as Chattopadhyay argues in his essay titled *Anukaran*, there was no other way but to

> learn ... by imitation. Just as children learn to speak by imitating the speech of adults, to act by imitating the action of adults, so do uncivilised and uneducated people learn by imitating the ways of the civilised and the educated. Thus it is reasonable and rational that Bengalis should imitate English.
> (translation quoted in Chatterjee 65)

Such arguments substantiate Ashis Nandy's claim that by the late nineteenth century, "the West ... came to represent, for many Indians, the more valued aspects of Indian culture" (22), thereby evoking the desire to "reorder Indian culture" (18) and make it more compatible with the values which the superior West stood for. Anglicisation, therefore, was at the heart of the middle-class nationalist quest for a new Indian identity.

Gandhian critique of anglicisation

With the emergence of Mohandas Karamchand Gandhi as the leader of the middle-class Indian nationalism in the 1920s, the linkages between the urge to become English and the quest for the true Indian identity were radically altered. Gandhi rose to prominence as a political leader in India in the years following the First World War, and his rise drastically changed the character of Indian nationalism from what it had been during the previous century when the version of Bengali Hindu nationalism was dominant. The cultural position that Gandhi championed undermined the earlier intertwining of the English self-fashioning and Indian nationalism in two different ways: first, through interpreting the Indian history and the role of British colonialism by using a different discourse about civilisation than the one prevalent among the middle class till the first two decades of the twentieth century, and second, by making nationalism mass based. The late nineteenth-century argument that in order to become a true Indian/Hindu, it was imperative to learn from the English and become more like them was necessarily informed by an ambiguous attitude towards British rule in India. Thus, someone like Bankimchandra Chattopadhyay, in spite of being "convinced that anyone with a dark skin had little hope of fair treatment in any employment under the Raj" (Raychaudhuri 119), was also equally convinced that the rule of the British was essential to teach the present-day Indians elements of civilisation that they once possessed but have now lost. Gandhi in his turn completely rejected this argument. For him, the loss of true Indianness did not date back 700 years but rather coincided with the importation of "Western civilization" in the subcontinent during the course of the British colonialism.[21] Hence, whereas for Chattopadhyay, it was important to learn from the colonisers, for Gandhi it was important for India to "unlearn [...] what she has learnt for the last fifty years" (letter to Polak 129). According to Gandhi, Western civilisation was essentially different from Indian civilisation and was therefore fundamentally incompatible with it. Thus, in his *Hind Swaraj* he argues: "The tendency of Indian civilisation is to elevate the moral being, that of the Western civilisation is to propagate immorality. The latter is godless, the former is based on a belief in God" (69). He further states that the essence of this deeply moral and theistic Indian civilisation had been perfected by "our ancestors" (66) and "found true on the anvil of experience" (64). Therefore, for Indians, there was "nothing to learn from anybody else" (65). To Gandhi, any attempt to emulate Western civilisation was, for an Indian, tantamount to becoming detached from his or her ancestral heritage and thereby deviating from one's true identity. Here we arrive at a fundamental critique of Indian self-fashioning as English which is now

INTRODUCTION: CONTOURS OF ENGLISHNESS IN COLONIAL INDIA

regarded not as a necessary step towards attaining true Indianness but as a departure from it which leads one to a culturally diseased state.

Gandhi, however, argues that the spread of this corrupting Western civilisation in the subcontinent was not complete but was limited merely to that section of the society who had, out of their own moral frailty, become enamoured with it and who now sought to get rid of the English so as to rule over India as the colonisers' anglicised representatives (27). The assertion near the end of *Anandamath* about English rule being beneficial for India because it would help the Hindus/Indians acquire the necessary knowledge to be ultimately able to rule themselves is here turned on its head. For Gandhi, a rule by the people who have transformed themselves into brown-skinned Englishmen by emulating the colonisers was inevitably going to be as foreign as the British Raj. Hence, the process of regaining true Indian identity did not involve being under colonial tutelage. Rather, it involved moving away from the sphere of Western influence and into the remote villages of the subcontinent "where this cursed modern civilisation has not reached" (68). As the "Editor" in the *Hind Swaraj* tells the "Reader":

> The inhabitants of that part of India will very properly laugh at your new-fangled notions. The English do not rule over them, nor will you ever rule over them. Those in whose name we speak we do not know, nor do they know us. I would certainly advise you and those like you who love the motherland to go into the interior that has yet not been polluted by the railways, and to live there for six months.
>
> (68)

This statement about not knowing those "in whose name we speak" and the appeal to try and connect with them leads to the second point regarding how Gandhi complicated the nationalist discourse of the earlier period that was underlined by a desire to fashion oneself as English. Indian middle-class nationalism as it developed in the nineteenth-century Bengal was, in essence, singularly elitist. As noted earlier, for someone like Chattopadhyay, becoming a true Hindu/Indian was to move away from the state of ignorance in which the ordinary Hindu/Indian has fallen at present. Even Rabindranath Tagore, who briefly led the nationalist Swadeshi movement, could only think of connecting to the masses through imagining such figures like the *shamajpati* who was to guide the people while himself remaining above and beyond them (I discuss this more elaborately in Chapter 1). The stress therefore was on the difference rather than on the commonality between the individual who was to lead the masses, and the masses themselves. Indeed, as I show in Chapter 1 of this book, in many of Tagore's writings idealised Indian individuals are regularly conceived as being detached from the common rung of people inhabiting the subcontinent. In contrast, as the

Indian leader who was most successful in channelising as well as containing mass protest against colonialism,[22] Gandhi repeatedly emphasised the need to integrally connect with the masses "in whose name we speak". Thus, instead of trying to elevate oneself from the masses, Gandhi's suggestion to the anglicised Indian elite was to try and become one with the peasantry. In his own words, "the so-called upper classes have to learn to live conscientiously and religiously and deliberately the simple peasant life, knowing it to be a life giving true happiness" (letter to Polak 129).

Anglicisation and the metropolitan audience

Apart from the Gandhian nationalist movement, what played an equally important role in marginalising the Indians who desired to anglicise themselves was the attitude of the metropolitan audience towards them. For all Indians fashioning themselves as English through their writings, the success of their anglicisation ultimately depended on their being accepted as part of the English community within the colonial system. For those anglicised middle-class Indians who sought to establish themselves as authors, such a sense of being accepted hinged on their being read and appreciated by the English metropolitan audience. Since the beginning of the twentieth century, this effectively signified getting published in the metropolis. However, even before there developed a strong relationship between Indian authors and the metropolitan publishing industry, the approval of a metropolitan audience was of paramount importance for validating the English self-fashioning of Indian authors. This explains why for someone like Michael Madhusudan Dutt, the attempt to anglicise himself was integrally associated with the desire to be lauded as a poet by his English/European "friends". Yet, as is exemplified by the career of Dutt, the attempt by anglicised middle-class Indians to gain validation of one's English identity from the responses of a metropolitan readership frequently led to a crucial contradiction. For a metropolitan audience, the voice of an author from the colonial periphery gained and still gains relevance only when it is perceived to be an authentic voice of a native informant who is embedded within a non-metropolitan cultural framework. In fact, Drinkwater Bethune's advice to Dutt to stop trying to be an English poet and write in a language that was his own is perfectly characteristic of this tendency of the metropolitan reader to insist on the cultural authenticity of the Indian author.

The insistence that an Indian author should write like an "Indian" and not pretend to be "English" remained equally valid even after the early decades of the twentieth century saw a steady surge in the number of Indian English writings being published from the metropolis. Thus, as I show in Chapter 2, an author like Cornelia Sorabji could only write for a metropolitan audience by assuming the identity of an "Indian girl". Similarly, Nirad Chaudhuri's claim that he embodied India was also crucial in his being accepted by a metropolitan readership. Dom Moraes too, in his turn, was asked by his literary agent to go back to India and write from there to become more acceptable to his metropolitan audience. As these instances reveal, an Indian author's desire to be English is always invariably buffeted by a compulsion not only to be Indian but also to be Indian according to the exoticised expectations of a metropolitan audience. Thus, Bethune's advice to Dutt about not to try to be English was also accompanied by a prescription on how to be Indian, which in this particular case was primarily constituted of the suggestion to write in vernacular. During the course of the twentieth century, the prescription of the metropolitan audience to the Indian author would change. It no longer contained Bethune's absolute interdiction about writing in English but nevertheless retained the expectation that Indian writers should write as Indians and by doing so reveal the real essence of their country which is otherwise apparently hidden from the foreigners. Such expectations of a metropolitan readership continue to influence the works of Indian English authors even today, making them strategically exoticise India through their writings so as to satisfy the taste of the metropolitan readership for an exciting dose of non-metropolitan otherness.

Importantly, while each of the anglicised individuals that I discuss in this book paid heed to the demand of the metropolitan audience to act and write like representative Indians, they also remained acutely aware of the discriminatory attitude that underlined such a demand. This is not surprising given that the sense of discrimination was crudely reinforced for them by the everyday racism that they were all subjected to while in England. As Radhika Mohanram has observed, during the nineteenth century, whiteness became a key element in the British perception of self-identity. Similarly, from the nineteenth century onwards, white skin acted as one of the main markers through which Indians identified the colonising English/British/Europeans and distinguished them as foreigners (Raychaudhuri "Europe in" 156). Hence, with the white body playing such a crucial role in defining the English identity both for the coloniser and the colonised, it was imperative that an attempt to become English also involve an attempt to become white-skinned. Indian efforts at English self-fashioning came up against an insurmountable barrier here. None of the Indian authors who tried to fashion themselves as English had an answer to this dilemma of skin colour, though they were persistently reminded of this epidermal barrier whenever they arrived in England. Thus, Michael Madhusudan Dutt, for example, was deeply unsettled at being treated as a "damned nigger" (Murshid *Lured* 162) in England and had to move out of the country where he always wanted to belong within just two years of his arriving there. Sorabji too, in spite of being "brought up English" (*India Calling* 15), faced similar racism in England near the end of the nineteenth century and writes in her autobiography how she was mistaken by English ladies as an illiterate "heathen" (*India Calling* 44) because of her skin colour. Among all the

INTRODUCTION: CONTOURS OF ENGLISHNESS IN COLONIAL INDIA

authors discussed here, it was only Nirad Chaudhuri who consciously tried to work through this dilemma by evolving an elaborate climatological argument which stated that he, along with all other Hindus in India who were descended from the Aryan race, was "actually" fair-skinned like the English but had turned brown because of the tropical climate of the subcontinent. Yet, irrespective of how convincingly Chaudhuri attempted to work out this theory, it did not prevent his being teased by an English boy on his first visit to England as an "African" (*Passage* 125).[23]

Overview of the chapters

Chapter 1 explores the intertwining of the quests for anglicisation and Indianness in nineteenth-century Bengal which framed the simultaneous origin of Indian middle-class self-fashioning as English and Indian middle-class nationalism. Here I primarily focus on the writings of Rabindranath Tagore who briefly became one of the most prominent leaders of the Swadeshi movement, the first significant middle-class-led anticolonial nationalist mass movement in India. Tagore remained involved with this movement from 1905 to 1907 and then abruptly withdrew from active politics to become one of the severest critics of the ideology of nationalism. This initial involvement with the politics of nationalism and the later denunciation of it was accompanied by a series of shifts in Tagore's cultural ideology. In the 1880s, he began from an ideological position that was harshly critical of Hinduism and sought to bring out its defects by "comparing ourselves to others" ("Prachya o Paschatya" 248), where the "others" stood for the English colonisers. However, by the next decade, Tagore came to occupy a position that closely resembled Bankimchandra Chattopadhyay's stance about the present-day Indians representing a degenerate species who have lost their ideal Hindu way of life that existed in the ancient times. Whereas Chattopadhyay in his *Anandamath* talks about the need for superhuman efforts in order to revert back to that ancient glory, Tagore speaks of "supermen" who would personify that lost ideal and would lead the present Hindu/Indian society out of the miseries into which it has fallen. Again, whereas for Chattopadhyay the superhuman effort involves learning from the English, for Tagore being the superman involves possessing qualities that characterise the "great men of Europe" ("Vidyasagarcharit" 480). Yet, as mentioned earlier, this position is inherently paradoxical because its basic argument is that one can become a "true" Indian or a "true" Hindu only by becoming less and less like the modern-day Hindus/Indians and more and more like the colonisers. It is a paradox that reaches its culmination in Tagore's 1910 novel *Gora* where the protagonist finally comes to embody the authentic spirit of Indianness when he realises that at the corporeal level, he is part of the community of white European colonisers and therefore socially unacceptable to all castes and creeds inhabiting the subcontinent.

INTRODUCTION: CONTOURS OF ENGLISHNESS IN COLONIAL INDIA

Chapter 2, which is on Cornelia Sorabji, focuses on the articulation of anglicised self-fashioning in the backdrop of Gandhian nationalism. Sorabji was "brought up English" (*India Calling* 15) in her parental home and later earned her fame as the Oxford-educated legal practitioner who worked for and wrote about the upper-caste Hindu *purdahnashins*. During the 1930s, she actively pursued the role of a Gandhi-baiter bent on proving the falsity of the contemporary anticolonial mass movements and Gandhi's duplicitous role as a leader. For Sorabji, the real people of India not only needed but also welcomed the benevolent patronage of the British Raj. In her 1934 autobiography, *India Calling*, Sorabji represents this relationship of patronage by speaking of her own association with the *purdahnashins* and her efforts to protect their traditional way of life from being swamped by the chaos of anticolonial mass movements. In her autobiography, the *purdahnashin* women of traditional Indian households are presented as the symbol of true Indianness, while Sorabji assumes the position of the benevolent English imperialist who was on a mission to protect the interest of these real Indians. However, despite claiming for herself the role of the English imperialist, Sorabji's text implicitly tries to avoid the Gandhian critique of not knowing the people "in whose name we speak" by trying to simultaneously position herself as an "Indian girl". This produces an inevitable contradiction between fashioning herself as an English and attempting to speak as an Indian who truly represents the real people of the subcontinent. In Chapter 2, I show how this contradiction is at the heart of Sorabji's career, and how it complicates the presentation of her anglicised self-identity in her autobiography.

Within two decades of the publication of Sorabji's *India Calling*, India achieved independence, thereby falsifying her argument about the real people of India being unaffected by the anticolonial movements and being still secure within the benevolent embrace of the British Raj. Indian anticolonial mass movement was clearly a triumphant force, and the political independence of India in 1947 was its ultimate vindication. Hence, by the time Nirad Chaudhuri started writing his *Autobiography of an Unknown Indian*, a few months before the British colonisers formally left India, he could not claim for himself a pro-colonial English identity like Sorabji did while simultaneously presuming to speak on behalf of the Indian masses. Consequently, in Chaudhuri's autobiographical writings, which I explore in Chapter 3, his declaration of being English is accompanied by a reversion to the late nineteenth-century Hindu nationalist argument of true Indianness being located above and beyond the deluded present-day inhabitants of the subcontinent. In fact, the elitist tendency that informed the nineteenth-century discourse becomes even more prominent in Chaudhuri's writings where he relentlessly criticises the seemingly debased character of the Indian masses—a character which apparently became more pronounced under the leadership of Gandhi. As Chaudhuri states:

INTRODUCTION: CONTOURS OF ENGLISHNESS IN COLONIAL INDIA

> I always had a profound distrust of indisciplined mass movements. It was strengthened in me when Gandhi made his deliberate attempt to draw the masses into his movement by playing on their xenophobia. ... I did not believe that his insistence on non-violence would make any difference to the long-established pattern of social behaviour of the Indian masses. It is true that the masses of India, both Hindu and Muslim, had a simple morality and piety. ... [B]ut ... this was their regenerate side, ... they [also] had an unregenerate side always prone to violent action.
>
> (*Thy Hand* 34)

This "profound distrust of indisciplined mass movements" obviously did not allow Chaudhuri to claim to represent the real people of India like Sorabji, but it did not stop him from claiming to be the very incarnation of the essence of India (*Autobiography* 488). The nineteenth-century Hindu nationalism, which asserted that true Indianness was foreign to the present-day Indians, allowed Chaudhuri to argue that though he represented the quintessential Indian, he was not part of the Indian masses. To this argument, Chaudhuri added a further elaboration by mobilising the theory of Aryan migration. This nineteenth-century theory proposed that Hindus originally belonged to that Aryan stock which had moved East from near the Caucuses to settle in India. It also proposed that the Indian Aryans had their counterparts in the modern-day Europeans who descended from the race of Aryans but moved West from their original homeland. In referring to this now debunked theory of Aryan migration, Chaudhuri was not being original. As I show in Chapter 3, this theory was originally proposed by European Orientalists like Friedrich Max Müller and was hugely popular among the colonised Indians, or at least Hindus, during the late nineteenth century as it enabled them to think of themselves as the equals of the white colonisers. However, the conclusions that Chaudhuri draw from this theory are uniquely his own. Chaudhuri argues that though the present-day Hindu was indeed the progeny of the civilisationally superior race of Aryans, the climate of the subcontinent had caused their character to degenerate, and the long absence from their original homeland had made them forget that they were actually a European race. Based on this assumption, Chaudhuri defined his life's project as recovering his lost Europeanness/Englishness which he claimed to be the true core of his Indian Hindu identity, and to migrate to his real homeland in the West. Thus, when at the age of 72, Chaudhuri finally settled down in England for good, he claimed that he did not feel detached from India. Rather, his writings from this period suggest that for him, it was akin to a return to the true essence of India, which was otherwise irrevocably lost in the subcontinent where the unregenerate masses clamoured to sever ties with their European masters under the influence of leaders like Gandhi.

INTRODUCTION: CONTOURS OF ENGLISHNESS IN COLONIAL INDIA

In Chapter 4, I follow this claim of Chaudhuri to have finally found his home in the metropolis with an analysis of a volume titled *Why I Mourn for England*. It collects together all the major essays and lectures of Chaudhuri in which he articulates his grievances against the colonial metropolis and its approach to the colonised subjects. Interestingly, though this book is one of the most stringent criticisms of England produced by an Indian, it is not critical of the ideology of colonialism. In other words, this collection, even though it criticises the colonial metropolis, cannot be categorised as an example of the Empire writing/striking back to dismantle the colonial project. Chaudhuri's articles here not only announce the historical inevitability of empire formation but also strongly advocate its moral necessity. Chaudhuri's criticism of England stemmed from what he believed to be Britain's inability to fulfil its mission as the possessor of the largest empire ever created and its duty towards the colonised subjects. Chaudhuri argues that England, having taken up the mantle of civilising the parts of the world it colonised, reneged on its promise and refused to accept in its rank as equal citizens those who came forward to anglicise themselves. According to Chaudhuri, this denunciation of the Indians who fashioned themselves as English was a great betrayal on the part of the metropolitan community which ultimately marred the entire moral legitimacy of the British colonial rule.

For Chaudhuri, Britain's decision to withdraw from its colonies after the Second World War only deepened this betrayal as it meant renouncing the civilising mission and abandoning that entire section of the Indian middle class which had sought to fashion themselves by imitating the colonisers. In Chaudhuri's opinion, Britain's turn towards multiculturalism during the late twentieth century completed this task of dismantling the empire. Thus, whereas giving up the overseas colonies in the mid-twentieth century meant ending the supremacy of the civilised Englishman outside Britain, the embracing of multiculturalism in the late twentieth century ended the supremacy of the Englishman within the metropolis. For Chaudhuri, whereas colonial Britain was guilty of not accepting anglicised Indians as English, the multicultural Britain was guilty of making the entire concept of Englishness superfluous, thereby undermining the kind of identities that anglicised middle-class Indians had painstakingly cultivated for themselves.

In Chapter 5, I focus on the writings of Dom Moraes to explore the issue of racism and the problematic relationship that an anglicised Indian invariably has with his brown body. Moraes, who was a poet, journalist, autobiographer, and travel writer was also, like Sorabji, "brought up English" in a thoroughly anglicised family in Bombay. Again, like all the other authors mentioned above, he too suffered from a sense of being not quite accepted by the metropolitan audience as a full member of their community. For Moraes, as for almost all the other anglicised Indians trying to make England their home, this feeling of being treated as an outsider was reinforced by instances of racism. As he writes in his first autobiography,

INTRODUCTION: CONTOURS OF ENGLISHNESS IN COLONIAL INDIA

My Son's Father, it "filled [him] with sudden rage and hatred" (223) when he had difficulties in finding accommodation in London because of the existing colour bar there. However, to Moraes, his brown body posed a problem not just because it did not allow him to readily become part of a white metropolitan community but also because it constantly threatened to dissolve the difference that he felt distinguished his inner English identity from the identity of other Indians. Chapter 5 investigates how Moraes in his writings tries to sustain this precarious difference, especially after returning to India, and how he seeks to engage with his land of origin and his fellow countrymen while still trying to remain English.

The concluding chapter addresses the question of whether the phenomenon of Indian self-fashioning as English has finally come to an end. As I have argued at the beginning of this Introduction, the desire to anglicise one's self was inextricably bound with the presence of the English colonisers in India as the political, social, and cultural elites. With the disappearance of those colonisers as the reference group for the Indian middle class, the phenomenon of anglicisation started to wane during the second half of the twentieth century. However, the very fact that a number of contemporary Indian English novelists have chosen to prominently focus on anglicised Indian characters in their writings signify that the desire for English self-fashioning has not become entirely irrelevant in modern times. Even though it has ceased to be a viable mode of self-fashioning in independent India, it survives as a cultural cul-de-sac that needs to be worked through in order to progress beyond its barren promises. I explore such an attempt to engage with and ultimately displace the phenomenon of Indian self-fashioning as English by reading Salman Rushdie's *The Satanic Verses*, which attempts to go beyond the colonial era binary of "Englishness" and "Indianness" and open up a new space of cultural possibilities.

Notes

1 For an elaboration of how within the colonial context English education was necessary for pursuing either government employment or professions, see Anil Seal (114–130).

2 For instance, in the Bombay presidency, the middle class had some degree of involvement in business primarily because the indigenous entrepreneurial spirit was not as completely stifled here by the colonial authorities as in Bengal. For an explanation of why colonial Bombay provided a more congenial atmosphere for the growth of Indian business than the rest of India, see A.K. Bagchi and Markovits.

3 I use the phrase "colonial middle class" to distinguish this group from the "new middle class" which emerged in India after independence and has risen to economic and social prominence since the 1990s. For an analysis of this new middle class and the ways in which it resembled and differed from the old colonial middle class, see Pavan K. Varma's *The Great Indian Middle Class* and Leela Fernandes's *India's New Middle Class*.

INTRODUCTION: CONTOURS OF ENGLISHNESS IN COLONIAL INDIA

4 Chakrabarty illustrates this conflict by referring to Vidyasagar's efforts to initiate widow remarriage within middle-class Hindu Bengali society to address the conflict between a young widow's sexual desire and the society's injunction against a husband-less woman's engaging in sexual activity (131–133)
5 For an elaboration of this term, see Merton (287–440).
6 In this context, also see Girija K. Mookerjee who observes that for a long time Indians did not distinguish one European country from another and one European people from another in spite of participating in and often cannily manipulating the Franco-British rivalry that unfolded in the subcontinent during the eighteenth century (15).
7 Macaulay is as fuzzy as the colonised Indians in his use of such words like English, British, European, and Western. In the 1835 Minute, all of these four words are used almost interchangeably without any significant distinction.
8 Gauri Viswanathan has famously referred to this strategy of using literary studies to bolster the colonial rule in India as a "mask of conquest". See her *Masks of Conquest*.
9 Even before the establishment of the Hindu college, there were private establishments like the Sherbourne's Academy and the Drummond's Academy which were offering Western-style education in Calcutta and counted among their students such celebrated figures like Rammohun Roy, Dwarkanath Tagore, and Henry Derozio.
10 Arvind Mehrotra's *The Oxford India Anthology of Twelve Modern Indian Poets* is perhaps the only significant exception.
11 Meenakshi Mukherjee's essay "The Anxiety of Indianness", first published in 1993, is also of significance here. It makes the interesting point that Indianness has primarily been a preoccupation of Indian English novels, whereas novels produced in the vernacular languages of the subcontinent have by and large remained untouched by the "anxiety" of Indianness. This turns the argument that an essential Indianness makes Indian English literature a part of the broader category of Indian literature on its head. Indianness is here regarded as a mark of peculiarity that separates rather than binds Indian English literature, or at least Indian English novels, with other varieties of contemporary literature produced in India.
12 The title of one of the founding texts of postcolonial literary criticism written by Bill Ashcroft, Gareth Griffiths, and Helen Tiffin is *The Empire Writes Back*.
13 Apparently no student of Hindu College, which was known for its Westernising influence on its pupils, had ever worn Western clothes before Dutt. One of the more eminent fellow students of Dutt, Bhudev Mukhopadhyay, notes in his memoir that Dutt spent an extraordinary sum of money just to copy a hairstyle that was then popular among the English colonisers (Murshid, *Lured* 31).
14 The first lady was named Rebecca whom Dutt had met while he was in Madras to escape persecution after converting to Christianity. Though Dutt boasted in a letter written from Madras to one of his friends that he was living happily with his "fine English wife", Rebecca's ancestry was in fact Eurasian (Murshid *Lured* 77). His second wife Henrietta, whom Dutt had known during his sojourn in Madras and whom he had married after breaking up with Rebecca and coming back to Calcutta, was also a Eurasian.
15 Apart from the epic, Dutt also composed a number of celebrated plays and sonnets in Bengali. He was in fact responsible for introducing the sonnet form in Bengali literature.
16 See Murshid *Lured* (89–90) and Mukherji (51).
17 See Kopf (22–42) and Trautmann (62–98).

18 See Chatterjee (56).
19 For Chattopadhyay, the three terms, Hindus, Indians, and Bengali, were largely synonymous. See Chatterjee (55). Also see Kaviraj's *The Unhappy Consciousness* (107–157) for an exploration of the uneasiness in Chattopadhyay's writings that resulted from this conflation of the terms "Indian", "Hindu", and "Bengali".
20 For an interpretation along this line, see Chatterjee (54–84).
21 It is important to note here that for Gandhi, not every Westerner was tainted by the "Western civilization". In fact, in his *Hind Swaraj*, Gandhi specifies that he derives a significant part of his critique of "Western civilization" from the works of such Westerners like Tolstoy, Ruskin, Thoreau, and Emerson. However, Gandhi's text also makes it evident that these intellectuals represent a minority that stands beyond the pale of the "Satanic civilization" (37), which has otherwise "taken such a hold on the people in Europe that those who are in it appear to be half mad" (36).
22 For an elaboration on how Gandhi both led and contained anticolonial mass movements, see Sumit Sarkar's *"Popular" Movements and "Middle Class" Leadership in Late Colonial India*.
23 For a more general account of how colour prejudice affected Indians, or more specifically Indian students, in England in the late nineteenth and first half of the twentieth centuries, see Lahiri (50–59).

1
NINETEENTH-CENTURY BENGAL AND THE EMERGENCE OF INDIAN MIDDLE-CLASS ANGLICISATION

In this chapter, I trace the genealogy of the phenomenon of Indian self-fashioning as English to try and open up some of the key complexities that the concept of Englishness had come to acquire among the Indian middle class by the time authors like Cornelia Sorabji, Nirad Chaudhuri, and Dom Moraes started writing about their anglicised selves. One of the goals of this chapter is to show that these later authors were not maverick figures writing from the margins of the Indian literary mainstream. Rather, the desire and the anxiety that animated their efforts to fashion themselves as English were part of an established sociocultural phenomenon that had started crystallising around the imaginary figure of England/Europe from the nineteenth century onwards. In India, two events initially shaped the desire as well as the fear of becoming English. First was the introduction of institutionalised Western education during the early half of the nineteenth century, and the second was the growing assertiveness of Hindu cultural indigenism in the late nineteenth century which ultimately grew into the middle-class nationalist discourse and anticolonial mass movements of the twentieth century. Since nineteenth-century Bengal was the epicentre from where both these historical trends originated, a discussion of the intellectual backdrop provided by this period and this region offers the best starting point for a study of the phenomenon of Indian self-fashioning as English. In what follows, I explore this milieu by especially focusing on the writings of Rabindranath Tagore who represents almost the entire plethora of arguments both for and against anglicised self-fashioning that were in circulation in nineteenth-century Bengal.

Anglicisation and the fear of losing one's true self

Though eighteenth-century history provides stray examples of Anglophile Indians like Mirza Lutfullah and Mirza Abu Talib Khan,[1] Sake Dean Mahomet stands out as the only pre-nineteenth-century figure to have sufficiently anglicised himself not only to move to London and settle down there but also to use the English language to fashion his autobiographical narrative.[2] With the establishment of Hindu College in Calcutta as the first major Indian institute of Western-style education in 1816, the scenario started to change. Instances of conscious attempts to become culturally like the colonisers gradually started multiplying among the English-educated Bengali middle class. Bankimchandra Chattopadhyay, writing about how significant the impress of such new education was on this social group, observes:

> That, in outward circumstances of social and personal life, English-educated Bengalis are rapidly getting Anglicised, few English-educated Bengalis will deny. The stamp of the Anglo-Saxon foreigner is upon our houses, our furniture, our carriages, our food, our drink, our dress, our very familiar letters and conversation. He who runs may read it on every inch of our outward life.
> ("The Confession" 137)

The transformation wrought by the English/Western education, however, ran far deeper than the "outward life". It dramatically restructured the intellectual make-up of the middle-class Bengalis through what Nirad Chaudhuri has described as a "wholesale transplantation of the modes of thinking evolved by one culture-complex to a society belonging to and inheriting a different one" (*The Intellectual* 8). According to Chaudhuri, the product of this transformation was a new kind of human being who was "quite different in personality from anything that had previously been seen in India" (*The Intellectual* 9). For Chaudhuri, this was "the consequence of the impact of European civilization on India, which in turn was brought about by the establishment of British political power" (*The Intellectual* 8). However, as we have discussed in the introductory chapter, it is problematic to read the impact of European civilisation in terms of a simple causal relationship. Indeed, some critics have also found problematic the argument of "wholesale transplantation" of cultural modes within the context of nineteenth-century Bengal. Tapan Raychaudhuri, for instance, has cautioned against such exaggerated notions of cultural transplantation and has suggested in its place "an alternative concept, that of a catalytic or chemical reaction generating phenomenon which do not represent the synthesis of two cultures or any simple importation of artifacts from one culture into another" (*Europe Reconsidered* xvii).[3] Yet even while denying a "wholesale transplantation", Raychaudhuri too agrees with the fact that Western learning and the glimpses of European civilisation that it offered to the Indian middle class produced "jagged discontinuities with earlier patterns of perception and, to some extent, even emotions" ("Europe in" 161).

Any such radical departure from the existing patterns of how life is lived and experienced, even if the departure is guided by a desire to "improve" one's social and cultural standing, triggers certain anxieties. It is, therefore, unsurprising to find that the desire for anglicisation among the colonial middle class was accompanied by a deep-seated fear about losing one's innate identity. This anxiety is repeatedly encountered in the writings of Bankimchandra Chattopadhyay, who, in spite of being an eloquent advocate of the need to learn from the colonisers, also feared its consequences. Thus, it is difficult to read any substantial part of his oeuvre without coming across instances of severe censure directed at his compatriots for turning themselves into grotesque imitators through a constant attempt to emulate "the best and the most recent English teaching concerning individuality and non-conformity" ("The Confession" 140), and "eat, dress and conduct ... in society exactly like an Englishman" (140). Chattopadhyay feared that English education, with its potential to turn Bengalis into English, might result in a loss of the true Indian self. This fear is particularly evident in his essay titled *Prachina o Nabina* (literally "The Traditional and the Modern Woman"), which is a scathing criticism of the attempt to "reform" the traditional Bengali woman by educating her and turning her into a "memsahib":

> Educate the women, permit widows to get married again, emancipate them from their domestic cage and let them fly up to the sky, abolish polygamy and do whatever else you can to make proper "memsahibs" out of our Panchi and Rami and Madhi. If you can do it well and good. But if Panchi grows into an English woman by and by, we may look forward to our *shal* trees turning into oaks one fine morning.[4]
> (translation quoted in Bagchi "May the" 51)

Chattopadhyay's comparison of turning Panchi into a memsahib with the *shal* tree turning into an oak tree suggests the impossibility of the attempt to "reform" the lot of women. At one level, the argument here is that just as a *shal* tree cannot become an oak, so "our Panchi" cannot be turned into a memsahib. But in the essay, Panchi, Rami, and Madhi represent the *prachinas* or traditional Hindu women who are contrasted with *nabinas* or the modern women, thereby suggesting that a new breed of women has already emerged in Bengal following attempts to educate and "reform" them. Thus, the comparison between Bengali women becoming memsahibs and *shal* trees becoming oaks also suggests an underlying anxiety generated by the perception that such a transformation, in spite of its apparent impossibility, was actually taking place in contemporary society.

For late nineteenth-century intellectuals like Chattopadhyay, Bengali Hindu women in their avatar of *Deshmata* (literally "land which is the mother") had come to represent the essence of indigeneity.[5] Hence, the very prospect of "our Panchi" turning into the alien figure of a memsahib evoked the fear of altogether losing the essence of indigeneity and becoming transmuted through the absorption of European influences into something totally different from what is one's essential nature—an indigenous *shal* tree grotesquely turned into a foreign oak. However, when such anxiety about Bengalis turning into English is contrasted with Chattopadhyay's essay *Anukaran* where, as I have shown in Introduction, he urges his fellow Bengalis to imitate the English, we come across a paradox. Are the colonisers to be emulated, or are their civilisational influences to be shunned? If one is to choose the latter, then how is the Bengali race ever to emerge out of the sorry state in which it has fallen, a state represented through the image of goddess Kali in *Anadamath*? If, on the other hand, one chooses the former option, how is the true indigenous nature to be preserved against the possibility of deracination? As we have already seen, Chattopadhyay sought to overcome this double bind by arguing that in acquiring Western education and by trying to become more and more like the coloniser in his civilisational attainments, an Indian/Hindu/Bengali was not becoming alienated from his or her true self, but was actually drawing closer to it. This paradoxical argument, where becoming anglicised was in essence becoming truly Hindu/Indian, was, however, not unique to Chattopadhyay. In fact, it can be traced back to the 1820s when emulating the English colonisers and being true to one's Hindu/Indian identity started getting entangled.

It was during the second decade of the nineteenth century that the group of Hindu College students known as "Young Bengal" came to prominence. They were among the first products of Western learning in India and were also some of the earliest Indians to consciously try and anglicise themselves in every aspect of their lives. They hailed mostly from high-caste orthodox Hindu families. But as students of the Hindu College, they were deeply immersed in European philosophy and politics, and in their bid to become as much like the English as possible, they sought to radically break away from the rituals and customs of their ancestral religion. This created a considerable furore in contemporary Bengali society. Peary Chand Mittra, one of the members of the Young Bengal group, later described how their attempts to flout the Hindu customs and taboos earned them a reputation of "cutting their way through ham and beef and wading to liberalism through tumblers of beer" (quoted in Rosinka Chaudhuri "Young India" 427). It is, however, important to note that the individual who most influenced the Young Bengal, both in their iconoclasm and their enthusiasm for that imaginary figure of England/Europe, was the Eurasian teacher of Hindu College, Henry Derozio.[6] Derozio (1809–1831) is better remembered today as the person who initiated among the nineteenth-century middle class in Bengal the quest for Indianness. In fact, Derozio was one of the earliest middle-class Indians to forge a language of nationhood, which finally developed into the late nineteenth-century Hindu nationalist discourse that we encounter in Chattopadhyay.[7]

Interestingly, Derozio's nationalist ideas of a Hindu India were articulated through a body of poems heavily borrowed from European literary traditions. "The Harp of India", one of his more famous compositions, is a case in point. It allegorises India as a harp, which had once been known for its "notes divine", but now

> Silence hath bound thee with her fatal chain;
> Neglected, mute, and desolate art thou,
> Like ruined monument on desert plain.
>
> (53)

The poem ends by speaking of the poet trying to "waken" the harp once again and recreate the divine melody that it had produced in the past. The circular teleology underlying the poem—a glorious past symbolised by the harp entwined by "many a wreath ... [of] Fame" (53), a dismal present symbolised by the unstrung harp bound in "fatal chains", and a hopeful future in which the harp is to be brought back to life again—is essentially the same pattern that Bankimchandra Chattopadhyay later uses in his *Anandamath* to depict the regeneration of Hindu India through the symbolism of the three different mother goddesses. This makes evident how strongly Derozio's writings prefigured the discourse of Hindu nationalism. A more thorough investigation also reveals how clearly Derozio's poem prefigures the idea of an India that is English/European. Structurally, Derozio's poem is a sonnet, and one of the earliest instances of this European form being adapted by an Indian.[8] However, what is more important is that conceptually too the poem is as European as its structure because the notion of a glorious Indian past that underpins the poem is essentially a European or more specifically an English colonial construct developed during the late eighteenth and early nineteenth centuries by orientalists like William Jones and H.T. Colebrooke to provide the inspiration for a new Renaissance in Europe.[9] This idea of an India that is English at its core finds its perfect objective correlative in the metaphor of the harp, which, in spite of representing India in the poem, is an English/European instrument that is unknown within the musical traditions of the Indian subcontinent. In the sections that follow, I will show how this curious idea of an India that is essentially English/European is deeply rooted in many of Rabindranath Tagore's writings produced between the last two decades of the nineteenth century and the first decade of the twentieth century.

The necessity and impossibility of fashioning oneself as English

Rabindranath Tagore (1861–1941) became a dominant figure within the Bengali middle class more than half a century after Derozio had died. What connects them, however, is the language of nationhood. This language which started emerging in Bengal in the poems of Derozio reached its culmination in the writings of Tagore produced in the years surrounding the historical watershed of the Swadeshi movement (1905–1908). Swadeshi (literally "of one's own country") was the first major anticolonial nationalist mass movement in India to be led by the middle class. Tagore was one of the guiding spirits of this movement till 1907, when widespread communal riots finally disillusioned him and led him to withdraw. His short-lived involvement in this nationalist movement was bracketed by a rich corpus of writings in which he negotiates the complexities of emulating the English and being "truly" Indian. Within this body of works, Tagore's novel *Gora*, serialised between 1907 and 1910, is undoubtedly the fullest expression of his attempt to think through the conflict between adopting the civilisational mores of the colonisers and remaining true to one's Indian identity. However, before I go on to discuss this novel, it is important to situate it within the broader context of Tagore's oeuvre. *Gora*, indeed, marks the culmination of Tagore's thoughts on cultural identity that he had started developing as early as the 1880s, and it is thus necessary to read the novel against the backdrop of these earlier strands of social, political, and cultural beliefs that first led the author to participate in the Swadeshi movement and then to disengage himself from it and write this novel. There are numerous studies of *Gora* available in English that tries to interpret it, with varying degrees of plausibility, in the light of contexts as diverse as the Swadeshi movement (Rege 41–48) and the Second Anglo-Afghan War (Mehta). Yet, none of these studies, including the perceptive readings of Ashis Nandy in *The Illegitimacy of Nationalism* and of Meenakshi Mukherjee in her introduction to Sujit Mukherjee's translation of the novel, work out in any detail the more obvious relationship between *Gora* and Tagore's writings on India and Indianness that immediately preceded his active participation in the Swadeshi movement.[10] What follows is thus an exploration of the essays produced between 1880 and 1905 in which Tagore elaborates the concept of authentic Indianness and studies its relationship both with the contemporary Bengali middle class and with the notion of Englishness or Europeanness.

To begin with, however, a few biographical details need to be stated. Tagore was born into a family that was exposed to English influences quite early during the colonial period. As Tagore would later recount, his ancestors had come "floating to Calcutta upon the earliest tide of the fluctuating fortune of the East India Company" (*The Religion* 168). By the nineteenth century, the family already boasted of a leading jurist with "a command of English language equal to that of London lawyers" (Dutta and Robinson, 19) and a musicologist who became the first Indian to receive an honorary degree from the University of Oxford. It was, however, Tagore's own grandfather, Dwarkanath, who was at the centre of that early nineteenth-century Bengali social milieu where everything, from social mores to dress codes, was "gradually being clipped and curtailed to Victorian manners" (Tagore, *The Religion* 168). Indeed, Dwarkanath's associations with English merchants were so intimate, and his attachment to elements of English culture so strong, that it alienated from him his orthodox Hindu wife who abjured all physical contacts with her husband. The most profound way in which England/Europe influenced the life of the Tagore family following Dwarkanath was, however, less through its association with merchants and more through the religion of Brahmoism.

Dwarkanath's friend Rammohun Roy, who founded this religious movement, was one of the great "westernizers" of early nineteenth-century Bengal and had famously pleaded with Lord Amherst to employ

> European Gentlemen of talents and education to instruct the natives of India in Mathematics, Natural Philosophy, Chemistry, Anatomy and other useful Sciences, which the Nations of Europe have carried to a degree of perfection that has raised them above the inhabitants of other parts of the world.
> (111)

Brahmoism, which was one of Roy's lasting contributions to Bengal, also reflected this faith in England/Europe and derived from it "the ideas of organized religion, a sacred text, monotheism and, above all, a patriarchal godhead"[11] (Nandy *The Intimate* 21). As a product of the nineteenth-century Bengal's encounter with Western ideas, Brahmoism was also characterised by that typical quest for Hindu Indianness which I have identified before. Thus, Rammohun Roy presented Brahmoism as a reform movement that sought to revert to a putatively more authentic and non-ritualistic form of Hinduism as conceived in the *Upanishads*. However, when by the late nineteenth century Hindu orthodoxy started gaining prominence among the Bengali middle class, Brahmoism came to be regarded more and more as purely an effect of anglicisation and less as a revival of Hinduism. Bankimchandra Chattopadhyay, for instance, clubbed Brahmoism with the other ideological importation from the West like "Deism" and "Compteism" while arguing, "what are all these *isms* at bottom but merely so many different embodiments of a strong desire to exempt ourselves from the obligations of Hinduism" ("The Confession" 140). For the orthodox Hindu revivalists who tried to argue for the more ritual-based version of the religion, Brahmos thus did not represent authentic Hindus in spite of their faith in the ancient Hindu scriptures like the *Upanishads*. Rather, they represented individuals who had become deracinated through imitating English values. In other words, they were the *shal* trees who had perversely turned themselves into foreign oaks.

It was in 1884, during the ascendency of this Hindu orthodoxy, that Tagore was appointed the secretary of the branch of the Brahmo organisation over which his father, Debendranath, presided.[12] This active involvement with Brahmoism strongly influenced the way Tagore conceived the idea of emulating the English and commented on its significance over the next decade. The other major event that shaped his idea of England was his stay there which preceded by a few years his becoming the secretary of the Brahmo organisation. In 1878, Tagore had gone to England to train as a barrister and had stayed there for about a year and a half. During this period, he was enormously influenced by European culture in general and European music in particular. This is evident from the fact that soon after returning to India in 1880, he composed two musical dramas, *Balmiki Pratibha* (1881) and *Kal Mrigaya* (1882), borrowing significantly from the European operatic structure and Irish and Scottish folk melodies.[13] Consciously, however, in spite of these influences, the attitude that Tagore adopted towards England during his stay was almost hostile. Later, in his memoir, *My Reminiscences*,[14] Tagore would state that while in England, his "youthful bravado" made it difficult for him to readily acknowledge his admiration for the European culture that he encountered there:

> At that age ... [a]dmiration and praise are looked upon as a sign of weakness or surrender, and the desire to cry down and hurt and demolish with argument gives rise to this kind of intellectual fireworks. These attempts of mine to establish my superiority by revilement might have occasioned me amusement today, had not their want of straightness and common courtesy been too painful.
> (156–157)

This concurrent acceptance and rejection of English influences marks the contradictory pull of desire and anxiety which, as I have noted above, framed the nineteenth-century Bengali middle-class's attempt to learn from the coloniser. It is this opposition between accepting and rejecting, desiring and fearing that was to set the pattern for Tagore's subsequent engagement with the notion of Englishness in the following years.

As noted above, by the late nineteenth century, there was a concerted effort underway in Bengal to reassert Hindu orthodoxy and its ritual practices. The proponents of this revivalist movement ranged from the ludicrous figure of Sashadhar Tarkachuramani, who claimed to have found a scientific rationale for every Hindu ritual and superstition, to more sophisticated intellectuals like Swami Vivekananda and Bankimchandra Chattopadhyay. Tagore's initial response to this Hindu revivalism was consistent with his anti-ritualistic Brahmo upbringing, and he published a number of essays during the 1890s criticising, to borrow the title of one of these pieces, *Acharer Atyachar* or "the torture of ritual observances". In his essay "Prachya o Pratichya" (literally "Orient and Occident") written in 1891, Tagore identifies Western education as the liberating force that will cut through the obscurantism of these dead rituals and usher in enlightenment:

> So what will come of the English education? We will not turn into English, but we will become strong, uplifted and alive. ... By

comparing ourselves with others, we will be able to rid ourselves of any callow rusticity, or undue excess regarding anything as ridiculous or corrupting. ... Those dead observances that have been polluting the air of our home or restricting our movements will be penetrated by the lightening of our intellect, and [as a result] some will burn out and certain others will be revitalised.

(248)

It is important to note that this paean to English education comes near the end of an essay, more than half of which is devoted by Tagore to decry the crass materialism of the English. Indeed, throughout the essay, Tagore tries to delink the effects of English education from the process of getting anglicised. Thus, he argues that those who think that there would be a radical change in the essential nature of the Bengalis through receiving English education are wrong because

> whatever kind of education we receive, our absolute transformation is impossible. English education might bring us certain ideas but can never bring the [material] conditions propitious to it. We might get English literature but how shall we get England. It is possible to acquire the seeds but difficult to acquire the soil.
>
> (240)

Intriguingly, the reasoning that Tagore employs in this passage runs counter to the logic of the passage quoted just before it. In the earlier of the two passages, Tagore's arguments typically resemble the case for English education as advocated by early nineteenth-century anglicists like Rammohun Roy. This argument is that English education is necessary to reform the claustrophobic world bound by rituals and superstitions. However, in the later passage, Tagore effectively undercuts the discourse of social reform by arguing that the full transformative influence of English education would be impeded anyway by the fundamental sociocultural alterity of those who are receiving that education in the colonial periphery. In this essay, Tagore suggests that the difference between the English preceptor and the Indian society is so vast that little can be communicated and understood across this barrier of difference and all attempts on the part of the former to reform the latter is doomed. In fact, he compares it with the absurdity of philanthropic fishes trying to save humans by drowning them in water (239). The reason for this self-contradiction is the same fear of deracination that problematised Bankimchandra Chattopadhyay's acceptance of English influences. To rephrase the conundrum: if an Indian/Bengali/Hindu is to become uplifted by comparing himself or herself with the English "others" and learning from them, then how is s/he to retain his or her "ownness"? And if it is argued that s/he can never lose his or her inherent nature because s/he is radically different from the English "other", then how is s/he to be uplifted from his or her plight as a colonised subject? Needless to say, we are here again confronted with the same double bind that we encountered in the writings of Chattopadhyay.

Tagore would tentatively try to resolve this dilemma in the years immediately following his writing of "Prachya o Pratichya" by completely jettisoning the discourse of Brahmo reformism and making his response to the idea of emulating the English closely allied to the position of radical sociocultural alterity. Thus, he would now argue that trying to reform "ourselves" by comparing our beliefs and thinking habits with those of the English "other" is not only impossible but also positively harmful. In an 1898 essay titled "Coat ba Chapkan" (literally "Coat or Chapkan"), discussing the adoption of English attires within Bengali society, Tagore rephrases some of the basic arguments contained in "Prachya o Pratichya" to support a very different conclusion about the nature of the English influence in the life of the Bengali middle class. In this later essay, Tagore writes:

> A great disadvantage of English clothing is that the source of its fashion is in England. We do not know what modifications are being undertaken there and for what reasons, and neither do we have any direct contact with it. ... The costume of every country has its ideal of civility. [But] from where shall we gather this ideal of the English formal wear? It is not present in our home or our society. We cannot create that ideal out of our own sense of civility, taste and better judgement. [Therefore] we have to pretend to be civil by researching the ideals of civility of others.
>
> (224)

Here is repeated the same logic about the radical difference that separates "our" lives from that of the English. But whereas in "Prachya o Pratichya" Tagore had argued that the foreignness of the English ideals was reassuring because these imported ideals could only act as catalysts within the native society without becoming integrally incorporated within it, in "Coat ba Chapkan" he argues that it is precisely because of the foreignness that elements borrowed from abroad must be avoided. These English elements are now perceived to be completely incompatible with the indigenous identity: "The day poor India would stand decked in the discarded rags of England, what a loathsome alien shape its poverty will assume" (226). His earlier counsel "to rid ourselves of any callow rusticity" by comparing the native ways with those of the English thus soon comes to be abandoned by Tagore and all such attempts are looked down upon by him not merely as unseemly affectations but as positively antinationalist. Tagore admits that his views in this regard are not guided by rationality, which he had preached so eloquently in his earlier essays, but by sentiments. Nevertheless, he insists that they are the noblest of sentiments, which are as valuable as reason:

> We will die but tolerate no insult, that is a sentiment too. Those who completely leave us out of [their] ceremonies, festivities, social formalities will not be invited by us in [our] puja festivals, son's wedding [or] father's funeral, that is a sentiment too. [Their] foreign attire is the national pride of the English and therefore we will not insult our nation by being disguised in it, that is also a sentiment. These are the very sentiments that are the real strength, the real pride, of a nation.
>
> ("Coat ba Chapkan" 226)

By the beginning of the twentieth century, the pull exerted by these nationalist sentiments made it more and more difficult for Tagore to advocate the regenerative influence of Western ideals and English education, especially within the colonial framework where the superiority of all that is English and the inferiority of everything Indian were to be accepted as axiomatic truths. In his own words:

> [Our] English preceptors reduce us to baseness through their bestowal [of knowledge]. They give with contempt and disrespect and keep reminding us: "You have nothing comparable to what you are getting, and it is beyond your ability to repay what you receive". Daily, the poison of this humiliation enters our marrow and brings palsy, [thereby] making us dispirited.
>
> ("Bharatbarsher Itihash" 386)

The above quotation is from a piece that forms a part of a cluster of essays that Tagore wrote between 1901 and 1902, articulating a position of no compromise. In these essays, Tagore advocates a complete rejection of all English influences and ideals, irrespective of whatever inherent value they might possess:

> As long as we cannot give anything to a foreign country, we cannot take anything from it. Since there is no self-esteem in what we receive, it does not become our own. ... When we can give with pride, only then shall we receive with pride.
>
> ("Bharatbarsher Itihas" 385)

For Tagore, to make this equal exchange with England possible, it was imperative to discover the fountainhead of what is "our own" that will enable the Indians to give as well as to receive with pride. Thus, we return to the quest for Indianness—a quest that remained the central concern in almost all of Tagore's prose writings of the first decade of the twentieth century, including *Gora*.

The alien locus of Indianness

An interesting aspect of these early twentieth-century prose writings by Tagore is that the way they seek to construct the idea of Indianness is by making it appear to be elusive. A close reading of the essays he produced till 1905 reveals how Indianness, though copiously written about, is almost always articulated through concepts that are in their very nature beyond articulation. In "Nababarsha" (literally "New Year"), for instance, Indianness is expressed through terms like "grand silence" (*bishal stabdhata*) or "vast solitude" (*bistirna ekakitwa*) or complete "self-absorption" (*atma-samahita*), all of which have little external manifestation. This idea of an India that is mute and cloistered in its solitude was crucial for Tagore to sustain the argument that though the subcontinent has been regularly ravaged by foreign invaders, the most recent of whom were the English colonisers, the essence of India has survived whole and uncontaminated:

> Even when for centuries mighty foreigners traversed India like wild boars tearing it from one end to the other with their teeth, India had been preserved by its vast solitude—none had been able to wound its innermost core. ... India's essence ... had been enclosed by an innate covering. Amidst all hostilities and upheavals, an impenetrable peace keeps it constant company, which is why it does not break, nor dissolve, nor is devoured by anyone as it stands alone within a frenzied crowd.
>
> (371)

The flipside of Tagore's argument is that this "enclosed" India has not only survived the foreign invasions through its solitude but has now become equally impenetrable to the English-educated Indians:

> That which we are refusing to look at out of disregard, that which we are not being able to know, that whose very hint detected from the windows of the English schools is making us turn our blushing faces, that is the eternal India.
>
> ("Nababarsha" 369)

Indianness is thus construed here as something that is beyond the contemporary Bengali middle-class social milieu of the author. Hence, whatever is impenetrable, unknowable, and embarrassing to "us" becomes, paradoxically, the basis of "our" true identity.

This disconnect between the concept of an essential Indianness, which has survived through eternity, and Tagore's contemporary middle-class society is even further widened in his essays which attempts to concretise the idea of India by trying to perceive it through a special category of individuals. The best known among these is his 1904 essay "Swadeshi Samaj" in which Tagore expresses the need for a "shamajpati", literally a leader of the society, through whom the essence of the whole country can be realised, worshipped, and served by its people. In the essay, he deliberately remains vague as to who this ideal man should be and how he is to be selected and ratified by the nation as a whole. However, Tagore makes two interesting observations regarding the shamajpati and his role within the society that illuminates his idea of an Indianness that is disconnected not only from the Bengali middle-class society but also from the Indian society in general. Firstly, Tagore states that the shamajpati will need to follow the "traditional" ways of the society, which, within the context of Tagore's essays of this period, invariably means the Hindu tradition. This observation therefore connects the shamajpati with the image of the ideal Brahmin that Tagore had elaborated two years before. The Brahmin, he had argued, was the leader of the ancient Indian society on whom rested the duty of preserving its ideals and reminding it of its rules and regulations that have been handed down through the ages in the form of tradition. Tagore had also argued that this position of leadership in the society could only be maintained by remaining detached from the travails of the society:

> To always show the right path to the workers, to always maintain unwaveringly the right note amidst the bustle of [their] labour, it is necessary that a group of people keep themselves as free as possible from labour and self-interest [that animates the society]. These are the Brahmins.
>
> ("Brahman" 393)

Thus, the Brahmin, on whom the idea of "shamajpati" is clearly modelled, is a figure who will preserve the social traditions and guide the society in its action, but he will himself remain conspicuously absent from the society. The second observation that Tagore makes in his essay "Swadeshi Samaj" underscores even further this paradoxical relation between the idealised leader of the Indian society and the society itself. Thus, immediately after emphasising the need for a "shamajpati", Tagore cautions: "There is not a shred of doubt that in our country he would always have to put up with the opposition and humiliation from specific individuals and groups" (545). However, Tagore then goes on to increase the sphere of this opposition to include the whole of contemporary society which, "by not acquiescing to respect anyone from its heart" (545), cannot but be inimical to its leader. Tagore writes, "we cannot extend even for a single day any hope of happiness and comfort to the person whom we would greet with the highest honour of the society" (545). Thus, Tagore's shamajpati as the repository of Indianness comes across as an individual, who is not only absent from the Indian society but also in a relation of antagonism to it.

This idea of a hostile relationship between the Indian society and the unique individuals through whom it can apparently perceive its Indianness and be connected to its Hindu roots had its origin in some of Tagore's earliest writings on Indian society. It can be traced back, for instance, to the biographical sketches of nineteenth-century Bengali social reformers that Tagore produced during the 1880s and early 1890s. In these essays, he repeatedly stresses the antagonism that separates these great men from their society. For instance, in a lecture on the life of Rammohun Roy that Tagore delivered in 1885, Roy is presented as a man who preserved the decaying Hindu society from the "terrible flood of the sea of foreign civilization" (519), but who was shunned by the society he helped regenerate: "His countrymen did not join him and he too was very far from the countrymen of his time" (514). According to Tagore, similar opposition and alienation was also the fate of the other great nineteenth-century reformer, Iswarchandra Vidyasagar: "Vidyasagar was peerless in Bengal. ... In absence of a companion who could equal him in his ability he had lived the life of an exile till death" ("Vidyasagarcharit" 501). Ironically, in their inimical relation to the Indian society and in their isolation from it, Roy and Vidyasagar come very close to Tagore's image of the English foreigner in India who neither belongs to the country nor is considered by the Indian people as one of their own. What is more intriguing is that Tagore himself makes this connection explicit in these early essays by stating that both Roy and Vidyasagar, in spite of their contribution to the indigenous society, were *essentially* Europeans:

> As on the one hand they are Indians, so on the other hand we see a very close similarity between their character and the European nature. *Yet this similarity is not [the result of] imitation.* In their attire, demeanour and behaviour they were completely Bengali. In their knowledge of the scriptures of their country they had no equals. It was they who laid the foundation of teaching their countrymen in their mother tongue. Yet in fearless strength, truthfulness, philanthropy, firm resolve and self-reliance they were especially like the great men of Europe. *Even in the contempt that they have displayed towards the insignificant external imitations of Europeans we can identify a European-like profound self-respect.*
> ("Vidyasagarcharit" 480, emphasis added)

The argument in this passage is peculiarly complicated, but it is important to unpack it because it brings us to the crucial figure of an Indian who is essentially English/European who is at the heart of the phenomenon of Indian middle-class anglicisation. The passage argues that Roy and Vidyasagar represent the quintessence of Bengaliness/Indianness ("Bengali" and "Indian" are obviously synonymous terms in the above passage). This is evident from "their attire, demeanour and behaviour". The passage further argues that they have been able to retain this Indianness because they, unlike their countrymen who sit in English schools or who despise them in spite of their contributions to the Indian society, have not given themselves up to servile imitation of colonisers. Till this point the radical alterity of Indianness and Englishness/Europeanness is maintained. But then Tagore goes on to conflate these two notions and make them interchangeable. Thus, it is argued that the authentic Indianness that characterise such great men like Vidyasagar and Roy is marked by the possession of virtues like "fearless strength, truthfulness, philanthropy, firm resolve and self-reliance" which make them "like other great men of Europe". What is important to note here is that these virtues that form the kernel of their quintessentially Indian identity are not imbibed by Roy or Vidyasagar from the colonisers—"this similarity is not [the result of] imitation". In other words, Tagore is not suggesting here any form of synthesis between Englishness and Indianness. Rather, what he is suggesting is that the exceptional character of Roy and Vidyasagar, which represents true Indianness, is *essentially* English/European in nature. This makes them *like* the colonisers even when they are showing their contempt towards them and *unlike* ordinary Indians even when they are leading them and reforming the Indian society. Thus, both Roy and Vidyasagar represent that complex figure of an Indian who is an English or a European from within which would be the central focus of his novel *Gora*.

European embodiment of the Indian identity

Like the essays discussed above, *Gora* too revolves around the quest to identify essential Indianness. However, it marks a major stylistic shift in the way this theme is approached. In Tagore's essays, it is the single voice of the author that dominates. But, as Mikhail Bakhtin points out, novel usually have a dialogic character where

> [t]he living utterance, having taken meaning and shape at a particular historical moment in a socially specific environment, cannot fail to brush up against thousands of living dialogic threads, woven by socio-ideological consciousness around the given object of an utterance.
>
> (276)

The novelistic form of *Gora* allows Tagore to make manifest these "living dialogic threads" while elaborating his idea of Indianness. Interestingly, however, for all the multiple opinions that *Gora* seems to include, the novel is almost wholly restricted to the narrow social milieu of the late nineteenth-century urban Bengali middle class. Characters from beyond the pale of this miniscule social group, like English colonial administrators or Bengali peasants or people of low castes, appear only at the edge of the narrative and are never in focus for long. However, this urban middle class that *Gora* depicts is seen spread over a wide ideological spectrum ranging from the pole of Brahmo reformism on one side to the pole of Hindu revivalism on the other. The eponymous protagonist himself is depicted as someone who has traversed the whole range of this spectrum before the narrative opens, tracing an ideological journey very similar to the one undertaken by Tagore before he came to write this novel. Thus, like the author, Gora too is depicted as having been an enthusiastic member of the Brahmo movement and a severe critique of Hindu ritualism in his early life. But under the influence of a Sanskrit scholar and provoked by the arrogance of a Christian missionary reviling Hinduism, he had sharply changed position and become a staunch advocate of the very ritualistic beliefs that he had once criticised. Here again, Gora's adherence to Hindu orthodoxy is guided by the same sentimental nationalism that informed Tagore's advocacy of Hindu revivalism during the turn of the century. Gora declares:

> We will not allow our country to stand as a convict in the court of the foreigners and be tried by their foreign laws. We will neither feel abashed nor proud by meticulously comparing [ourselves] with the foreign ideals. We will not be embarrassed either to ourselves or to others for the customs, faith, scriptures and society of the country in which we are born. Only by accepting with force and pride all that belongs to our country shall we protect ourselves and our nation from insults.
>
> (138)

These lines of Gora closely echo the arguments that Tagore had forwarded just a few years before in essays like "Coat ba Chapkan". In the novel, however, this generalisation about "ourselves and our nation" is posited within a polyvocal field of social opinions. Gora's attempt to reach the absolute essence of India by rejecting every perceived form of Westernisation and by "feeling completely that we are indeed ourselves" (139) enters in this novel in "a dialogically agitated and tension-filled environment of alien words, value judgements and accents" (Bakhtin 276).

One of the first dialogic confrontations that Tagore stages in this novel, where Gora's view of Indianness confronts the "alien words" of someone else, is in the form of a conversation with Binoy. Binoy is the closest friend of Gora and had kept him company throughout his university days before becoming his active collaborator in the efforts to organise the Hindu revivalist movement in India. He diligently echoes Gora's views on Hindu orthodoxy and the glory of ancient Hindu India, and often articulates them better than their original proponent. But in spite of this, Binoy lacks the conviction with which Gora adheres to his beliefs about India and Indianness. Though he is readily swayed by Gora's arguments, he finds it difficult to apply Gora's ideology to his lived reality and to the complex network of human relations that surround him: "Whatever a doctrine might sound like, when it comes to applying it on humans, it loses its absolute certainty—at least it loses it for Binoy, who is strongly influenced by his heart" (129). Unable to resolve this contradiction between abstract doctrines and the concrete reality of human society, he confronts Gora with his doubts:

Binoy: Where is that India of yours?
Gora placed a hand upon his chest and said, "It is there where the needle of this compass points at night and day".
(132)

The answer does not convince Binoy, who still remains sceptical about the actuality of the India that Gora speaks of. Thus, to his persistent questioning, Gora now excitedly replies:

> Of course there is ... [a] complete India—complete in riches, complete in knowledge, complete in *dharma*. Do you think this India does not exist! What exists is [merely] this falsehood that surrounds [us]! This Calcutta of yours, these offices, these law-courts, these few bubbles of bricks and woods! Fie!
> ... This place where we are studying, soliciting for jobs, meaninglessly slaving away from ten to five, is an illusory India that has been mistaken by us to be true. That is why twenty-five crore people are deludedly roaming about, believing [their] false honour and false labour to be real. ... There is [however] a true India—a complete India, and unless we come to rest on it we will not be able to draw the vital sap for our intellect or for our heart.
> (132–133)

It has been noted by Ashis Nandy that Gora "reifies the idea of India" (*The Illegitimacy* 40) and perceives the nation in terms of "political and cultural abstractions" (*The Illegitimacy* 40). However, what the above excerpts demonstrate is that this reified notion of India is enunciated in the novel within a dialogue where it is under constant challenge. In this particular set of quotations, for instance, Binoy's fundamentally different concept of India, which is realised in terms of personal human relationships rather than in terms of a doctrine, keeps countering the abstraction that is Gora's India. The persistent scepticism of Binoy regarding the substantiality of Gora's idea of India makes it impossible for the latter to merely state the abstract notion. Rather, as a speaker within a dialogue, Gora is required to "break [...] through the alien horizon of the listener, [and] construct [...] his own utterance on alien territory against his, the listener's apperceptive background" (Bakhtin 282). To do so, Gora has to spell out the relationship between his abstract notion of India and the more mundane Indian society that surrounds him. Gora's attempt to answer Binoy thus oscillates between the poles of a "true India" and an India of "falsehood"—poles within which he tries to locate the concepts of reality and concreteness.

In the conversation quoted above, the things that constitute for Gora the notion of "false India", namely Western education, ten to five clerical jobs in the colonial bureaucracy, law courts implementing the legal system introduced by the Raj, and most importantly the colonial city of Calcutta, all typically represent zones of contact where the nineteenth-century Bengalis came in touch with Englishness mediated by the framework of colonialism. Consequently, they were sites that also represented for the exposed section of Bengalis the anxiety of becoming deracinated through anglicisation. They symbolised the fear of turning "false" by losing one's indigeneity and forfeiting the essence of ownness to the foreign other. This precarious play between the sense of indigeneity of the colonised self and the foreignness of the colonising other that these contact zones opened up gave rise to a desire for an unchangeable centre of identity—a kernel of the authentic native self which was above and beyond this play with the other. Writing about this desire for an unchanging centre that is characteristically generated from within any structure that is open to play, Jacques Derrida states:

> As center, it is the point at which the substitution of contents, elements, or terms is no longer possible. At the center, the permutation or the transformation of elements ... is forbidden. ... Thus it has always been thought that the center, which is by definition unique, constituted that very thing within a structure which while governing the structure, escapes structurality. This is why classical thought concerning structure could say that the center is, paradoxically, *within* the structure and *outside* it. The center is at the center of the totality, and yet, since the center does not belong to the totality (is not part of the totality), the totality *has its center elsewhere*.
>
> (352, emphasis in the original)

The way Gora describes his version of "true India" in his dialogue with Binoy is a typical example of this concept of the centre located "elsewhere", and as such reflects Tagore's earlier construction of Indianness as the elusive ideal from which the contemporary English-educated Bengali society is completely alienated.[15]

What is unique in Gora's presentation of this concept of "true India" in his conversation with Binoy is, however, the physical gesture that accompanies his speech. While explaining to Binoy the idea of an India that is beyond the matrix of human relations and mundane social interactions of the urban Bengali middle class, Gora suggestively places his hand on his own chest. This pointing towards his own body, while arguing that India's true identity is outside the sphere of the surrounding commonplace, is significant. Indeed, one of the key themes that emerge early in the novel is the metaphoric relationship that exists between the idea of an Indian essence located "elsewhere" and the unique body of Gora. The readers are supplied with a detailed description of this unique body near the very beginning of the narrative:

> He has incongruously outstripped everyone around him. ... His skin colour is somewhat aggressively white, unsoftened by any tinge of yellow. He was almost six feet in height, broad-boned, with the clutches of his hands as big as a tiger's paws. ... Gour[16] cannot exactly be described as good-looking, but there was no way one could avoid looking at him. He is sure to be noticed amidst all.
> (119–120)

In contrast to the physique of his friend Binoy, who is as ordinary-looking as any other "educated Bengali bhadralok" (120), the above account of Gora's body stresses its distinctiveness. It is this distinctiveness that makes Gora stand out within the Bengali society with the conspicuousness of an alien outsider. All along in the novel, this visual salience of Gora's body is foregrounded every time he discourses on the nature of "true India", till at the end, his transcendental notion of Indianness and his white body, which "incongruously outstrip[s] everyone around him", becomes a single entity.

Gora, however, himself remains largely impervious to the uniqueness of his body. In fact, he attempts throughout the novel to make his body representative of the Indian community as a whole by making it mundane and typical. Thus, early in the novel, Gora decides to leave Calcutta and go to Triveni, a confluence of three rivers considered sacred by the Hindus, to literally merge his body with the crowd of Indians:

> By making himself one with that crowd of ordinary people he wants to submit himself to a great flow of the country and feel in his heart the heartbeat of the land. ... [B]y forcefully rejecting all his prejudices he wants to come down to the level of the commoners of the country and declare, "I am yours, you are mine".
> (143–144)

Like his version of "true India", Gora's claim to be one with the "commoners of the country", whom he romantically presumes to be the repository of authentic Indianness, is placed in the novel within a dialogically agitated environment of alien words and counterarguments. This dialogic confrontation occurs when Gora, on returning from Triveni, goes to the house of Pareshbabu, a Brahmo, who was once a friend of Gora's father. In his effort to make himself bodily resemble the commoner and feel within him the "heartbeat of the land", Gora decides to reject "all the conventions of the educated people acquired through books and imitations" (157). Hence, he dresses himself in a peculiar outfit of a coarse *dhoti*, a lace-tied shirt, and a quaint pair of shoes with upturned toes while painting his body with clay from the Ganges. Thus clad, Gora visits the household of Pareshbabu with the intention of refuting the ideology of Brahmoism, the major bastion of the nineteenth-century middle-class led social reform movement.

On entering the precincts, Gora immediately finds his adversary in Haran, an overzealous advocate of Brahmo reformism and a frequent visitor in Paresh's house. Haran challenges Gora's deeply felt nationalist sentiments by arguing that the contemporary Bengali society is in a degenerate state and therefore cannot be readily sympathised with (162). This conviction did indeed inform much of the reformist zeal of the English-educated Bengali middle class during the greater part of the nineteenth century and is also evident in the early essays of Tagore on Indian society like "Acharer Atyachar" (1892) or "Samudra-jatra" (1893). However, when uttered by the slightly caricaturish figure of Haran, such a generalised view about the Bengali society held by one of its own members sounds ridiculously sanctimonious. It becomes even more ridiculous when later in the novel this view is juxtaposed to the abject sycophancy that Haran exhibits towards a British magistrate in his attempts to show how remarkably "reformed" he is in comparison with the rest of his fellow countrymen (282–287).[17] Gora locks horns with Haran by claiming that all attempts to reform the native society following the prescriptions of "English books" (162) are bound to be repudiated by the native population, or at least by Gora who considers himself to be their representative:

> Those whom you people are calling illiterates I am on their side. That what you all consider to be superstition is my belief. As long as you do not love the country and cannot stand alongside the people of the country in the same place, till then I will not tolerate a single word of condemnation about the country from your mouth.
> (170)

What undermines Gora's arguments in the house of Pareshbabu is, however, not so much the discourse of social reformation (whose principal spokesperson, Haran, is made too laughable by the author to be taken seriously) as his own body. Gora's strange costume donned over his excessively fair-skinned body smeared with clay, rather than making him a spokesperson of the "people of the country", marks him out as an oddity. Indeed, within the urban middle-class household of Pareshbabu, the peculiar exoticism of Gora's body turns the notion of the authentic Indian community of "illiterate" and "superstitious" commoners that it seeks to represent into something as elusive as his notion of "true India". It becomes similarly located "elsewhere" from the social milieu of the urban middle class to which all the major characters in the novel belong.

This "elsewhere" that is the locus both of Gora's concept of "true India" and his notion of the authentic Indian community, however, keeps on shifting endlessly through a chain of what Derrida would call eternal différance. Thus, when Gora decides to journey to the villages to connect with the "crowd of ordinary people" he finds the centre of Indianness to be as distant from there as it was in the midst of the colonial city which he had earlier described to Binoy as the site of "false" India. His first attempt to penetrate into the rural society leads him to a Muslim village where he is unable to be at home even in its sole Hindu household because the poor barber to whom it belongs has broken the caste taboos and has sheltered a Muslim child (278). Hence, ironically, the rigorous adherence to the rules and prohibitions of the caste system, which he had supposed would make him feel at one with the "crowd of ordinary people" of India, proves to be the greatest obstacle for him to accept and be accepted within the village community. This alienation is further intensified when, during his subsequent travel through the villages, Gora comes to realise that the various customs and prejudices, which he had earlier regarded to be the pillars of the true Indian society, are nothing but the dead weight of obscurantism that stifles courage and undermines individual initiative:

> Apart from being guided by the customs they know of no other good. ... Through punishment and through sectarianism, they have come to regard prohibitions as the highest truth. The consciousness of what not to do has tied up their whole character with nets of interdictions.
>
> (530)

Gora discovers that there is no "great flow of the country" that courses through these village communities riven with sectarian strife and obscure fears. His journey through this landscape, fragmented by religious and caste differences, rather than leading him to the imagined India "complete in riches, complete in knowledge, complete in *dharma*", only confirms the sense of alienation that he had always experienced in Calcutta. Moreover, his body, which had made him conspicuous in the urban Bengali middle-class social milieu, makes him even more of an outsider among the peasants who cannot comprehend why such a huge and unusually fair-skinned Brahmin is roaming amongst them and interfering in their lives (529).

Gora's frustrating quest to connect himself with the "true India" comes to a head when he finally learns from his father, Krishnadayal, the history of his parentage. He discovers that his biological parents were Irish, and that during the Indian Revolt of 1857 in which his father was killed, his mother had sought refuge in the house of his foster parents. She had died there while giving birth to a child whom Krishnadayal and his wife Anandamayee had then adopted. It was these foster parents who gave the child the name Gora which is a word commonly used in many vernacular languages of India to refer to the white colonisers in the same generic way in which terms like English, British, and European were used within the colonial context. This news of being born of the colonisers completes Gora's alienation from India. Yet, this moment of anagnorisis also ironically brings him to the threshold of realising his idea of "true" India. Thus, the novel ends with Gora declaring:

> Today I am, what in all these days I have wanted to be but had not succeeded in being. Today I am [truly] Indian. Within me there is now no conflict between communities, be they Hindus, Muslims or Christians. Today all the castes of India are my caste, what everyone eats is my food.
>
> (570)

It is possible to read this declaration of Gora as an assertion of an ideal of inclusive secularism. Gora becomes "Indian" by becoming impervious to all the different castes, creeds, and religious communities that make up the sociocultural landscape of the subcontinent. Reading the novel in the shadow of the 1992 demolition of the Babri Masjid in Ayodhya and the communal violence that followed in its wake, this is precisely how Jasodhara Bagchi chooses to interpret the culmination of Gora's quest for self-identity—a journey from narrow religious sectarianism to a secular inclusivity:

> The secular outlook that Gora regains at the end of the novel is not just a narrative ploy, a happy ending that rounds things up in a spirit of reconciliation. Taking Gora and his discursive prose written right through the first and second decade of this [twentieth] century, we see Tagore fighting religion as a basis of political life. While not denying the importance of the search for self-identity, he searches for a secularism that is inclusive and indigenous at the same time.
>
> ("Secularism" 57)

The problem with this interpretation is its stress on inclusivity. Gora's claim in this final moment of the novel to be truly Indian is based on his realisation that he, as a European "infidel", is equally shunned by all castes in

India: "Today, I am debarred from all the temples in India from its north to south. Today, I have no place in the rows of my countrymen when they sit together to eat" (569). In other words, Gora's identity as a true Indian is based on a principle of alienation, which makes him an outsider to all the indigenous society, rather than a principle of secularism that is inclusive and indigenous. Supriya Chaudhuri in her reading of the novel's denouement has highlighted this note of alienation. Chaudhuri has pointed out that Tagore in a letter written in 1922 to the English translator of the novel had described his original intention of ending the novel by making Gora's social exclusion even more starkly evident. Referring to this possibility of an alternative ending, Chaudhuri writes: "I would like to suggest that this figure of radical alienation, however intolerable in moral terms, might indeed have better represented the homelessness of the novel's protagonist" (110). However, Chaudhuri's emphasis on Gora's radical alienation, though it balances Bagchi's stress on inclusivity, ends up, I think, by slipping into an equally fallacious reading. Whereas Bagchi misses out the note of isolation that frames the identity that Gora finally claims for himself, Chaudhuri underplays Gora's claim to have, at long last, come to properly identify himself with India. "Today I am Indian", declares Gora, but for Chaudhuri this is at best an empty claim because "there is no assurance of what, by way of productive action, Gora's discovery of his new 'identity' with India, as the casteless product of India's diversity ... can achieve" (110–111).

Both Gora's radical alienation and his claim to have become truly Indian can, however, simultaneously make sense if he is read as the figure of the "Indian who is English". Viewed from this perspective, it does not appear ironic or contradictory that it is precisely at the moment when Gora realises that he is the son of a colonial officer, and therefore radically alienated from the Indian society at large, that he comes to identify himself with a whole and unfragmented Indianness. As I have shown above, for Tagore, individuals who truly represent India are always alienated from the Indian society. Indeed, it is this very alienation that makes them "great men" and this greatness in turn makes them more like great Europeans rather than the crowd of ordinary Indians whom they try to lead or reform. Within this ideological framework, it is not at all surprising that the secret identity of Gora's "English" body, which always made him incongruous among common Indians, when revealed, ultimately makes him the perfect embodiment of Tagore's idea of "true India" that is located "elsewhere".

Conclusion

It is important to note here that though Gora represents an intertwined identity that is simultaneously English/European and Indian, he is not an example of an anglicised Indian. Yet, the figure of Gora is important in our understanding of the cultural history of Indian efforts at anglicisation primarily because what he represents is an idealised resolution of some of the fundamental conflicts that plagued the Indian desire to be English. Gora is presented as an individual whose credential as "English" cannot be questioned because of his white body and yet who can claim for himself the mantle of true Indianness. Gora therefore emerges as an ideal that the anglicised Indians throughout the nineteenth and early twentieth centuries would aspire to be—a figure who is able to represent the compound identity of an "Indian who is English" without being buffeted either by the anxiety of being deracinated or by the anxiety of not being recognised as an equal member of the colonising elites who formed the reference group.

However, the ideal that Tagore presents through Gora of a "true" Indian who is also essentially an English/European and spectacularly alienated from the "degenerate" masses of India was already being put under erasure even as the novel was being written. By then the Indian middle class had already started to position itself as the voice of the Indian populace. In fact, with the beginning of the twentieth century, the Indian middle class was convinced that their role as petitioners to the colonial authority for political reforms, which constituted the chief activity of the Indian National Congress during the late nineteenth century, was not going to earn them a hegemonic status within the people of India. As Ranajit Guha explains:

> [F]or any class "to present its interest as the common interest of all the members of the society" means, simply, to represent them. But how was such representation to be achieved in a polity [where] ... representation ... amounted to little more than a selective recruitment of collaborators by ... [the colonial] bureaucracy [?]
> (101)

Guha writes that under these circumstances, the only way the middle class, or what he calls the indigenous bourgeoisie, could sustain their legitimacy as representatives of the Indian population as a whole was by "mobiliz[ing] the people in a political space of its own making—that is, to enlist their support for its programs, activate them in its campaigns and generally organize them under its leadership" (110). The Swadeshi movement, which was triggered off by Lord Curzon's decision to partition Bengal in 1905, was the first major attempt by the middle class to mobilise the people under its banner. This marked a significant shift from the elitist attitude of the early nationalist leaders associated with the Congress. These leaders shared "feelings of mingled contempt and fear of the 'lower orders'" (Sumit Sarkar *Modern* 92) and might therefore have been able to sympathise with the transformed Gora who tries to embody Indianness while asserting his alienation from most Indians. But, with the beginning of the Swadeshi movement, the masses gradually started occupying for the middle class the locus of the "true India" that they sought to represent. With the arrival of Gandhi on the political scene during the following decade, this process reached its culmination. Gandhi, while making mass mobilisation the chief form of middle-class political self-assertion, upheld villagers and peasants from whose custom-bound lives Gora had recoiled in disgust as the main repository of authentic Indianness. Within this context of the emergent mass-based nationalism, the two ideas—being fundamentally an English who is alienated from the people of India and being the representative of true Indianness—which Tagore tries to bring together in the figure of Gora, come asunder. Thus, an author like Cornelia Sorabji, who started writing against the backdrop of mass-based nationalism in India, had to renegotiate the notion of being English and its connection with the idea of authentic Indianness. The next chapter explores the dynamics of this renegotiation.

Notes

1 The fascination of these two individuals with England in particular and Europe in general is dealt with in Tapan Raychaudhuri's essay "Europe in India's Xenology".
2 *The Travels of Dean Mahomet.*
3 For a similar criticism of the idea of wholesale cultural transplantation, see Sudhir Chandra's *The Oppressive Present.*
4 Chattopadhyay's typical ambivalence towards acquiring English education and imbibing European cultural influences is gathered from the fact that he himself wrote and published in the same journal which had brought out the original essay angry letters purportedly composed by three emancipated and Europeanised women. These women, who had been the target of Chattopadhyay's ridicule in the earlier essay, now defend themselves by targeting in turn the Europeanised Bengali males, including the author of the offending essay (see Jasodhara Bagchi "May the" 52-53).
5 For a discussion on this point, see Tanika Sarkar.
6 Apart from Derozio, there were others like David Hare, Alexander Duff, and to an extent even Rammohun Roy who exerted an influence on this group, and these influences were often contradictory to the ideals received from Derozio (see Sumit Sarkar "The Complexities of Young Bengal"). Yet, it was Derozio who remained the major guiding figure for the Young Bengal, at least while its members were still in their youth.
7 For a discussion on Derozio and the construction of the nationalist discourse in the nineteenth century along communal lines, see Rosinka Chaudhuri's "An Ideology of Indianness".
8 It is in fact a very close imitation of Thomas Moore's sonnet "The harp that once through Tara's hall".
9 For a discussion on the influence of the orientalist discourse on Derozio's sonnets, see Rosinka Chaudhuri's *Gentleman Poets in Colonial Bengal* (27-28).
10 The only exception is perhaps Sumit Sarkar's brief comments on the novel in *The Swadeshi Movement* (52-53).
11 These ideals were not merely derived from Christianity but also, as Ashis Nandy has pointed out, from the European colonial discourse of "masculinity" and "maturity" through which Christianity was refracted in nineteenth-century India. See Nandy's *The Intimate Enemy* and also his essay on Sati.

12 By the 1860s, the Brahmo movement had become divided into an orthodox and a progressive group. Debendranath was the leader of the orthodox faction known as the "Adi Brahmo Samaj".
13 Tagore would, however, later insist that his appreciation and understanding of European music during his stay in England was limited and that the essence of European music was fundamentally irreconcilable with Indian music (*My Reminiscences* 188-191).
14 This memoir was published in Bengali under the title *Jibansmriti*. A free translation of this memoir titled *My Reminiscences* was published in 1917, but it does not contain the translator's name. All quotations from this text are from the 1917 translation.
15 For an analysis of this complexity of Gora's identity as someone who represents "India" and yet stands aloof from its masses through the lens of a guest–host dynamics, see Gayatri Chakravarty Spivak's *Aesthetic Education in the Era of Globalization* 301-315.
16 "Gour" and "Gora" are both diminutives of the full name of the protagonist, Gourmohon.
17 In spite of the caricaturish exaggerations through which Haran is portrayed, his sycophancy does reflect the excessive loyalism towards the British rule for which some of the late nineteenth-century Brahmos were notorious. See Sumit Sarkar's "The Radicalism of Intellectuals" (66).

2
IMAGES OF INDIAN WOMANHOOD AND THE "ENGLISH" SELF OF CORNELIA SORABJI

In Chapter 1, I tried to elaborate how Tagore attempted to reconcile the idea of being English with an essentialist notion of authentic Indianness. In this chapter, I seek to provide a counterpoint by focusing on the self-fashioning of Cornelia Sorabji who sought to assert her anglicised identity in opposition to the essentialist notions of Indianness. Thus, whereas Tagore's Gora seamlessly merges the two identities of being an English and a quintessential Indian, Sorabji, as I would argue, spent her life dissociating her English self-image from what Antoinette Burton has referred to as "the overarching, homogenizing category of 'the Indian woman'" ("Cornelia Sorabji" 111). Born in 1866, Sorabji was the first woman to practise law in India and is best remembered today for her role as a legal advisor to orthodox Hindu *purdahnashins*,[1] whom she guarded against being cheated out of their inheritance and legal rights. However, although the field of her legal work was primarily India, she belonged to that select group of nineteenth-century Western-educated individuals from the subcontinent who not only spent a significant part of their lives in England but also considered it to be their home (or at least one of their homes). Thus, throughout her life, she frequently travelled between England and India and positioned herself as an interpreter of the East to the West. Sorabji wrote extensively for a metropolitan audience narrating her experiences among *purdahnashins*, and when she died in London at the age of 88, she left behind a large number of fiction, non-fiction, and journal articles.

In spite of her unique historical position as the first woman lawyer from India, and in spite of the abundance of documents that she left behind, Sorabji was almost completely forgotten during the five decades following her death. However, more recently, she has emerged as one of the most researched Indian women writers in English. In the significant amount of scholarship produced on her during the span of the last few four decades, Sorabji has been typically celebrated as a hyphenated figure who coexisted in two worlds—an anglophile Indian who "paradoxically and simultaneously ... [belonged] both at the margin and at the centre of metropolitan life" (Rastogi 743). Richard Sorabji, the nephew of Cornelia Sorabji, states in the biography of his aunt that she was "wholly Indian ... but otherwise brought up ... in English style" (3). Leslie Flemming argues that Sorabji had a "sense of herself as both English and Indian at the same time" (90). While Ellen Brinks finds proof of Sorabji's in-betweenness reflected in "Miss Sahib", the narrator of Sorabji's *Sun Babies*, "whose age, social position, and profession bear a strong likeness to Sorabji's own" (125) and who stands for "a 'Presence', both British and Indian simultaneously" (127). I would, however, like to argue that Sorabji's self-fashioning as English was predicated on a strategic denial of Indianness. Indeed, as I argue here, her career from a very early stage was marked by attempts to distance herself from the role of the "Indian woman" and to project this role outside, particularly onto the *purdahnashins* amidst whom she worked, to offset her own image as an individual who belonged to the metropole. This makes it difficult, if not impossible, to understand her life and career from within the framework of simultaneous belongingness. It therefore becomes imperative to unpack the various denials and disavowals that inform her identity to reach a more comprehensive understanding of the intricacies of her self-fashioning. In what follows, I attempt to do this by focusing on Sorabji's 1934 autobiography *India Calling*.[2]

The "very real isolation" of being brought up English

The claim that Sorabji is a figure who is simultaneously British and Indian apparently finds substantiation in the very opening paragraph of the introduction of her autobiography where she writes: "I have been privileged to know two hearthstones, to be homed in two countries, England and India" (5). To elucidate this statement, the introduction brings together a cluster of images relating various emotions and sensations that both Britain and India have evoked in Sorabji's life, shaping the way it has been led and experienced. However, a careful reading of these images shows that rather than substantiating, they problematise Sorabji's claim of being equally at home in England and in India. For instance, the images of her childhood home with which she begins her record of mental and physical impressions seem to be located neither in England nor in India, but in a landscape that eludes geographical rootedness. Her descriptions of the space where "we played as children" (5), amidst "the branches of the forest trees on moonlit nights" (5), looking up at "the stars hanging like lamps out of an indigo sky" (5), though thickly detailed, are strangely evasive in producing a geographically determinate image of a homeland. They depict the vision of childhood that is still not framed by the coordinates of space and time. This indeterminacy sharply stands out when contrasted with the following lines where Sorabji records her impressions of India gathered during her years spent there as a legal practitioner incessantly moving across the length and breadth of the entire subcontinent. In these lines, every snippet of physical sensation—her experience of the "[d]awn at Darjeeling" (6), her sighting of the "green paroquets at Budh Gaya" (6)—is meticulously labelled with place names, thereby locating each of them within concrete geographical spaces.

The Indian images are distinguished from the images of Sorabji's childhood home not only in terms of their specific geographical rootedness but also in terms of their impersonal objectivity. The personal pronouns and possessive adjectives that characterise Sorabji's description of her parental home at the edge of the woods, and firmly situate her own self within each of these images, completely disappear in this latter section. What the reader is presented with instead is a series of impersonal tableaux sketched by a detached traveller, who is enamoured of the picturesque, during the course of her interminable "cross-country journeys by palanquin or elephant, in canoe or dugout" (6). Sorabji's absent self in the Indian images, however, reappears when she proceeds to describe London and the English countryside—places where the intimately possessed landscape of her childhood home finds its counterpart in her experiences of "*My* first robin: *my* first fall of snow: ... The Irish crossing-sweeper with her bonnet awry, who smiled at *me* ...: the lion in Trafalgar Square with whom *I* shared all *my* jokes and *my* anxieties" (6, emphasis added).

The brief introduction, thus, depicts not only the sights, sounds, and fragrance of the different places that Sorabji inhabited during her lifetime, but also the different ways in which she identified with these places. It traces a variegated pattern of intimate belongingness and objective detachment. The childhood home, distinctly remembered but indistinctly moored within a specific geographic location, the impersonal images of India, strung together by a travel motif recalling Kiplingesque colonial adventures, and an England, where Sorabji is acutely aware of her own self that is simultaneously alienated and at home ("knowing one's self utterly insignificant and alone, yet alive and perfectly companioned") (6), hint at the radically diverse ways in which the various locales are mapped and represented in Sorabji's life history. It makes evident how England and India along with her childhood home were, for Sorabji, distinctly nuanced territories within which she integrated herself in markedly different ways.

While contrasting Sorabji's belongingness to her childhood home and to England with her sense of detachment from India, it is important to note that she grew up with her parents in the Indian town of Poona (now Pune) in the erstwhile Bombay Presidency. This contradiction in both belonging to and being detached from India is, however, explained by what Sorabji describes as the strong sense of "apartness" (13) that characterised her family. In her own words, though her home was in India, "there was an invisible circle drawn round it which brought us [the family] very close to one another, and which made it untypical of the Indian home of the period" (15). This "untypical" home belonged to Cornelia Sorabji's father, Sorabji Kharsedji. He was originally from the community of Zoroastrian Parsees that had emigrated from Iran and had settled in the western part of India. Kharsedji had, however, distanced himself early in his life from the orthodox section of the community by converting to Christianity under the influence of his English tutor George Valentine. The English influence was also very strong on Sorabji's mother, Franscina. Though born a Hindu[3] into a tribal family in the Nilgiri Hills, Franscina was brought up as a Christian by missionaries working in the area and was later adopted by one Cornelia Ford, the wife of a British colonel posted in India. Sorabji recounts in her biography of her parents that Franscina "learnt from [Lady Ford] everything which an English child would learn" (*Therefore* 43). This later reflected on how Franscina raised her own children. In her autobiography, Sorabji remembers how she, along with her siblings, was "'brought up English'—i.e. on English nursery tales with English discipline; on English language, used with Father and Mother, in a home furnished like an English home" (15). The all-encompassing "Englishness" of the parental home in the midst of India, as Sorabji describes it in her autobiography, gives a clue as to why the sense impressions that she records from her childhood in the introduction do not appear to be rooted within a specific geographic locale.

While elaborating on her life as an "English" child, Sorabji, however, also points out that her parents compelled her and her siblings to

> learn the languages of the Peoples among whom we dwelt. We were told tales of our ancestors in Persia, and of our forebears and immediate family in the Parsee community in India. We were made proud of that community; but from our earliest days we were taught to call ourselves Indians, and to love and be proud of the country of our adoption: while the history of our Parents made us love also the people and country to which George Valentine and Cornelia Ford belonged.
>
> (15)

These various affiliations and allegiances, conceived in terms of harmoniously interlocking concentric circles—the first taking in the Parsee community,[4] the second taking in India, and the third and final taking in imperial England, so as to build "a unity which did not at the time exist in India" (15)—bring us back to the concept of simultaneous belongingness. However, here too a closer examination of the text reveals that the idea that Sorabji equally shares all these separate identities is only tenuously held, and ultimately gives way to a variegated pattern of identification and dissociation similar to the one found in the introduction of her book. In fact, in the very same chapter in which she lays claim to these multiple identities, Sorabji also makes evident the impossibility of simultaneously belonging to the separate communities. For instance, Sorabji asserts that she is a "Parsee by nationality" (12) and then goes on to stress, with persistent repetition, how the Parsee community has kept itself distanced from the rest of the people of India even centuries after their immigration. She narrates how, on coming to India, the Parsees were forced to do away with their ancestral ways of dressing and their Persian language in favour of the local costume and the Gujarati tongue. But rather than using the local language and costume to get assimilated, the Parsees, according to Sorabji, turned them into signs of their "apartness": "Our women wear a *sari* certainly, but it is of silk, and draped differently from the Hindu *sari* ...; while the Guzerathi spoken by the Parsees is '*Parsee* Guzerathi'" (13, emphasis in original). Sorabji also underlines the Parsee reluctance to adopt the customs of other Indian communities by stating that unlike the Hindus and the Muslims in India, "our women have never been secluded" (13) and that "[t]here is no parallel among us to the Hindu caste system" (13).

Having made her point about how she shared with the Parsee community its sense of distinctness from the rest of India, Sorabji goes on to describe the detachment of her own family from the Parsee community which, as she narrates, had its roots in her father's conversion to Christianity, accomplished "in the manner of the Early Martyrs of the Christian Church, at peril of death" (14). The full import of this statement is understood from the more detailed account of the episode that Sorabji provides in the biography of her parents, where she describes the huge furore within the Parsee community that was sparked by her father's decision to renounce the ancestral faith. Protecting the Zoroastrian religion was, according to Sorabji, an all-engrossing absorption for the Parsees of the Bombay Presidency (*Therefore* 30), and as a result her father's conversion to Christianity meant that "the hostility of the entire community was directed ... against *the convert*" (*Therefore* 30–31, emphasis in original). These tales of exclusivity and persecution weave in *India Calling*, a narrative of what Sorabji herself describes as "very real isolation" (14), which complicates her assertions of multiple belongingness. Indeed, the history of "apartness" empties out the concept of Sorabji's being an "Indian" almost to the point where the term becomes a free-floating signifier. Though occasionally used in her autobiography, it remains unconnected to any specific aspect of her childhood life that was, in Sorabji's words, "spent in much the same ways as those of children in England" (16–17).

What is interesting to note, however, is that though Sorabji's account of her family history in the autobiography destabilises her Parsee and Indian identities, her sense of being an "English" remains undisturbed. As noted above, Sorabji repeatedly uses the word "English" to describe her experiences of growing up. Yet this Englishness is never elaborated in the same way as Parseeness or Hinduness or Muslimness is elaborated in her narrative. Thus, whereas Parsee costumes (13), Zoroastrian religion (13–14), and the layout of Hindu and Muslim households (17) are described in minute ethnographic details, the reader is never made aware as to what exactly constitutes "an English home" or how precisely the "children in England" spend their childhood days. Indeed, in Sorabji's autobiography, Englishness is described only with further repetition of the word "English". Thus, for instance, the "English manner" of eating, which the Sorabji family was used to, is simply described as the way in which meals are partaken from "English plates, and with English adjuncts" (16). A Parsee meal in contrast is explained through rich and exotic particularity—"luscious stews flavoured with pineapple or preserved mangoes, the sweet 'motif' beloved of the community" (16). The suggestion implicit in this narrative strategy of selective elucidation is that "Englishness" represents the self-evident norm—a norm which Sorabji shares with her metropolitan readers and which makes her one of them. On the other hand, every Parsee or Hindu or Muslim element that might add up to and constitute the idea of Indianness is particularised and thereby made non-normative, exotic, and "other".

Enacting and resisting Indianness in England

Ironically, the non-normative Indianness, which Sorabji implicitly but cautiously distinguishes from her normative English self while describing her childhood days, was precisely what was foisted on her when she proceeded from Poona to Oxford at the age of 23 to pursue her higher studies and to get "England into [her] bones" (26). Having secured the highest marks in the whole of Bombay Presidency in her B.A. examination, Sorabji was entitled to a Government of India scholarship to study in an English university. This scholarship was, however, denied to her on the ground that she was a woman. Nevertheless, her study in England was made possible by the generosity of some English friends who raised enough funds to enable her to undertake the journey and to enrol at the University of Oxford. The major figure among Sorabji's English benefactors was Lady Mary Hobhouse who publicised Sorabji's arrival in England by writing a letter to *The Times* in London (published on 13 April 1888) describing her as a young lady "of pure Indian birth" (52). Burton has observed that the motive behind Hobhouse's labelling Sorabji as the archetypal "Indian woman" was "to 'sell' Cornelia Sorabji to an English metropolitan audience that was sympathetic to the plight of Indian womanhood" ("Cornelia Sorabji" 111). I will have to come back to this idea of "the plight of Indian womanhood" when discussing Sorabji's career among *purdahnashins*. Here, however, I would like to note how this categorisation of Sorabji as a disadvantaged "Indian woman" is markedly in contrast with her own account in *India Calling*, where she takes pain to underline her atypical condition amidst the women of India. As already mentioned, Sorabji emphasises in her autobiography that as a Parsee she belonged to a community where women were never secluded behind the constraining purdah like Hindu and Muslim women. She also stresses that as a child of Franscina, she apparently never felt disadvantaged within her family. As Sorabji notes, Franscina "was proud of having seven daughters, in a country where the birth of a daughter was considered a calamity" (19), and she looked upon them as "women that India wanted, just then, for her service" (19). The image of Sorabji as the emblem of Indian womanhood, which sharply contrasts with this self-image of being singular and even anomalous in India, was formed in England almost as soon as she arrived. With some degree of irritation, Sorabji notes in her letters to her parents how she was repeatedly invited to lecture on "the position of Indian woman" (*An Indian Portia* 110) in public meetings as well as asked to discourse on anything and everything "Indian" in private gatherings. In one of her early letters, Sorabji relates how, within a month of her coming to London, she was in the "formidable Drawing Room" (*An Indian Portia* 79) of one Mrs Gilmore, reviewing

> the development of the mind of young Indians, depict[ing] some Indian scenes, [and] display[ing] the growth of Indian thought with regards to the work being done by Missionaries in India.
> (*An Indian Portia* 79)

That Sorabji was frustrated by the situation is easily gathered from these letters written while she was in England as a student, and this note of frustration also subtly informs her autobiography. Thus, in *India Calling*, she devotes a significant portion of the chapter describing her stay in England to recount the numerous ways in which her "real" identity was misjudged by those who insisted on viewing her through the lens of Indianness. She describes, for instance, how the librarian of one of the colleges where she studied in between her lectures "seemed to think that I must always be cold" (30). As a consequence,

> The kind man used to have a rug for my knees, which he pressed upon me even in Summer: and on the closest of days he would call to the boy in attendance as I entered the Library—"Pile on more coals, Horsley!"
> (30)

The tone here is mildly sarcastic which, even while acknowledging the librarian's concern, makes fun of his fixed notion about Sorabji being an "Indian woman" and therefore perennially in need of extra warmth even in summer and even on the closest of days. The sharpness of the critical edge in Sorabji's sarcasm, however, increases as she goes on narrating further instances of being stereotyped as "the Indian woman". She describes with more than a touch of derision the "Dear old ladies" (44) who were "always trying to convert me …—the heathen at their gates" (44), and who insisted on speaking to her very loudly in pidgin-English—"Calcutta

Come?" "Bombay Come?" (44). Her scorn is also clearly palpable in her mocking depiction of the Christian cleric who felt "[s]o like Home" (44) on seeing her because, as he explained, he had worked "among the Coolies in South Africa!" (45).

By clustering together such diverse stories of "mistaken" identifications, Sorabji makes it evident that all attempts to pigeonhole her identity within the preconceived image of a typically disadvantaged Indian woman—who must necessarily be a "heathen", necessarily be ignorant of English, and necessarily always feel cold—are equally absurd and invariably lead to her being misrecognised. Nevertheless, in spite of her use of sarcasm while narrating these stories, the depiction of her response as a student in England to the stereotyping of her identity is complex and ambivalent. Whereas the tone in which she narrates the stories of the various "misrecognitions" makes it clear that she is rejecting as false all those identities that portray her as a typical "Indian woman", she does not make this rejection explicit.[5] This ambiguity of Sorabji towards her false image as "the Indian woman" can be traced back to her student days in England when her financial dependence on her English benefactors made her feel duty-bound to act out her part as the resident "Indian". She was also cannily aware of "the happy fact that I am Indian is an advertisement in itself" (quoted in Burton "Cornelia Sorabji" 126), and was therefore awake to the possibility that her lectures on India could "be the tickets to help towards my expenses" (*An Indian Portia* 80). At the same time, Sorabji also wrote back home about her annoyance at being "placarded about" (*An Indian Portia* 111) in meetings organised around the topic of India and Indian women. This complexity of her attitude at having to play the Indian "other" amidst an English society where, ironically, she found "companionship outside [her] family for the first time" (30) is best reflected in *India Calling* in the episode that relates how Sorabji once came to write a play at the behest of her English friends.

The play was commissioned by Graham Alexander, one of the major late nineteenth-century theatre producers in London, and Sorabji was expected to write "an Indian play" (40) with an oriental appeal that was to satisfy the English audience's craving for oriental exoticism and the English heroine's "long[ing] to play in Indian draperies" (41) and resemble "an Indian dream" (41). Understandably, the offer marked one of the high points in Sorabji's student life in England and she does describe it in her autobiography as "a great moment" (40). However, what she then goes on to narrate is not the story of how she fulfilled her expected role as an "Indian" playwright but rather how she distanced herself from it. Apparently, Sorabji accepted the offer only by first making it clear that she was no playwright and therefore could not and would not author an original play. Instead, she "would put into suitable form for the English stage a Sanskrit play, reputed as of the second century" (40). This marks an effort to redefine her role from being an "Indian" playwright, expected to generate Indianness from within herself, to being an "English" translator who, much like the two Oxford University orientalists Monier Monier-Williams and Friedrich Max Müller whom Sorabji intimately knew, "made suitable" ancient Indian material for the metropolitan audience without personally embodying India. Sorabji's attempt to distance herself from the "Indian" substance of the play is further emphasised by her underlining how strongly she refused to take on board any suggested alterations to its content even while readily acquiescing to change the English language from prose to blank verse. The play, she stresses, was most definitely not hers:

> I told our little group that night that I was afraid it was no good. The changes could not be made. *The play was not mine*, and its value lay in keeping it as close as possible to the original.
> (41, emphasis added)

This account of Sorabji's early effort to narrate "original India" for a metropolitan audience is important because it provides a framework to understand her later attempts to recount the tales of *purdahnashins*. In these tales, which form the bulk of her oeuvre, one witnesses the same desire to maintain a separating line between her Indian subject matter, on the one hand, and her metropolitan "English" self on the other. It is this central concern in Sorabji's writings on India that I would try to unpack by focusing on the long second section of *India Calling*, which narrates her work among *purdahnashins*. However, before doing so, I would like to dwell on how *purdahnashins* became a career choice for Sorabji, and how this career was framed by the imperialist ideology of the nineteenth century.

"The object of her ambition"

During the course of her legal career in India that spanned more than three decades, Sorabji's name became inextricably associated with the secluded women of aristocratic Indian families who observed purdah and did not expose themselves to the sights of strange men. However, according to Sorabji's account in *India Calling*, her association with secluded *purdahnashins* was already strongly established when she was a child. At a very early age, she witnessed a Gujarati Hindu widow visiting her mother Franscina in a thickly veiled wagon. This was Sorabji's first intimate encounter with a *purdahnashin*. The Hindu lady, she learnt, had once owned a considerable amount of landed property but was cheated out of it by her man-of-business. By the time she visited Franscina, the lady had become penniless. With no access to legal aid except through men like the one who had swindled her, the *purdahnashin* had little hope of regaining her possession. It was after witnessing the plight of this widow that Franscina apparently urged Sorabji to study law so that she could "help in this kind of trouble" (22). According to her autobiographical narrative, it was from this moment onwards that the plight of the secluded women of India became Sorabji's overwhelming concern, deciding the course of her future career.

In spite of the tremendous significance that Sorabji attributes to the case of the Gujarati Hindu widow in deciding her vocation as a legal advisor dedicated to help *purdahnashins* in their plight, the episode remains somewhat dubious on at least two accounts. First, it has been argued that Sorabji showed no intention of studying law till she arrived in Oxford. In fact, she started off to England with the express purpose of studying medicine.[6] Secondly, before returning from Oxford, there was no indication that Sorabji wanted to choose a career through which she could serve the cause of *purdahnashins*. In fact, prior to her going to Oxford, she was engaged as the principal of a men's college in Gujarat. Thus, the Gujarati widow could not have inspired Sorabji either to become a lawyer or to commit her life to the service of the secluded women of India. On the contrary, there are strong indications that it was Sorabji's patrons in England who primarily steered her towards a legal career and determined her role as the alleviator of "the plight of the Indian women". Burton has extensively discussed in her essay, "Cornelia Sorabji in Victorian Oxford", the nature and extent of the intervention of Sorabji's English benefactors in deciding the course of her study. I will therefore confine myself to the discussion of how these benefactors forged the link between Sorabji's future career and the women of India.

Lady Hobhouse's letter to *The Times* introducing Sorabji to the English public (dated 13 April 1888) helps understand the kind of role among Indian women that was imagined for her by her patrons. In the letter, Lady Hobhouse declares Sorabji's education to be an "experiment" which, if successful, would open "a new era and sphere for the women of India, whose energies and capacities have been so closely suppressed hitherto" (52). This statement clearly forms part of the rhetoric of imperialism as a civilising mission and is underlined by two of its basic beliefs. First, India is a primitive country, representing one of the earliest rungs in the "scale of civilization"[7]—a primitiveness best reflected in the degraded condition of Indian women whose "energies and capacities" have been "closely suppressed".[8] Second, the degraded state of Indians, especially Indian women, necessitated colonial intervention to rescue the barbarous people from themselves and make them more like the British by subjecting them to English education. Sorabji, a meritorious student who had been brought up within an English environment by parents, themselves newly converted to Christianity through successful intercession of English missionaries, was, for her English patrons, a glowing testimony to the civilising and reforming influence that British imperialism had been able to exert in the colonies. Interested English friends like Lady Hobhouse[9] who were paying for the "Sorabji experiment" were thus convinced that she in her turn would use her higher education to reform her fellow countrywomen and draw them out of their present pitiable condition and into the light of modernity and progress. Indeed, so committed was Lady Hobhouse to this image of Sorabji as a pioneer who would beat out a path for other Indian women that she considered it wise to downplay the fact that before joining Oxford, Sorabji was serving as a principal of a men's college and was not directly involved in addressing "the plight of Indian womanhood". Hence, in another letter to *The Times* written the year Sorabji arrived in England and published on 12 June 1889, Lady Hobhouse sought to assure the English audience by spelling out on behalf of Sorabji the "real" ambition of her life. Sorabji's education in England, Lady Hobhouse stated, "will enable her to be more useful to her countrywomen in the future, *for that is the object of her ambition*, though circumstances and her own abilities have led to her beginning her professional career by the teaching of men" (55, emphasis added). Thus, whatever Sorabji's goal in life might have been before coming to Oxford, by the time she arrived in the metropolis, she was already fitted out as the champion of the suppressed women of India. Sorabji on her part accepted the role but did not quite play it along the line her English patrons like Lady Hobhouse expected her to. She rejected the ideology of reform and redefined her position vis-à-vis Indian womanhood along the more conservative line of imperialist thought that had come to prominence during the late nineteenth century.

Following the Indian Revolt of 1857, the efficacy of the reform-oriented interventionist approach of imperialism was largely discredited. In place of the civilising mission that sought to radically transform the Indian society, the British rule in India now came to be defined in terms of its commitment to protect the "traditional" societies of the colonised subject and preserve its various customs and rituals.[10] Consequently, within this late imperial ideology, there was no room for the anglicised native whom earlier ideologues like Macaulay had tried to create—the figure who was "Indian in blood, but English in tastes, in opinions, in morals and in intellect" ("Minute"). Indians and English were considered as separated by an unbridgeable gulf, and it was deemed neither practicable nor admissible to transform the colonised subject into the colonisers' self-image. In fact, any colonised subject who sought to extract himself from the "traditional" basis of his society was considered not an exemplar but merely a deracinated pretender.[11]

While in Oxford, Sorabji regularly attended the lectures of Sir Alfred C. Lyall (Richard Sorabji 122), one of the chief architects of the late imperialist ideology, and soon internalised this discourse of "protection" and "preservation". She came to support wholeheartedly the desire to conserve rather than modernise the "traditional" Indian society and shared the reluctance to see Indians transform themselves into English. Sorabji made evident her newly found ideological conviction in an article written for the journal *The Nineteenth Century* while she was still at Oxford. This piece was written in the wake of the enactment of the 1891 legislation that raised the age of consent for Indian girls from 10 to 12 years. This Age of Consent Act was one of the late attempts by the colonial authority to demonstrate the need for a civilising mission in India that would intervene to reform "barbarous" practices within the native society (Sinha 102). In her article, Sorabji strongly opposes such intervention. Faithfully reproducing the late imperial rhetoric of "preservation", she contests the mission to reform "traditional" customs in accordance with English standards of morality. Indeed, she undermines the whole concept of the in-between space (as represented by Macaulay's Indian men with English tastes, opinions, morals, etc.) that the reform-minded ideologues of the Empire wanted to open up through their intervention, by arguing that "you might as well start a mission to clothe the children of tropical regions in *furs*, because *English* children suffer from the severity of a northern winter" (151, emphasis in original). According to Sorabji, "every nation has an individuality of its own" (153), and she reminds the English that by imposing their own distinctive qualities onto the Indians what they had produced in the past is not an improved species of individuals but merely "faded and monotonous cop[ies] of themselves" (153).

This trenchant criticism shows that unlike some of her patrons, Sorabji did not consider herself as a woman pioneer who occupied the interstitial space between the Indians, bound to their antiquated traditions, and the English, representing the pinnacle of civilisational progress. But how then did she conceptualise her identity vis-à-vis Indians in general and Indian women in particular? The answer, I believe, can be teased out from the following passage in the above-mentioned article:

> Let us remember that India is the home of old traditions and long-founded beliefs, and we cannot ruthlessly raze ancient structure to its foundations. This is what many well-meaning reformers would do. They would demolish with one blow the whole system of female treatment in India. They would fling open the doors of the zenanas and let out the prisoners into the blinding brilliance of too rapid and ill-based reforms.
>
> (153)

It is important to note here the way Sorabji connects the "whole system of female treatment in India" with the idea of "imprisoning" women so as to conflate the "prisoners" of the zenana, i.e. *purdahnashins*, with the idea of Indian women as a whole. This allows her to articulate an image of Indian womanhood rooted in the "old traditions and long-founded beliefs" of India to which she, as the daughter of parents who had renounced their ancestral faith and converted to Christianity, as a girl who had been "brought up English", and as a student who had travelled from India to be educated in Oxford, clearly does not belong. In fact, Sorabji's paternalistic concern for hurriedly transforming the condition of "Indian woman" suggests that in the article she assumes the position of an English imperialist who is benevolently disposed towards the old customs of India and who intends to protect the time-honoured "tradition" that defines the Indian woman's location within zenana. Thus, in this article, Sorabji's position with regard to her countrywomen becomes articulated in terms of the same Manichean division between the coloniser and the colonised subject that underlined the ideology of late-nineteenth-century British imperialism.

However, assuming the position of a patronising English imperialist while speaking of the "traditional" Indian woman posed one serious difficulty for Sorabji. To the Western readers, towards whom the above article and indeed all of Sorabji's writings were directed, her accounts of Indian women were valid only when articulated from the position of a native informant. As Lady Hariot Dufferin noted in her introduction to Sorabji's first book, *Love and Life behind the Purdah*, her writings were expected to

> exhibit to us from the inside, as it were, customs and ways of living and of thinking which we usually contemplate from the outside only, and which we are apt to consider and appraise through the mists of our own European prejudices.
>
> (7)

Indeed, speaking as an "Indian" was the only authorial position available to Sorabji from within which she could possibly communicate with the metropolis. This resulted in a contradiction that is central to all of Sorabji's writings on *purdahnashins*. In them she articulates her views on "traditional" India and the lives led inside its secluded zenanas from the position of a conservative English imperialist. Yet, at the same time, she tries to occupy the position of an "Indian" author to partake the sense of authority that could only be gained by her in the metropolis by playing the role of an insider. This explains why, in spite of defining Indian women as traditional *purdahnashins*, Sorabji paradoxically ends the above article in *The Nineteenth Century* by claiming that the opinions she expresses are those of "an Indian girl, who has her country's good at heart" (154). This ambiguous authorial position of "an Indian girl" was sustained by Sorabji throughout her writing career and even prominently flaunted in such book titles like *Between the Twilights: Being Studies of Indian Women by One of Themselves*. But in each of these texts portraying "Indian woman", there can be witnessed a desire to distance the English authorial self from the subject that is being represented. The section in her autobiography, which deals with her journey back from Oxford after the completion of studies, and her life in India as a legal advisor working for *purdahnashins* mostly on behalf of the Court of Wards,[12] perfectly brings out the various textual strategies through which Sorabji tried to achieve this distance even while ostensibly writing as "an Indian girl".

Othering the "Indian woman"

The tales of the *purdahnashins*, which in a way constitute the heart of Sorabji's autobiography, are part of a vast profusion of such stories that Sorabji narrated across many decades and numerous volumes. These tales, as Sorabji explains in an introduction to one of her books, were much in demand in the metropolis: "I am always being asked in England alike by friend and chance-met stranger, how Indian secluded women live, what makes their lives, what ... is the status and position of such women in the body corporate" (*India Recalled* vii–viii). Such enthusiasm in the metropolis to learn about the secluded Indian women was due to the fact that by the nineteenth century, the zenana had come to represent for the English the quintessential site of true Indianness. As Sara Suleri writes, it was believed that only after penetrating the zenana could one "claim to 'know' India" (93). This process of "knowing" and representing the zenana was part of a colonial discourse that had as its "predominant strategic function ... the creation of a space for a 'subject peoples' through the production of knowledges in terms of which surveillance is exercised and a complex form of pleasure/unpleasure is incited" (Bhabha 70). In other words, to "know" the zenana fitted into the larger colonial project of constructing the image of Europe's "other", both as an object of learning and codification that allowed surveillance and as an object of desire and fantasy that elicited complex forms of pleasure and unpleasure.

During the course of the nineteenth century, the discourse of anthropology[13] gradually came to define this project of othering the Indians through the dual process of codification and exoticisation. By the early nineteenth century, men like Francis Buchanan and Colin Mackenzie had already initiated the process of travelling through India, observing the "subject peoples", and "scientifically" classifying them (Metcalf 114–116). After the revolt of 1857, when the colonisers' confidence about "knowing" the natives had been badly shaken, these early initiatives developed into an extensive and organised project to ethnographically chart the subject population onto a grid of static and singular identities so as to transform them into "things" that can be comprehensively understood and authoritatively ruled. These "things" of administrative surveillance were also equally objects of fantasy. Exactly how vague the separating line was between "scientific" enquiry and the quest for the exotic is gathered from the fact that Watson and Kaye's *The People of India*, which was originally commissioned as a quaint picture book that the viceroy Lord Canning and his wife could take back home as an Indian souvenir, was ultimately published as the most important nineteenth-century document of "official ethnography" on India (Cohn 29).

In the section of her autobiography dealing with *purdahnashins*, Sorabji carefully attunes her language to the rhetoric of otherness of colonial anthropology so as to confirm her position as an outsider in India and to distance herself from the world of the zenana that she represents.[14] Sorabji stresses her role as an anthropologist by confessing that "the delight of contact with the Indian *Purdahnashin*" was primarily due to the opportunities of ethnographic research that the zenana provided her with. Indeed, when she speaks of "the joy one had in the work itself" (132), she does not refer to the openings it presented to her as a lawyer. What she refers to is rather the opportunity it provided her for "studying the real people of India in their setting" (132). She made full use of this latter opportunity by observing the various ceremonies and rituals of the zenanas that she visited ("I was interested in all old ceremonies; and my Zenanas were kind enough to secure that the auspicious days for these should coincide with my ability to attend" 141), and by "collect[ing] the specimens" (146) of everything that "play[ed] a vital part in the life of the orthodox" (146). The zenana, thus, emerges in the autobiography as an anthropological "field" which Sorabji inhabits as an outside observer to learn "about manners and customs at close quarters" (53).

One of the most important ways in which Sorabji maintains the distinction between herself as the outside observer and the *purdahnashin* as her object of study situated within an anthropological field is through her use of what Arjun Appadurai has identified as the "language of incarceration" (37). According to Appadurai, the depiction of "natives" as being incarcerated within a particular space is a classic strategy that Western anthropologists use to freeze non-Western societies as their objects of "knowing", while portraying themselves as observers who are quintessentially mobile (37). This is precisely the strategy that is at play in Sorabji's depiction of the zenana as a jail that encloses a self-contained space untouched by the larger world beyond:

> Their [*purdahnashins'*] quarters were apart, with a courtyard attached into which they seldom entered. The outer walls were sometimes spiked like the walls of any gaol: and at the foot of the stairs an armed guard stood, back to the "Inside", facing the door which led to the outer courts. From this sanctuary they went not forth, except on pilgrimage, or ... to visit their father's house.
> (54)

In sharp contrast to the incarcerated *purdahnashins*, Sorabji presents herself not only as mobile but even excessively so. She records in a footnote that just during the year 1919, she had travelled 26,313 miles (133n). However, as a distancing strategy, what plays a more important role than this accurate quantification of her mobility is the way Sorabji describes her travels, transforming them into perilous expeditions across a strange territory that are undertaken to claim its people as objects of colonial knowledge. She speaks of setting off from Oxford with the mindset of "an explorer" (46) and then travelling through "unsophisticated water-routes" (163) infested with crocodiles and stretches of jungles that "seemed altogether unreal" (163) to arrive at a land that resembles the setting "of the Arabian Nights" (53). This India has at its core not Sorabji's own home but rather the exotic space of the heavily guarded zenana. Hence, by moving away from the metropolis in the direction of the zenana that holds the "real people of India", Sorabji does not arrive among her fellow countrywomen. Rather, she moves from the thoroughly known space of England to an unfamiliar and fantastic land that needs to be anthropologically coded.

Adopting the role of the colonial anthropologist enables Sorabji to distance herself from the exotic world of the *purdahnashin* not only spatially but also temporally. In *India Calling*, the zenana is thus typically presented as a world that is out of sync with the present time. The secluded *purdahnashin* who inhabits this world observes "ancient customs" (134) and "old ceremonies" (134) and is "bound to ... conditions and prejudices as old as Time" (153). Even when she tries to kill Sorabji, she does so by using her "mediæval knowledge" (66) of poisons, and by applying a method that was apparently used in seventeenth-century Europe by Catherine de Medici to murder her victims. The very fact that Sorabji identifies these customs, ceremonies, and practices as archaic suggests that she locates herself within a time frame that is distinctly separate. In this, Sorabji follows yet another anthropological convention where the anthropologist is aligned to a present that is geographically mapped on to the metropolis, and the native society represented by the Indian zenana is made to stand for a past whose temporal distance from the present is directly proportional to its spatial distance from the metropolis. According to Johannes Fabian, this geographical plotting of time, which he sees in operation throughout the history of anthropology as a discipline, "is made for the purpose of distancing those who are observed from the Time of the observer" (25) and thereby results in a "denial of coevalness" (31). In her autobiography, Sorabji similarly resists "coevalness" by consigning the zenana to the past and by refusing to accept the *purdahnashin* as her contemporary.

Another way in which the distance between herself and the *purdahnashin* is consolidated by Sorabji in her autobiography is through an ingenious utilisation of "gaze". Whereas Sorabji uses her anthropologist's gaze to defamiliarise her native country and her fellow countrywomen, she also uses the reciprocal gaze of the people whom she fixes as her objects of study to serve the same purpose. Indeed, the fact that Sorabji was herself an object of reciprocal surveillance is intimately coupled with her description of how she surveyed the zenanas. This is best evident in her depiction of her "first Bihar case related to a quarrel in three generations" (107). Sorabji had travelled to this estate in Bihar (which she refers to as "Raj") on behalf of the Court of Wards to make peace among the three generations of *purdahnashins* of the royal household. On her arrival, she realised that "[t]he countryside had never seen an official like me" (108). She was also quick to realise that the curiosity she aroused could be an aid to her work. Her assumption was proven right when on "[t]he very first day of my visit, the collateral representatives of the Raj and other leading men turned up to ask for interviews" (108). This results in a parody of the interviewer–interviewee relationship that underpins anthropological discourse, because, in this case, those who are supposed to be the objects of study are the ones who eagerly seek the interview so as to scrutinise the outsider. The scrutiny, however, does not stop with these initial interviews but continues more surreptitiously throughout Sorabji's stay in the estate. She writes, "I had not known that every action of mine was spied upon through the skylights in the roof of the Guest-house, the Rani's women being stationed there for the purpose" (110). Put under such surveillance, Sorabji's role as an anthropologist who pries open the secret of the private space of the zenana and fixes it as the object of her learning is inverted. The dynamics of seeing and being seen is reversed and this reversal produces a curious effect:

> One day they [the Rani's women] saw me using a pit of pumice-stone. The next day the Rani professed herself agreeable to Peace Making; her waiting-women had told my *ayah* that the Rani had said she would do anything that I wished, because I was a worker of magic!
>
> (110)

Here, the reciprocal gaze that is directed at Sorabji transforms her into an exotic object in much the same way as her own gaze exoticises the *purdahnashin*. By recording this process through which she is herself exoticised, Sorabji makes it clear that if to her, the *purdahnashin* is the denizen of a different world located in a different time, then, for the *purdahnashin*, she too is as strange a creature.

As a narrative strategy, this interweaving of the two very different kinds of gaze helps Sorabji to redefine her authorial position vis-à-vis her readers' expectations. As stated earlier, for the metropolitan readers, Sorabji was supposed to be a native informant who was herself part of the exotic and unfamiliar spectacle of India that she represents. In her autobiography, Sorabji partly fulfils this metropolitan expectation by making herself appear through the eyes of her *purdahnashin* clients as strange and exotic as the India and the Indians she depicts. But at the same time, she also undercuts this expectation by portraying her strangeness from a reference point that is diametrically opposite to the point of reference from which "the real people of India" (132) are exoticised. Indeed, the *purdahnashins* of her autobiography, by identifying Sorabji as an utter stranger to their world, who cannot be comprehended except as "mad or a *puja-in* (a religious)" (117), endorse her position as an outsider. Being perceived as an exotic object by those who are "truly" exotic from the metropolitan perspective confirms Sorabji's location within the domain of English normativity. It enables her to become identified with her English readers and "to share a wink" (148) with them as she passes "through every thrilling Zenana experience" (148).

One of the zenana stories in the autobiography in particular brings out the effectiveness of this strategy in identifying Sorabji as English without the authorial voice explicitly stating it so. Early in her career, Sorabji was involved in a case where the *purdahnashin* was a dowager Rani whose circumstances had forced her to live the life of a prisoner within a fortress. While describing the daring rescue operation that she had to plan and execute to save the Rani, Sorabji writes how her exploits aroused a great sense of wonder among the palanquin-bearers who were assisting her in the rescue. According to Sorabji, these palanquin-bearers, like the *purdahnashins* of her previously mentioned stories, were intrigued by who she was (88). They found that the best way they could explain to themselves the unusual figure of Sorabji was by comparing her to the Viceroy—a person who was even more strange and distant to them than the "worker of magic" or the *pujain*. Thus, as Sorabji records in her autobiography, in a song that the palanquin-bearers made while carrying the Rani and the rescue party to safety, she was declared to be the equal of the "Burra Lat Sahib" or the British Viceroy in India, who could miraculously make everyone around pliant to her authority: "She spoke like the *Burra Lat Sahib* (Viceroy) to the guard, turning the men in, shutting the gates on them. *And they obeyed*" (88, emphasis in original).

Gandhian nationalism and the image of Indian womanhood

What complicated Sorabji's English self-fashioning both in her real life and in her autobiographical representation of it was the advent of a mass-based anticolonial nationalist movement in India at the beginning of the twentieth century. As the above discussion has made clear, Sorabji's attempt to identify herself as English was heavily predicated on her authority to construct an image of Indian womanhood that would make her own distance from it obvious—so obvious, in fact, that she would not be mistaken as part of that Indian womanhood even when she articulates her views on it in the guise of an "Indian girl". This she achieved by fixing the identity of the *purdahnashin* as static and eternally frozen, and by presenting it as the "real" image of Indian women. The nationalist movement undermined this equation by bringing forward a very different image. By the late nineteenth and early twentieth centuries, "Indian woman" had become a crucial part of the Indian nationalist iconography and India was extensively imagined as a mother who needs to be liberated from the British rule.[15] Sorabji's attempt to present through the *purdahnashin* a fossilised image of the Indian woman, secluded from the outside world and detached from the flow of history, was thus in direct conflict with this nationalist attempt to evoke the image of an Indian woman as a powerful ideological motivation for bringing about political change. In her autobiography, Sorabji tries to minimise this conflict by emptying out the section that narrates her engagement with *purdahnashins* of all references to the ongoing Indian nationalist movement and by relegating discussion of the contemporary political scenario to a single chapter in the last part of the text. However, in spite of being so thoroughly truncated, the moment the context of the anticolonial nationalist movement enters the autobiographical narrative, it subverts most of the assumptions that underpin Sorabji's anthropological rhetoric of the previous section and calls into question her position and authority as an outside observer. Firstly, it destabilises the notion of a homogenous, fixed, and eternally frozen India. What constitutes "true" India and who are the "real people of India" become impossible to ascertain within the melee of the anticolonial movement, which, as far as Sorabji was concerned, "was a war by Indians upon, for the most part, the poorest of Indians" (185). What further enhances the confusion is the international character of the nationalist movement. Sorabji admits that

> ever since 1907 there have been underground forces at work—inspiration coming from outside India—from Berlin first, and since the end of the [First World] War from Soviet Russia. The movement is identifiable with the terrorism and communism which is sweeping the whole world.
>
> (194)

The picture of India that emerges here is fundamentally different from the image of an exotic land which lies with its "mysterious forests" and "unsophisticated water-routes" somewhere in the back of the beyond of the British Empire. Not only is this India spatially connected with other parts of the world like Berlin and Moscow through a steady traffic of political ideas, but it is also temporally connected with the simultaneous revolutions "sweeping the whole world". The "coevalness" that is denied by Sorabji's anthropological discourse is thus found unsustainable when placed within this historical backdrop of the contemporary political situation.

The context of anticolonial nationalism also shatters the myth of seclusion that Sorabji weaves around the zenana to fix it as an anthropological "field". Sorabji states that the nationalists "approached the Zenana directly" (189) to raise funds for their movements, and then proceeds to relate a "particularly glaring" (189) instance of such an activity. Sorabji writes that a certain number of widows, who were apparently on their way to a pilgrimage, were accommodated by the Rani of one of the estates that was being managed by her on behalf of the Court of Wards. These widows approached the Rani in her zenana, and after discussing various other things finally broached the topic of Swadeshi and demanded money for the cause. When the Rani proved unwilling to pay, they shed their widow's garbs and revealed themselves to be men in disguise. They threatened the Rani that they would proclaim to the world that her "purdah has been broken" (191) and then by forcing her to give the keys to her safe made away with all the money. This story, which Sorabji tells as a searing criticism of Swadeshi extortion, also ends up inadvertently suggesting that zenanas were already penetrated by the outside world of anticolonial politics by the early twentieth century. Hence, Sorabji's portrayal of the zenana in her autobiography written in the mid-1930s as a space that is hermetically sealed and detached from the outside world is questionable at the very least.

What the above story consciously elides is, however, even more interesting than what it inadvertently reveals. Following a footnote attached to this story, the reader is led to "other tales relating to the Zenana in this connection" (191n) that were published in the year before *India Calling* came out. These tales, which mainly concern the activities of a Bengali woman revolutionary, speak of how this woman political activist travelled all over India lecturing about the nationalist cause to *purdahnashins*. She apparently divided her audience into two categories:

> I had two lists of names. One list was of those entirely with us; to those persons I spoke openly. The other list was of those to whom we could not speak openly, but who could be asked for money to forward *Swadeshi* or Indian home-industries.
>
> (*An Indian Portia* 547)

This account, which Sorabji chose to omit from her autobiography, reveals, firstly, that those who intruded into the zenana were not always men, and secondly, that the money that was collected from *purdahnashins* was not always extorted out of them but was often given voluntarily.

The marginalisation of these "other tales" in Sorabji's autobiography hints at an anxiety regarding the active and willing participation of Indian women in the nationalist movement. This is fleetingly laid bare in *India Calling* through a brief and deprecating reference that Sorabji makes to the women picketers who played a prominent role in the anticolonial movement led by Gandhi[16]: "that women should lie flat in the mud in public streets, should scratch the faces of Indian tradesmen, set fire to their shops; should picket liquor shops and bandy words with the intoxicated—all this was against tradition" (187–188). As individuals who literally thrust their bodies into the public sphere of nationalist politics, these picketers present an image of Indian womanhood that is clearly inconsistent with Sorabji's idea of Indian women as incarcerated *purdahnashins* who are closeted within the private spheres of their individual zenanas and who consider getting out into the public to be as unthinkable as "run[ning] down the street in your skin" (54). By not being "traditional", these picketers do not fit into the role of Sorabji's veiled and secluded Indian "other". Rather they emerge as Sorabji's articulate equals in the public sphere. As a result, they erase the distance that Sorabji seeks to maintain in her narrative between herself and an ossified image of Indian womanhood.

In fact, by the time Sorabji came to write her autobiography, this distance was actually rendered even more tenuous by the movement to enfranchise women in India, which, though it was not exactly coterminous with the nationalist movement, had as its leaders women like Saraladevi Chaudhurani and Sarojini Naidu who were also dedicated Congress workers. By the second decade of the twentieth century, a concerted effort was launched to officially bring the women of India within the ambit of active politics by securing for them voting rights. By the early 1930s, most of the provinces in India had extended franchise to a section of Indian women and a second round of vigorous campaigning had already been launched by various women's organisations in India to secure universal adult franchise. In these decades, Sorabji had emerged as one of the harshest critics of enfranchising the women of India and had strongly argued that they were as yet unprepared for direct participation in the political process of democracy (Forbes *Women in Modern India* 99). Suparna Gooptu in her biography of Sorabji has suggested that even though she resisted the large-scale enrolment of women within the political process, she actively tried to open up an alternative public sphere for the *purdahnashins* whom she knew (163–178). Indeed, near the end of her autobiography, Sorabji does dwell upon her efforts to involve *purdahnashins* in various social welfare projects outside the zenana (170–173). But in these descriptions, Sorabji also equally dwells on how she meticulously maintained the taboo of seclusion for her *purdahnashin* clients by arranging for them "purdah-ed cars" (171) to go out of their homes, and by reconstructing "the inside" of their zenana in the middle of open courtyards when they went out for "village work" (171) so that "[o]ur village gatherings were held in strict purdah" (172). Hence, in terms of claiming for Indian women a space in the public domain, these efforts were fairly conservative and were marked by the paradoxical attempt to open up the outside world to the secluded women while at the same time reaffirming the rigid boundary of purdah that was intended to keep them away from that outside world.

Those trying to secure enfranchisement for women in India, on the other hand, sought to dismantle far more radically the barrier between the public and the private spheres that kept the Indian women separated from the political domain. To this end, one of their first steps was to put into proper perspective the whole notion of purdah and the seclusion of Indian women. Muthumeenakshi Reddi, the first woman legislator of India, argued that the purdah was an outmoded custom and a sign of the patriarchal oppression of women that needed to be abolished (Forbes *Women in Colonial India* 21);

while Sarojini Naidu explained to the Joint Select Committee responsible for framing the 1919 Government of India Bill that only a few upper-class women actually observed the purdah and were therefore by far a minority section of Indian women (Forbes *Women in Modern India* 98).[17] By the mid-1930s, the advocates of enfranchisement had so successfully redefined the prevalent image of the Indian woman from being a helpless prisoner of the zenana to an active participant in the nation's political process that the British administrators framing the India Bill of 1935 felt compelled to increase the voting strength of women to men to an unprecedented ratio of 1:5.[18] Sorabji, in spite of being deeply involved in the debate of women's enfranchisement in India, completely ignores this history of the past few decades in her autobiography and remains absolutely silent about the ongoing process through which Indian women were being transformed into citizens.

These silences, omissions, and marginalisation which characterise her representation of the contemporary political scenario betray Sorabji's deep-seated uneasiness about the rapidly changing position of Indian women. It suggests a reluctance to acknowledge them as her coevals in the public sphere. Consequently, when the repressed political context is made manifest, Sorabji's depictions of both the Indian woman as the *purdahnashin*, isolated within the "primitive" zenana, and her own self-image as the metropolitan ethnographer of this exotic realm are revealed to be deeply anachronistic and seriously out of touch with the contemporary reality.

Conclusion

The reluctance to accept contemporary reality, evident in Sorabji's inability to come to terms with the changing lives of Indian women, is also apparent in the way she sought to counter the tide of Indian nationalism. In the last decades of her life, Sorabji was engaged in an almost quixotic attempt to prove the "falsity" of the Indian anticolonial movement by trying to reveal Gandhi as a charlatan who only posed to be a leader of the Indian masses but who in effect did not have any significant following. "His truths", as Sorabji wrote in her autobiography, "were built upon deceptions, his loyalties upon verbiage" (193). She even met with Gandhi in 1931 when the latter was in London to attend the Round Table Conference and forced him to admit that he led no more than 30,000 followers, though he claimed to represent the 350,000,000 men and women of India (Richard Sorabji 343–347). Sorabji coupled this anti-Gandhi campaign of hers with extensive tours of America in 1930–1932 as a self-styled defender of the British Raj. There she tried to explain away the anticolonial movement in India as an "absurd propaganda against t[he British] as a nation" (*India Calling* 204) and sought to disabuse her audience by "stating facts" (*India Calling* 205). Her autobiography, published only a couple of years after her American tours, was a similar attempt to "state facts"—an attempt to expose the dark underbelly of the nationalist movement and to place against it the "traditional" space of the unchanging zenana where the "real people of India" actually live.

She was of course fighting a losing battle, and the only effect that such ardent attempts to separate "facts" about India from "fiction" had was to widen even further the gulf that separated Sorabji from contemporary reality. This gulf ultimately pushed her towards insanity, and from 1945 onwards Sorabji's mental derangement was clearly evident (Richard Sorabji 378). She was confined to a mental asylum in London during the last years of her life (Tharu and Lalita 160) where she died in 1954, possibly oblivious to the fact that India had become independent, and the British Raj was no more there. Her conscious efforts to maintain a distance between herself and India meant that after her death she was almost immediately erased from the memory of the people of her native country. On the other hand, her inability to firmly establish her English identity meant that she was also soon forgotten in the metropolis. What has followed this oblivion is an ambiguous resurrection. Ever critical of anglicised Indians whom she considered no more than "faded and monotonous copies" of the English, Sorabji is now ironically regarded as one of their most representative figures. Thus, she now occupies that very same space of in-betweenness, which, paradoxically, she had tried to undermine all her life.

Notes

1 Literally those who sit behind the veil.
2 In this chapter, I will be referring to the version of the text edited by Chandani Lokugé, which was first published in 2001.
3 This is according to Richard Sorabji, the nephew of Cornelia Sorabji and the grandson of Franscina (*Opening Doors* 9).
4 Interestingly, as Chandani Lokugé has pointed out in her introduction to *India Calling*, "although Cornelia was only 'half Parsee' she makes no mention of her maternal lineage" (xiv).
5 In *India Calling*, Sorabji speaks of trying to disabuse a person "only once" and that too not very successfully: "Only once did I try to undeceive a proselytizing old lady. She regarded me reproachfully, 'But you *look* so very heathen!'" (44, emphasis in original).
6 See Burton ("Cornelia Sorabji") and Banerjee. Suparna Gooptu has however argued that Sorabji "was determined to study law since her students days in India" (29) and that the account of always wanting to become a lawyer which she furnishes in *India Calling* is indeed accurate.
7 The belief that each civilisation could be scientifically graded along a "scale of civilization" was a product of the Scottish Enlightenment. It was later adopted by James Mill in his *History of British India*, one of the core texts articulating the principles of British liberal imperialism, to depict India as a country trapped in a low state of civilisational progress (see Metcalf 30–31).
8 For an elaboration of how the "degraded" condition of "Indian women" was used to justify British imperialism in the nineteenth century, see Uma Chakravarti (34–35).

9 Lady Mary Hobhouse along her husband Lord Arthur Hobhouse were leading figures of Britain's National Indian Association to which Sorabji had written for assistance to pursue her studies in England.
10 The concept that Indians belonged to a "traditional" society which, by being structured around kinship bonds, by prioritising community and social custom over individual agency, and by making rigid ritual codes determine every individual action and thought, essentially differed from the modern society of the West was primarily sketched out by Henry Sumner Maine. For a discussion on Maine's "traditional" society and how it influenced the post-1857 shift in the British imperial attitude to India, see Mantena.
11 The most notable instance of such attitude was the British aversion to the Bengali *bhadraloks*. See Metcalf (105–106).
12 The Court of Wards, for which Sorabji worked from 1904 onwards, was set up by the British administration in India to take under direct governmental control the management of the estates of secluded widows and minor children of deceased landed proprietors.
13 I use the term "anthropology" without distinguishing it from ethnography. In this I follow Pels and Salemink who have argued that the distinction between ethnography as a form of knowledge that is tainted by its association with the colonial power structure and academic anthropology as a "pure science" that is devoid of political utility cannot be sustained. On the contrary, they argue, there is a clear continuity between the ethnographic discourse as it developed under colonialism during the nineteenth century and the rhetoric of academic anthropology of the following period.
14 For a discussion on how Sorabji used her role as an ethnographer of the zenana to advance her career within the British administrative system and integrate herself as part of the colonial state, see Burton's "Tourism in the Archives".
15 The various metaphors of motherhood and their use in nationalist discourse have been most extensively studied in the context of colonial Bengal. See, for instance, Tanika Sarkar's "Nationalist Iconography", Jasodhara Bagchi's "Representing Nationalism", Sen's "Motherhood and Mothercraft", and Bose's "Nation as Mother". Charu Gupta's "The Icon of Mother in Late North India" explores the connection of images of mother and nationalism within the context of the United Provinces, and Sumathi Ramaswamy's "En/gendering Language" explores the theme of motherhood in relation to the discourse of Tamil nationalism.
16 For a discussion on Gandhi's use of women picketers, see Bald (89–990).
17 Forbes has, however, pointed out that there was a degree of discrepancy between the feminist rhetoric of "tearing the purdah" and the actual practice of the various women's organisations in India (*Women in Colonial India* 20–22).
18 This was of course a disappointment to those who were trying to secure universal adult franchise, but it was nevertheless a significant improvement over the 1:20 ratio that was initially proposed by the Lothian Committee in their white paper in 1934, which was supported by Sorabji in a letter dated 8 June 1934 written to *The Times* in London (*An Indian Portia* 557–558).

3
THE TRADITION OF NATIONAL AUTOBIOGRAPHIES AND NIRAD CHAUDHURI'S HOMEWARD JOURNEY TO ENGLAND

The key conflict that Sorabji tries and ultimately fails to resolve in *India Calling* is the conflict between her individual identity and the image of India. An attempt to negotiate between these two concepts was, however, not unique to Sorabji's autobiography. In fact, individual identity and the image of India were the two main concerns that dominated the Indian literary scene in general during the first half of the twentieth century (Das 417–418). The literary form in which these two concerns most powerfully came together was the political autobiography. The first half of the twentieth century saw a profusion of such autobiographies being produced by prominent Indian leaders like Surendranath Banerjea, M.R. Jayakar, M.K. Gandhi, Jawaharlal Nehru, and Abul Kalam Azad. In all these narratives written by politicians engaged in the anticolonial struggle, the personal life histories provide the template for inscribing the history of the contemporary nationalist movement and the "growth" of the nation towards freedom. According to Milton Israel, such a juxtaposition of life writing and national history had its precedence in the various nineteenth-century biographies of historical figures ranging from Shivaji to Rammohun Roy, which presented them as nationalist heroes and their lives as exemplary episodes in the national history. These hagiographies, which were part of an early effort to forge a nationalist discourse, soon gave way to the political autobiographies of the twentieth century as the conviction grew that the nationalist leaders themselves "were involved in extraordinary events that needed to be recorded" (Israel 83). These narratives, which I will be referring to as "national autobiographies" (I borrow the term from Philip Holden), were characterised by a fusing together of the project of individual self-fashioning and the political project of fashioning the destiny of the emerging nation.[1] In them, the articulation of the self-identity of the protagonist merges with the fate of the nation as a whole, and even in texts where the "I" of the autobiography and the image of India are not seamlessly joined, they are at least perceived by the authors to be significantly related.[2]

In this chapter, I argue that Nirad C. Chaudhuri is perhaps the last and definitely the most prolific representative of the tradition of national

DOI: 10.4324/9780367809492-3

autobiography. Such an assertion, however, might seem to be somewhat inaccurate given the fact that unlike the other practitioners of this genre, Chaudhuri was never a politician in the strict sense of the term. Yet, Chaudhuri himself claims that he was writing from within a social milieu where nationalist politics were all engrossing and, as he writes, "I could no more help absorbing politics than I could avoid breathing air" (*Autobiography* 332). What is even more important is that Chaudhuri makes extensive use of the tropes that characterise the Indian national autobiographies of the twentieth century throughout his writings making these narratives about his English self-fashioning legitimate examples of that genre. In what follows, I use these life writings of Chaudhuri to explore how they both use and subvert the form of national autobiography by complicating the connection between the authorial self and the image of India in order to create a discursive complement to his anglicised self-identity.

Autobiography as national history

Nirad C. Chaudhuri was born in 1897 in a small town called Kishorganj in East Bengal which is now Bangladesh. After graduating as a student of history from the University of Calcutta, Chaudhuri went on to take up a series of jobs that ranged from being a clerk in the accounting department of the Indian Army to being a staff in the news division of All India Radio in Delhi. His fairly inconspicuous existence till the first five decades of his life, however, took a sharp turn when, a few months before India attained independence, Chaudhuri was seized by the fear that "all our lives lived till yesterday" (*Autobiography* 141) were going to disappear without a trace. These lives were, as Chaudhuri believed, inextricably intertwined with the history of the British Raj. But he was convinced that "no true history of the disappearance of the British Empire in India will *ever* be written" (*Thy Hand* xvi, emphasis in original). Chaudhuri was of the opinion that on the one hand the more recent scholarly histories produced by people who had not lived through that period "are arid, shallow, uninspired, totally devoid of atmosphere, and at times even false" (*Thy Hand* xviii), on the other hand the nationalist versions of the history of British India were nothing more than "lurid myths" with "even their luridness ... made dull by the crudity of style of the writers" (*Thy Hand* xviii). His despair, however, soon gave way to motivation when "in the night of 4–5 May, 1947, an idea suddenly flashed into my mind. Why ..., I asked myself, do you not write the history you have passed through and seen enacted before your eyes [?]" (*Thy Hand* 868). This inspiration to write the true history of British India[3] as he lived through it ultimately gained the concrete form of *Autobiography of an Unknown Indian*,[4] which was published in 1951. This was to be the first in a series of several autobiographies and memoirs that Chaudhuri would go on producing literally till the very end of his life. Thus, in 1987, he published his second volume of English autobiography, *Thy Hand, Great Anarch!*. This was followed in 1994 by a book in Bengali titled *Amar Debottor Shampatti* containing a section telling his "Jiboner Kahini" (literally "The Story of [My] Life"). Finally, in 1999, the year he died, there was published in Bengali yet another autobiography, *Aji Hote Shatobarsho Age* (literally "Hundred Years Ago"), which in turn ended with Chaudhuri stating his desire to write one more account of his life in Bengali. This obsessive fascination with the details of his own life meant that Chaudhuri's literary career was almost entirely given to a single autobiographical project, with each successive writing supplementing and bringing up to date the life history as narrated in the previous one. It was, however, his maiden attempt, *Autobiography of an Unknown Indian*, for which he is primarily remembered today. *Autobiography* brought Chaudhuri to the attention of an international readership, but in his own country it made him one of the most reviled literary figures. The dedicatory lines of this book, published just four years after India attained independence, claimed, "all that was good and living within us was made and shaped by the ... British rule" (v). Unsurprisingly, this earned him among his fellow countrymen the lasting reputation of being a singular oddity, an anomaly, and even a "disease" (Chellappan quoted in Ranasinha 83) whose works are characterised by a "lonely and perverse intent" (Amit Chaudhuri 50). But as Chaudhuri himself notes, the label that has most persistently stuck to him since the publication of his first autobiography is that of being an "anti-Indian" writer (*Thy Hand* 917).

Ironically, this anti-Indian reputation of Chaudhuri sits in marked contrast to the way he conflates the image of India with the articulation of his anglicised self throughout his various life writings. For instance, in the very *Autobiography* which cemented his reputation as a traitorous anglophile, we find Chaudhuri claiming: "I have only to look within myself and contemplate my life to discover India ... I can say without the least suggestion of arrogance: *l'Inde c'est moi*"[5] (517–518, emphasis in original). More than three decades later, while writing his second major autobiographical work, *Thy Hand, Great Anarch!*, he re-emphasises this interweaving of his life story with India and its national history:

> Actually, this book has three elements in it: first, my personal life which I have made the framework of whatever history I wish to offer; second, my thoughts and feelings about the public and historical events through which I have passed; and third, an account of what happened in India in the political and cultural spheres in the period from 1921 to 1964, free from the current myths.
>
> (xiv)

This close intertwining of the personal with the national reveals that Chaudhuri's autobiographies are integrally associated with the tradition of national autobiographies. However, in his writings, Chaudhuri's use of this typical trope of the national autobiography is complicated by his attempt to significantly modify the underlying structure of this genre along which the graph of the personal life is plotted. In the following sections, I show how Chaudhuri achieves this modification by transforming the poles of "home" and "exile" between which the genre of national autobiography conventionally operates to suit the orientation of his English self-fashioning.

National autobiographies and the trajectory of homecoming

Philip Holden in his book on postcolonial life writings notes that "[n]ational autobiographies as a genre ... follow a common structural 'grammar' of a journey, a time in the wilderness of exile, and then a return" (5). The two spatial points between which this circuitous journey of exile and return takes place in such representative Indian national autobiographies as the ones written by Gandhi or Nehru are, of course, England and India. Both Gandhi and Nehru had journeyed to England as students and had spent a substantial part of their formative years there. There are, obviously, differences in the way each of them experienced the colonial metropolis, but in both their autobiographies their stays in England are depicted as marked by false pursuits and extravagant wastefulness. For instance, Gandhi writes how, while in England, he spent lavishly on clothes and "other details that were supposed to go towards the making of an English gentleman" (43), and though he soon realised that he "was pursuing a false ideal" (44), his extravagant "punctiliousness in dress persisted for years" (44). Nehru in his turn speaks of similar prodigality and "a vague kind of Cyrenaicism" (33) informing his life in England. Their return from England to India (via South Africa in the case of Gandhi) is depicted, in contrast, as a journey to a more purposeful life, a life identified with the unfolding of contemporary national history.[6]

Within the broader context of Indian postcolonialism, the spatial dimension that underpins the journey of exile and homecoming in the autobiographies of such pre-eminent national leaders like Gandhi and Nehru evokes deeper resonances. Indeed, the journey that they trace between India and England is in many ways the paradigmatic Indian journey between the native village and the colonial city writ large. Such journeys to the colonial city began in the subcontinent during the nineteenth century when cities in India came to be defined primarily as centres of colonial political economy rather than as important sites of pilgrimage. The new cities, built by the colonisers, were effectively spatial representations of the metropolis in India. London was the archetypal city of the British Empire and colonial cities like Calcutta were, to quote Chaudhuri, the "half-caste offspring of London" (*A Passage* 64). Hence, if for a privileged few the journey from home to exile involved a physical journey to England, for the overwhelming majority this journey took the form of a journey to the city.

Writing about the lure of these comparatively new colonial urban spaces in India, Ashis Nandy in his book *An Ambiguous Journey to the City* states that these Westernised modern spaces wove and continue to weave for the inhabitants of the subcontinent "a dream of total freedom for the individual and the reasoning self" (viii). Nandy continues to say that a journey to the city from the village thus came to signify in India, "a journey from a self buffeted by primordial passions and an authoritarian conscience—the village is seen as the repository of these—to a self identified with fully autonomous ego function" (viii). However, the city, in spite of assuring a "fully autonomous ego", has also been seen in India since at least the nineteenth century as a place of moral and even physical degeneration. Absolute freedom carries with it the fear of absolute depravity, and in this the city is perceived, again like the metropolis, as a space of indulgence in excesses. Gandhi in his *Hind Swaraj* repeatedly juxtaposed the immorality of the Western civilisation with the immorality rampant in the cities from where one contracted the "disease" of Westernised education and of modern technocratic civilisation. This negative connotation of the city as a place of exile, a place where allured by the dreams of autonomy the self becomes atomised and fragmented, has persisted. As Nandy observes, "[f]ew seem to love the city in its own terms in India, even among those who would prefer to lose their identity among its anonymous masses and seem eager to extol that loss" (28). Hence, the journey to the colonial cities within India, like the journey to the metropolis, becomes a journey into the "wilderness of exile". Consequently, it gives rise to the desire of making a return journey home, which, as an antithetical space to the impersonal and anonymous city, gets associated with a utopic village of imagination. A journey to the village is thus a nostalgic return journey from a city of atomised individualism to a pastoral home that is imagined as, to quote Nandy again, a "utopia of an idyllic, integrated, defragmented self" (13), as well as "a prototype of Indian civilization" (29).

The journey of Nirad Chaudhuri's life, narrated in his several autobiographical works, uniquely transforms these trajectories of exile and homecoming that underline the journey from India to England or from the village to the city. Firstly, the direction of Chaudhuri's journey does not trace the familiar pattern of homecoming to India that frames the Indian national autobiographies. Rather, it begins from India and ends on the English shores. Secondly, it also does not trace the Gandhian journey from the city to the village but rather narrates a journey from a very small country town located in the far-flung colonial periphery of East Bengal to the centre of the British Empire. Thirdly, far from being a journey towards "Indian civilization", Chaudhuri's journey is unabashedly motivated by his desire to rescue his English self from the corrupting influence of India and its hoi polloi. However, in spite of this singular curve of Chaudhuri's journey that presents itself as an absolute antithesis to the journeys underlining the national autobiographies, I would argue that his life's trajectory nevertheless conforms to the same pattern of exile and homecoming. I would suggest that this is achieved by Chaudhuri through radically redefining such constructs like "home" and "foreign land" and thereby geographically realigning the poles of home and exile. I trace below the vicissitudes of this unique journey of homecoming to the metropolis which forms one of the central facets not only of Chaudhuri's own peculiar self-fashioning but indeed of the Indian middle-class anglicised self-fashioning in general.

Village homestead and the distinction between living and lodging

To begin with, it is important to note that at a very superficial level, Chaudhuri's autobiographies do present his journey from the village to the city through the trope of the archetypal journey from home to exile. But Chaudhuri then goes on to uniquely problematise this conventional trope by reversing its underlying grammar. However, before I explore this problematisation that Chaudhuri brings about, I would like to discuss the ways in which he presents the more familiar pattern of the journey between a village home and a city of exile in his first major piece of life writing, *Autobiography of an Unknown Indian*. Chaudhuri begins this text with a description of Kishorganj, "the little country town in which [he] was born" (1). However, having identified his birthplace as a "country town" located in East Bengal, Chaudhuri immediately clarifies the statement by declaring that the "place had nothing of the English country town about it" (3). Rather, it was

> only a normal specimen of its class—one among a score of collections of tin-and-mud huts or sheds, comprising courts, offices, schools, shops and residential dwellings, which British administration had raised up in the green and brown spaces of East Bengal.
> (3)

Just 16 years before the publication of *Autobiography*, R.K. Narayan had evoked the image of such a semi-urban settlement, established by the British administrators, when he published his first novel *Swami and Friends*. His fictional town of Malgudi, with the statue of its British founder overlooking it, was to become the most popular small town in Indian English literature. It depicted an ambiguous space between the city and the village where the two spatial polarities, along with the psychological associations they evoked, merged and blended together.[7] Much like its fictional predecessor, Kishorganj too marks an ambiguous space in Chaudhuri's writing where the urban is shown to be precariously located at the edge of the rural while constantly tending to merge and disappear within it:

> Altogether, the town did not mark too hard a blotch on the soft countryside. Besides, the huts were flimsy. They creaked at almost

every wind, and one strong cyclone was enough to obliterate the distinction between country and town.

(*Autobiography* 3–4)

The river that flowed across the country town and gave it its identity also attracted people from villages, and Chaudhuri narrates how "peasant women with earthen pitchers appeared off and on out of the dark jungle, walked into the water and bent over it, filling their gurgling vessels" (5). Yet this physical proximity to the villages and the villagers in Kishorganj did not reduce its "self-consciousness" of being an urban centre and Chaudhuri recalls that even as children, "we had a sense of the city and citizenship in a very specialized form" (40).

This sense of urbanity was reaffirmed with every visit to his ancestral village of Banagram, which, to Chaudhuri as a child, was an absolute contrast to the spirit of city life that characterised Kishorganj. One of the major differences that distinguished the urban life as led in the country town from the life at the ancestral village was the distinct daily routine of the former, which was governed by the disciplinary clock time. Sumit Sarkar explains that the introduction of clocks in colonial Bengal ushered in this sense of a disciplinary time, which "manifested itself primarily in the form of clerical jobs in British-controlled government or mercantile offices" ("Renaissance" 90). This was essentially the urban time of colonial cities, introduced by the government to optimise the labour input in running its bureaucratic machinery.[8] But as Sarkar points out, the disciplinary time also controlled the lives of the urban students enrolled in the new Western educational institutes and "the reasonably successful English-educated religious and social reformers, writers, journalists, lawyers, doctors, teachers, or politicians" (190). Kishorganj, in spite of its physical proximity to the villages, was a subdivisional headquarters of the British administration and was strictly guided by this urban disciplinary time. Interestingly, Chaudhuri remembers the Kishorganj of his childhood being almost entirely bereft of old men. He explains that this was because only those who were pursuing some profession or were employed in the government offices inhabited the country town. Anyone who had retired would normally have gone back to his ancestral village. As a result, the entire parental generation of the author consisted of middle-aged professional men. The children of these men were all school-going kids and they too did not have a great variation in age. This demographic character of the town had a profound impact on its daily life, tuning it to the urban clock time of work and studies: "It was a routine of steady, unremitting and regular work for everybody, all round the year, except during the two yearly vacation" (*Autobiography* 46–47).

In contrast to this urbanised daily routine of hard work, Chaudhuri portrays the ancestral village, which he regularly visited as a child during his vacations, as a place of uninterrupted leisure. As Chaudhuri recalls, in the kind of feudal landowning family to which he belonged, "work" was entirely the domain of "serfs, who gave us domestic service as a matter of hereditary obligation" (*Autobiography* 64). The family members, at least the males, are thus described in *Autobiography* as spending their time lounging in the hut especially decorated to serve the purpose of a retiring room:

> The main hall was occupied for the most part by an immense bed, spread with white sheet and provided with cushions, pillows and bolsters. This was the place for every lazy fellow, and everybody was lazy. There was always a bunch of sprawlers throughout the morning, and the most assiduous were my brother and I.
>
> (65)

Apart from this labour-less existence, which was unperturbed by any regimentation of clock time, there was another thing that distinguished Banagram from Kishorganj. This was the difference in intra-personal relationship that framed life in these two places. In the ancestral village, there was no purely social relationship, and everyone with whom one could socialise belonged to the family. In contrast, the urban life of Kishorganj was completely devoid of such extended family ties, and Chaudhuri explains that what brought the people together was not a common bloodline but a sense of loyalty to the city and the idea of a shared citizenship.

However, in spite of this bond of citizenship that Chaudhuri felt at Kishorganj, he states that an essential part of growing up there was to learn that it was not his home but only a place of temporary residence:

> I hardly remember one single adult who thought of his Kishorganj life as his whole life, who considered it in the light of anything but a sojourn.... In our perception of duration Kishorganj life was ever fleeting present, and the past and the future belonged to the ancestral village.
>
> (55)

Following the grown-ups, the children too had to carefully bear in mind the different answers to the questions: "Where do you lodge?" and "Where do you live?" The distinction was important because the words "lodge" and "live" are connected to two very different Bengali words evoking not only different spatial but also emotional resonances. In Bengali, the act of "living" or being "at home" somewhere is associated with the word *bari*. This is opposed to the Bengali noun *basha*, which is generally translated as "lodge", and conveys, as Chaudhuri puts it, "the suggestion of temporary lodgings" (55). In other words, one never "lives" in a lodge or *basha* but merely uses it as a sojourner. Chaudhuri recollects that in his childhood, he had to diligently learn how to answer the questions about living and lodging separately even when speaking in English: "In our English lessons and attempts at English conversation we replied 'Banagram' when asked 'Where do you *live*' and 'Kishorganj' only when the question was put in the form, 'Where do you *lodge*?'" (56, emphasis in original).

According to Chaudhuri, this consciously cultivated feeling of living away from one's true village home got even more accentuated when he finally moved from the semi-urban space of Kishorganj to the city of Calcutta and stayed there continuously from 1910 to 1942. When he first went there as a student, Chaudhuri writes that he observed the same sense of a missing but ever-present ancestral homestead in the village informing the consciousness of all the resident students who had come to Calcutta from outside. He describes the institution of "messes" or boarding houses where students like him would stay. They were typically *basha* or lodges where one resided only temporarily, but even this temporary residence bore the unmistakable stamp of the more permanent provincial homes of the students. "Thus", Chaudhuri writes, "the messes could be regarded as little colonies in Calcutta of the different districts of East Bengal" (330). They replicated the model of the ancestral houses in the villages inhabited by large extended families where everyone was related through family ties, "and even when a young man was personally a stranger his family was sure to be known to the others by report" (330). Chaudhuri makes it evident that these ties of belonging to common districts in East Bengal were important in order to retain one's provincial identity, which was regarded as one's true identity. It was from these rural provinces that one came to the city, and it was there that one went back. Thus "the shedding of provincialism was considered 'unpatriotic'" (330).

Indeed, as Chaudhuri notes, this provincial identity had to be held on to in spite of the many disparagements which it attracted from the "gentry of Calcutta" (401) who looked upon every Indian coming from provinces outside the city as an absolute country bumpkin. He tells how, depending upon whether one travelled back to his village home via the railway station located in the east or west of the city, the person would be branded either a *bangal* or a *rerho*—both contemptuous adjectives, with the first used to describe people from East Bengal and the second used to describe people who spoke Hindustani and came from places like Bihar and the United Provinces. To the natives of the city, who appeared to young Chaudhuri as "amazingly parochial" (402), "the world beyond the Hoogly river and Mahratta Ditch[9] was a wilderness" (402). However, Chaudhuri, true to the teaching he received in Kishorganj about always regarding the village as the real home, states that he appropriated these abuses of the city gentry and flaunted them as the badge of his identity. Thus, in the Calcutta section of *Autobiography*, Chaudhuri proudly declares that he "was semi-savage when [he] came to Calcutta" (283), and though the city polished off the rough edges, he was successful in retaining the "rustic core" (283). The city, he tells, made him "dependent upon urban sanitation and urban amenities" (283), but it could not reconcile him to the city life. Rather, Calcutta turned him into a loner and developed in him "a violent dislike for crowds" (283). Hence, in spite of staying there for more than three decades, Calcutta, like Kishorganj, never became home to him. Chaudhuri writes that he shared this feeling of homelessness with almost every other sojourner in the city who came there from East Bengal to study and who were perfectly happy to go back to their village homes "the same rough diamonds they had been ... [with] a diploma of some kind to earn a living" (330).

As mentioned earlier, though this journey between Banagram, Kishorganj, and Calcutta gives the impression of conforming to the paradigmatic trajectory in which the village represents the home and the city the wilderness of exile, this impression is problematised by a more careful reading of Chaudhuri's autobiographical works. Thus, one of the first things that a more perceptive reader of *Autobiography* notices, for instance, is that in the sections of the narrative discussed above, Chaudhuri presents himself as part of a larger community. Consequently, the emotions that he describes in these sections as being associated with spaces like the ancestral village or the country town or the city are primarily emotions of this larger community which Chaudhuri mimics in order to fit in. Hence, when he is in Kishorganj, Chaudhuri feels obliged to consider his ancestral village as his home and the country town as a place of exile because he is meticulously coached by the adults who surround him to do so. Similarly, when in Calcutta, Chaudhuri feels obliged to carry the badge of his provincial identity because it was considered to be part of one's duty to remain loyal to one's village roots, and because acquiring a taste for things like "Calcutta speech and Calcutta cuisine were ... most emphatically frowned upon" (330) by his fellow students of the messes. Thus, in the sections of his autobiography quoted above, the association of home and exile with particular spaces is clearly framed as emotions acquired through socialisation. They are emotions that Chaudhuri internalises while learning how to function from within the values and norms of his particular social milieu. However, Chaudhuri in *Autobiography* also describes a world of private emotions and personal associations which deeply complicate the socially sanctioned ideas of home and exile discussed above.

Never at home in India

An attempt to explore this private world of emotions and associations finally brings us to the peculiarities of Chaudhuri's anglicised self-fashioning and his engagement with that imaginary figure of England/Europe which presented itself within the colonial society as a set of prioritised values absorbed by the colonised subjects through their Western education. For Chaudhuri, one of the most influential figures that Western education exposed him to was Henry James Sumner Maine. Maine, who is most well known for his theory of social evolution, argues in his treatise on *Ancient Law* that "the movement of the progressive societies has hitherto been a progress *from Status to Contract*" (165, emphasis in original). Maine explains this evolutionary movement from "status" to "contract" by proposing that the more primitive forms of society are bound together by kinship status, making the extended family the sine qua non of their social unity. The progress towards modernity, on the other hand, is defined as the gradual dissolution of family dependency, which informs the concept of "status", and the growth of individual obligation in its place, which forms the basis of "contract" (163). Thus, according to Maine, in the more modern societies which formed the hallmark of the West, individuals come together voluntarily and are bound not by kinship but by social contract:

> Starting, as from one terminus of history, from a condition of society in which all the relations of Persons are summed up in the relations of Family, we seem to have steadily moved towards a phase of social order in which all these relations arrive from the free agreement of Individuals.
>
> (163)

Though Maine claims that the direction of this social evolution is universal, he argues that the rate of progress has not been the same throughout human societies. He therefore suggests that while "primitive" societies like those in India have remained largely organised around kinship status, "in Western Europe the progress achieved in th[e] direction [of social evolution] has been considerable" (163).

Maine was one of Chaudhuri's lifelong heroes, and the reverence in which he held Maine becomes evident on reading these following lines from *Thy Hand*:

> Had there been more Englishmen of Maine's type at the top in British Indian administration, the history of British rule in India would have been different. It would not have failed to produce all the good it was capable of doing, nor would the Indian Empire of Britain have come to an untimely end.
>
> (671)

One major aspect of Chaudhuri's anglicised self-fashioning constituted of his internalising Maine's prioritisation of the individual as citizen whose social position is determined by his freely agreeing to enter into a social contract, over the individual whose social position is determined by his placement within a web of family relations. This led Chaudhuri to attach himself with Banagram, Kishorganj, and Calcutta in ways very different from what he was otherwise socially conditioned to do. For instance, if family ties made it socially imperative that he regard Banagram as his true home, then it was precisely these family ties that made it difficult for him to be completely at home in Banagram where no social interaction was possible outside the kinship group. Thus, the idyllic picture of Chaudhuri, lazily sprawling in an immense bed in Banagram, cushioned by pillows and bolsters and away from the regimentation of the urban clock time of Kishorganj, is undermined in *Autobiography* by the picture of Banagram as "the empty shell of the past" (84). To understand the full implication of the latter comparison, we need to turn to Chaudhuri's essay "The Joint Family", which was published as part of his 1971 anthology *To Live or Not to Live*. In this essay, Chaudhuri argues, à la Maine, that the "joint" or "primitive patriarchal family" (89),[10] which for him was only a "smaller and more closely knit replica of the village community" (89), was an extension of the tribal existence of the past where one's status and identity were determined by one's position within a network of blood-ties. According to Chaudhuri, such a kinship structure does not foster, and indeed actively destroys, "individuality and the spirit of self help" (90). He perceives both the village community and the joint family through which one belongs to that community[11] as anachronistic in modern times. This suggests that for Chaudhuri, considering his ancestral village as his home was buffeted by the fear of a retrogression to a more primitive state of being—a fall from "contract" to "status".

If Maine's influence made Banagram "unhomely" for Chaudhuri, the same influence made him regard Kishorganj, the place in which he was explicitly taught to be in exile, as the place where he belonged. Chaudhuri states in his *Autobiography* that each time he returned to Kishorganj after his trips to the village, "we felt as if we had come back to our native element" (40). This was because Kishorganj was completely devoid of the despised ties of the extended kinship network. As noted above, the bond in Kishorganj was the bond of being fellow citizens of a shared urban space, brought together by a "cohesive power belonging to the town in the abstract and exerting its influence on everybody who came to live in it" (40–41). Thus, for Chaudhuri, the existence in Kishorganj was "social as distinct from tribal" (40), and within the scheme borrowed from Maine, this meant being closer to the ideal of human progress that has been perfected in the West in general and England in particular. Hence, Chaudhuri proudly asserts that while living in Kishorganj, he felt himself to be a "citizen" who was bound to the community by the kind of feeling "which lay at the root of the Greek loyalty to the *polis*" (41).[12]

The same kind of home and exile ambivalence, which problematises Chaudhuri's sense of belonging to both Banagram and Kishorganj, also complicates his stay in Calcutta. As noted above, the colonial city of Calcutta is described by Chaudhuri as the place where he felt the most exiled, but it was also the place where he chose to stay the whole of his adolescence and his youth as well as a considerable part of his middle age. Thus, in each of the three places, Banagram, Kishorganj, and Calcutta, the idea of exile and home overlapped so problematically that his journeys between these three places were apparently never journeys of homecoming but always journeys from one kind of homelessness to another. Consequently, when Chaudhuri describes in *Autobiography* his permanently leaving Kishorganj in 1910 to go to Calcutta via Banagram, he states that the journey was marked by a peculiar sense of rootlessness. Kishorganj had never been home to Chaudhuri. It had always been the place where he temporarily "lodged", not "lived". But the Banagram towards which he was moving did not seem to be his home either: "Although I was coming to the village of all my known ancestors, where Chaudhuris had lived for no one knew how many hundred years, I felt as if I had left home to trudge forever along a public road" (281). With his coming to Calcutta, the sense of homelessness was complete:

> [O]nce torn up from my natural habitat I became liberated from the habitat altogether; my environment and I began to fall apart; ... It is said that to be once bitten is to be twice shy, I suppose to be once *déraciné* is to be forever on the road.
>
> (285)

Hence, whereas a national autobiography begins and ends with the home in India, in Chaudhuri's autobiographies, all the spaces in India that he inhabits are equally replete with a sense of exile. The desire to return home, which is strongly evoked in each of these spaces, cannot be satisfied by moving into any of them. Interestingly, the journey that Chaudhuri describes as ultimately connecting him with a sense of "home" is his journey to England, and it uniquely reverses the underlying pattern of exile and homecoming that forms the "grammar" of the national autobiography.

England as the imagined pastoral home

Chaudhuri wrote *Autobiography* quite a few years before he was able to visit England. Nevertheless, in its very opening section, there is a whole chapter dedicated to that country. Chaudhuri explains this inclusion by stating, "England, evoked by imagination and enjoyed emotionally, has been as great an influence on me as any of the ... places sensibly experienced" (1). The most obvious physical way in which England was encountered in such administrative centres as Kishorganj was through meeting the local British officials. Yet such encounters were seldom pleasant, and Chaudhuri tells that "the normal reaction of the unsophisticated Indian villager in the face of an Englishman is headlong flight" (128). The fear of such representatives of England was even greater among children who were brought up on various bizarre stories about the idiosyncrasies of the English. Chaudhuri recalls how, when young, he and his brothers jumped into a roadside ditch on sighting an Englishman not so much to protect themselves as to protect the bananas they were carrying, for they were made to believe "that Englishmen were as fond of bananas as any monkey could be and that they swooped on the fruit wherever and whenever they saw it" (128). However, Chaudhuri encountered England in a different, more benevolent, and more enchanting way inside his parental home. The names of Queen Victoria and Prince Albert were familiar to him from his early childhood and the imperialist propaganda following the Diamond Jubilee celebration of Queen Victoria had ensured that they were represented throughout the empire as "the paragon of every virtue" (111). English heroism was made incarnate for Chaudhuri by such Boer war veterans like General Roberts and General Kitchener who were not merely familiar names but also known faces from the two "panoramic pictures of the Boer war" (29), which hung in one of the huts of their Kishorganj house. Another object that evoked a reverential image of England and its civilisational attainments was the collection of English books that was proudly exhibited in a glass-fronted cupboard decorated with China vases, flowers, and various other knick-knacks. The volumes in the collection ranged from Charles Annandale's *English Dictionary* to the works of Shakespeare and Milton. All these familiar names, pictures, and books created the impression in young Chaudhuri of an England which in spite of its distance was as ever-present as the sky itself "without, however, the sky's frightening attitude of vast and eternal silence, for it was always speaking to us in a friendly language in the knowledge of which we were improving day by day" (109).[13]

This imagined England, stretching above the head like the sky, not only spoke the language of "improvement" to Chaudhuri but also provided him with a sense of security and order. As a son of a *muktear*, or a lawyer dealing in criminal cases, the world that lay around Chaudhuri was "a world of murder, assault, robbery, arson, rape, abduction" (51). A sense of order and justice was maintained in such a violent world of crimes by a faith in religion and inherent moral values. But Chaudhuri states in *Autobiography* that even more crucial than these was apparently the faith in British imperial authority:

> Overhead there appeared to be, coinciding with the sky, an immutable sphere of justice and order, brooding sleeplessly over what was happening below, and sweeping down on it when certain limits were passed. Its arm seemed to be long and all-powerful, and it passed by different names among us. The common people called it the Company, others Queen Victoria, and the educated the Government.
>
> (52)

Interestingly, however, this sense of an all-powerful British Empire did not evoke for Chaudhuri the corresponding image of the city of London as the great imperial metropolis. In fact, the visual image that accompanied his conceptualisation of England was not urban at all but almost wholly rural, and these pastoral images were supplied by English literature. Chaudhuri mentions that Mary Mitford's *Our Village* was one of his favourite reads as a boy. This popular children's book, first published periodically between the 1820s and 1830s, vividly describes the rural life of a village in a home county, and begins with the assertion, "Of all situation for a constant residence, that which appears to me most delightful is a little village far in the country" (3). Such evocations of the image of a village as home exerted a strong pull on Chaudhuri as a young man and presented, in contrast to his ancestral home at Banagram, a redemptive vision of rural dwelling.

This redemptive pastoral space that was located in the England of imagination was even more powerfully visualised through the aid of another of his favourite childhood books, *Palgrave's Children's Treasury*, which introduced him to the world of English poetry. As Chaudhuri writes in *Autobiography*, Ariel's song "Full fathom five" from Shakespeare's *The Tempest*, coupled with Webster's "Call for the robin-redbreast and the wren" and poems like Wordsworth's "Lucy Gray" and "Daffodils", "set our imagination bestirring" (126).

> What a magic country it was where the drowned were transformed into pearl and coral and where the robin and the wren covered the friendless bodies of unburied men with leaves and flowers, and the ant, the fieldmouse and the mole reared hillocks over them. Reading these lines of Webster, our hearts warmed up with a faith that could be described as the inverse of Rupert Brooke's. He was happy in the conviction that if he died in a distant land some part of that foreign soil would become for ever England. We had the feeling that if we died in England what would become for ever England would be a little foreign flesh, and with that faith there was happiness in perishing in an English glade, with the robin and the wren twittering overhead.
>
> (126–127)

These lines, packed with literary allusions, can be easily regarded as sheer exhibitionism on the part of an anglicised Indian who was writing his autobiography to impress a metropolitan audience. It can also be regarded, following one critic, as "[a]bject colonial self-obliteration ... exaggerated to the point of parody" (Sabin 38). Yet, none of these critical judgements quite explain why the pastoral image evoked by British poetry would cast such a spell on a boy from a small country town in the backwater of the British Empire so as to make him dream of dying in the English glades. The reason is, however, explained if this pastoral space is read as an anxiety-free rural haven, that is familiar like the ancestral village yet free from the fear of regressing into a rustic backwardness, which was associated with Banagram. This bucolic vision is located at the heart of England from where was spoken the "friendly language in the knowledge of which we were improving day by day" (109), and in Maine's scheme of evolution, it represented the most progressive of human societies. This English countryside of the literature thus became, for Chaudhuri, the village of nostalgia to which it was possible to "return" without the fear of losing either individuality or affiliation to the ideal of human progress as represented by the West.

This juxtaposition of rural England with the idea of home is further emphasised in *Thy Hand*. In this second autobiography, Chaudhuri tells of a moment of epiphany when the known landscape of rural East Bengal—the landscape of his "home"—gets magically transformed into the landscape of the English countryside. However, this time the catalyst is not poetry but the paintings of John Constable. The moment of epiphany, which, as Chaudhuri states, occurred in 1927 during his very last stay in Kishorganj, apparently proved to be so significant a turning point that he describes it as "an experience which I can regard as 'conversion' in the religious sense" (210). Chaudhuri writes that while strolling at the edge of the town, he suddenly came across a cluster of huts hedged in by bamboo clumps, with a pond before it reflecting the clouds that had taken on the red and pink tint of the setting sun:

> The whole scene was like one of Constable's landscapes, and I can confirm the impression after seeing the Constable country. It came to me in a flash that the Bengali scene too had a particular beauty of its own, very intimate, but not less moving for that. ... [I]t was like enlightenment bestowed in a blessed moment.
>
> (210)

It is significant that Chaudhuri refers to an English painter in relation to the Indian rural landscape not in an attempt to exoticise what is mundane and already familiar. It is also significant that the specific English painter evoked in this passage is John Constable who is more renowned for his depictions of thoroughly familiar rural homesteads like the Willy Lott's cottage in *The Hay Wain* than for exotic scenes of medieval ruins or of wild desolations which were more common in the early nineteenth-century English landscape painting. The reference to Constable, therefore, transforms this Bengali landscape not by making it look foreign, but rather by making it appear even more homely and more intimately known to Chaudhuri. Thus, in this passage too, as in the previously quoted passage referring to Rupert Brooke's poem, there is a juxtaposition of home and the metropolis as the English pastoral landscape is merged with rural East Bengal. The moment of "enlightenment" dissolves the home/exile binary, as the iconic village homestead, which marks the place for return in the conventional journey of exile and homecoming, is perceived not located in the anxiety-laden space of the ancestral village of Banagram but in "Constable country".[14]

Once the poles of home and exile are reversed, the journey too changes direction. Hence for Chaudhuri, a journey to England becomes not a journey into the wilderness of exile but rather a journey of homecoming. What is interesting, however, is that Chaudhuri does not make this journey guided by his intimate subjective realisation alone. His conviction that his anglicised self is indeed the true representative of the Indian self (*"l'Inde c'est moi"*) and his desire to script his life as the life of the nation as a whole makes him search for a more objective basis in the history of India which would justify this reversal of the familiar direction of the homeward journey. Chaudhuri finds this justification in a discourse that had gained prevalence during the nineteenth century—the theory of Aryan migration. A rephrasing of this hotly disputed theory in his autobiographical writings provides Chaudhuri the ideological ground from which to argue that as a putative Aryan, he was racially akin to the Englishmen. Whereas Mary Mitford and Constable had magically transformed Chaudhuri's idea of village home, the Aryan migration theory and its proponent Friedrich Max Müller help him transform himself racially, thereby taking him beyond the ultimate barrier that had kept the identities of the coloniser and the anglicised Indian middle class separate and distinct.

Of mythic ancestors and foreign homelands

When William Jones in the late eighteenth century discovered the similarities between Sanskrit on the one hand and Greek and Latin on the other, there was already a racial element informing the research. Jones, working within an ethnological framework derived from the Bible, regarded the common ground shared by the classical languages of the East and the West as proof that the Europeans and the Indians both had their ancestor in Ham, the son of Noah.[15] However, it was not until the emergence of Friedrich Max Müller during the nineteenth century that this theory of kinship was placed on a more solid philological foundation. By the first half of the nineteenth century, the study of Indian languages by European Orientalists like F.W. Ellis, Alexander D. Campbell, Brian Houghton Hodgson, and John Stevenson had arrived at the consensus that Sanskrit, and the Prakrit languages deriving from it, were not the only linguistic unit in India, but rather there existed another linguistic unit comprising the Dravidian group of languages. The speakers of Dravidian languages were considered to be the original black aborigines of India and the speakers of Sanskrit were taken to comprise the three groups of high-caste Hindus—the Brahmins, the Kshatriyas, and the Vaisyas. It was argued by scholars like Stevenson that the Sanskrit speakers possessing a higher level of civilisation came to India from outside and inhabited the northern planes by pushing the dark Dravidian natives to the South. Those aborigines who stayed back were made into slaves and they formed the caste of Sudras. This two-race theory was, however, soon discredited by Robert Caldwell who in his seminal study *A Comparative Grammar of the Dravidian or South-Indian Family of Languages*, published in 1856, showed that there exists a third linguistic entity in India comprising the Munda languages of Central India and Bengal which have no similarity either with Sanskrit or with the Dravidian group of languages. In effect, this was to argue that the theory of a race of proto-Sanskrit speakers coming from outside and colonising an India that constituted of a homogenous ethno-linguistic group of people was unsustainable. However, Max Müller subscribed to the earlier two-race theory, and grouped all Indian languages under two categories—the Aryan group, constituting Sanskrit and its derivative languages, and Turanian group, constituting all the other languages. His theory of Aryan invasion, based on these two broad divisions of Indian languages, proposed that Aryans, who were a race of fair-complexioned people speaking a proto-Indo-European language that was still not differentiated into Greek and Sanskrit, migrated from their common homeland to two different directions. The group migrating to the north entered Europe while the other group migrating to the south entered India through Iran. There they conquered the dark-skinned Turanian speakers who were made into *dasas* or slaves from whence apparently came the distinction between *arya-varna* and *dasa-varna* in *Rigveda*. The term "*varna*" was interpreted by Max Müller as "colour", which was regarded by him as the physical marker that differentiated the Aryans and the non-Aryans as two segregated social groups with different languages and different religious practices. He extended this same theory to the contemporary period and argued that the English colonisers were Aryans returning to India for a second time to be reunited with their Hindu "brethrens" who had come as colonisers thousands of years ago:

> [I]t is curious to see how the [English] descendants of the same [Aryan] race, to which the first conquerors and masters of India belonged, return[ed] ... to their primordial soil, to accomplish the glorious work of civilization, which had been left unfinished by their Arian brethren.
> (Max Müller quoted in Trautmann 177)

As Romila Thapar observes, Max Müller in proposing this theory of Aryan invasion "used a number of words interchangeably such as Hindu and Indian, or race/nation/people/blood/—words whose meanings would today be carefully differentiated" (6). Yet it was perhaps because of this ambiguity, which allowed one term of reference to effortlessly slip into another, that Max Müller's myth of Aryan invasion had such widespread appeal in India, especially among the Hindus. Tapan Raychaudhuri writes about this in his *Europe Reconsidered*:

> Max Mueller's scholarly theories concerning the common origin of all Indo-Aryan races based on his linguistic studies were received with incredible enthusiasm [in India]. The belief that the white masters were not very distant cousins of their brown Aryan subjects provided a much needed salve to the wound of the dependent elite. A spate of Aryanism was unleashed. The word "Aryan" began to feature in likely as well as unlikely places—from titles of periodicals to the names of street corner shops.
>
> (8)

In his biography of Max Müller, Chaudhuri too refers to this phenomenal popularity that the German Orientalist enjoyed in India in the nineteenth century, and he mentions how, even as a child growing up in East Bengal, he was acquainted with Max Müller's achievements:

> My father ... explained to me how Max Müller had established that our languages and the European languages belonged to the same family ... and that Hindus and the Europeans were both peoples descended from the same original stock.
>
> (*Scholar Extraordinary* 5)

This lesson learnt in childhood that the English coloniser and colonised Hindus had the same blood running through their veins later became pivotal in shaping Chaudhuri's self-identity as well as his relationship with the Indian society and with England. Thus, in 1965, Chaudhuri published a book titled *The Continent of Circe* which centres on Max Müller's thesis that Aryans were foreign colonisers who, like the recently arrived English colonisers belonging to the same race, had come from outside to conquer and rule India. In the book, Chaudhuri relies on this myth to understand the character of the Indian people in general and the Hindus in particular. But, more importantly, he tries to explore his own identity as a modern-day Aryan. This personal aspect is emphasised at the very beginning of the book where the motto "Know Thyself" appears in five languages, all belonging to the Indo-European family. To Max Müller's myth of Aryan invasion, Chaudhuri, however, adds two very unique elaborations of his own—first, a "climatological philosophy" (136), which argues that the climate of India has proved to be thoroughly different from the climatic conditions of the Aryan homeland which was "somewhere between the Danube and the Volga" (48), thereby making the Indian Aryans brown-skinned, and second, the idea that Hindu life to its present day is informed by a subconscious longing for the Aryan homeland which they have had to leave behind. In *Autobiography*, Chaudhuri had described the Indo-Gangetic plain as "the Vampire of geography, which sucks out all creative energy and leaves its victims as listless shadows" (554), and in *The Continent of Circe*, he argues that it was this "vampire" which sucked out the vitality of the invading Aryans, thereby degenerating them mentally and physically. According to him, for the Aryans coming down from the temperate heights of Europe, the heated plains of India offered only unmitigated suffering. Exchanging the word Hindus for Aryans he writes:

> Even after living in the country for thousands of years the Hindus have not got used to the heat. I have never seen a people so mad for ice in the hot season as the inhabitants of the Gangetic plain are. They put up the price of ice in June, even beggars rush for it, and they remind me of polar bears in our zoos.
> (137)

Chaudhuri adds that in spite of this suffering, the Aryans could not return to their putative homeland because they had completely forgotten their original home during the course of their long journey: "coming to India after many wanderings and finding there something like their old plains, they made themselves at home, and indeed so much so that they completely forgot that they ever had another country" (135). With the memories of their homeland almost completely erased, the Aryans were apparently doomed to suffer forever in India, which, like Circe, had invited them with open arms only to trap them in:

> She has taken them in, given them seats, and served food. But with the food she has also mixed the drug which makes them forget their country. Then she has turned them into brute beasts.
> (306)

Chaudhuri claims that even in this land of imprisonment and everlasting sorrow, the Aryans unconsciously held on to some symbols of their pre-Indian existence, and he mentions four such things to which they "have clung with desperate tenacity" (151). Firstly, he mentions the *Vedas*, which, according to him, are the scriptures describing the "original" Aryan life and are therefore among the most precious connections that the Aryans have with the pre-Indian existence. Secondly, he refers to the Hindu fascination with fair complexion, which he attributes to the original Aryan complexion that had initially separated them from the non-Aryan *dasas* in India and helped them retain a distinct identity. Thirdly, Chaudhuri speaks of the sacredness of rivers in the Hindu consciousness, which in its turn he traces back to the nostalgia for the original Aryan homeland situated between the two great European river systems of Danube and Volga. Finally, Chaudhuri mentions the cult of cow worship, which too he connects, with some degree of ingenuity, to the faded memory of the lost Aryan homeland. He argues that the hump-backed cows were brought to India by the Aryans and were not indigenous to this land. Thus, the cows were "as much a part of their Aryan heritage as the Vedas" (172). According to Chaudhuri, this is the reason the scenes of cows returning home in dusk have been immortalised in Indian miniature paintings, and the "Aryan hero Krishna" (175) is depicted as a cowherd. This is also apparently the reason why in the daily routine of a Hindu, there is so much emphasis given to the care for cattle:

> [I]n the cult of cattle the deepest reverence and the most poetic quality were to be found in the daily routine, and that routine of care was at its best in relatively humble homes, for instance, a homestead of thatched cottages with yellow corn ricks, by a sluggish and reedy stream or a large shinning tank, in which ducks swam about, a place in which the sons of the family, home from their hostels in Calcutta could forget not only examinations but also time.
> (176–177)

Though Chaudhuri does not explicitly mention it, the village home portrayed here is clearly a composite image drawn from his childhood memories of Kishorganj and Banagram. In this image, the river of Kishorganj with its reeds and ducks merges with the ancestral home of Banagram where the urban clock time strictly regimenting work and studies gave way to uninterrupted leisure and where "the sons of the family, home from their hostels in Calcutta could forget not only examinations but also time". He goes on to describe the daily routine of caring for the cattle in this village home by vividly depicting a scene of a girl going to put the lamp in the cowshed—a scene that must have been very familiar to Chaudhuri from his childhood days:

> The girl goes in, puts the lamp on a pillar of mud near the pen of the calves …. Then she stands still in reverie, minding neither the reek nor the pungent smell of oilcake.
> The cows on their part stare at her, with their large liquid eyes, … [and] tears of all things appear to gather in those eyes. At last a very faint voice comes borne on the darkness, and if it is piercing that is because of its pain. It says from ever so far away: 'Daughter! Come back to me from your dread Hades. Come back to Europe of the living. Come where you like—to the snow-covered Russia, pine-covered Germany, or corn-covered Sicily. Only come back Persephone, Persephone, Persephone!'
> (178)

This description of a village girl in East Bengal, moved to tears along with her cattle on remembering the Aryan homeland that has apparently been left behind some 3,000 years ago, is a ludicrous flight of fancy, but it is also something more. This image, like the previous quotation describing the village home, reveals the personal subtext to the more impersonal narrative of Aryan invasion as elaborated in *The Continent of Circe*. The village girl in her cattle pen might not have heard the voice calling her back to Europe, but this voice was most definitely heard by Chaudhuri as a child in his Kishorganj home, coming from his *Palgrave's Children's Treasury*, urging him to return to England and assuring him that "there was happiness in perishing in an English glade". The village home where the girl takes her lamp to the cattle pen is thus a site doubly laden with nostalgia. It is not only the place where she listens in her reverie the call to come back to her "real" home in Europe, but it is also the village home that the Calcutta student in his hostel—and Chaudhuri was just such a student—dreams of returning to. Thus, here again, as in the passage on finding Constable country in Kishorganj, the nostalgic urge to return home is juxtaposed with an urge to return to England/Europe. Chaudhuri makes this personal aspect even more evident in the concluding chapter of *The Continent of Circe* where he refers to his own journey to England as an attempt to "return" to the Aryan homeland:

> [T]he memory of some past which I could not bring up to the surface of consciousness lurked within me and kept me struggling, until I remembered one day who and what I was. The notion that we Hindus were Europeans enslaved by a tropical country became a conviction when I paid a short visit of eight weeks to the West in 1955 at the age of fifty-seven.
>
> (*Continent* 307)

With this short visit, which produced the memoir *A Passage to England*, began the process of Chaudhuri's unique homecoming, predicated on a recovery of the lost "Englishness/Europeanness" of his "true" identity:

> I have rescued my European soul from Circe, to whom it was a kind of happiness to be in thrall. I have recovered my Ariel's body from Sycorax, the terrible and malevolent hag who stands behind Circe in India.
>
> (*Continent* 309).

After publishing *The Continent of Circe*, Chaudhuri went to England again to collect the Duff Cooper Prize in 1966. He returned to England yet once more a few years later to research for his biography on Friedrich Max Müller. Finally, when he went there in 1970 to work on a book on

Hinduism, he settled down in Oxford and never returned to India again. But did Chaudhuri's physical journey to England actually lead him to the redemptive pastoral home of his imagination? Chaudhuri's writings on his life in England provide an ambiguous answer. As scholars like John Thieme and Pallavi Rastogi have shown, *A Passage to England* betrays signs of a deep conflict arising from Chaudhuri's inability to perfectly fit the England of his imagination with the post–Second World War England which he physically confronted. We will be looking into this conflict in more detail in the next chapter. Yet, what is important to note here is that in his later writings, produced after he had permanently shifted to Oxford, Chaudhuri never ceases to stress on the fact that his move to England did indeed bring him back to his "home". However, the image of "home" that the reader comes across in these later writings is no more the pastoral England that he had imaginatively constructed while he was in India. The home that he writes about from Oxford is an imagined version of his childhood home in East Bengal. What helps him (re)construct this new idea of the old home is not books of English poetry which he first encountered within the charmed glass-fronted cupboard of his father in Kishorganj, but rather Bengali books that his mother used to read. In his last autobiography, *Aji Hote Shatobarsho Age* (literally "A Hundred Years Ago"), Chaudhuri writes of his mining the Bodleian library in Oxford to retrieve these other books that informed his childhood: "In my childhood days my mother used to have a book—*Helena Kavya* written by Ananda babu. I have found that in the library here" (76). This rediscovery of his Indian childhood in the shelves of Bodleian is coupled with his rediscovery of Kishorganj in the fields of Oxford. In his Bengali essay "Ami Keno Bilete Achhi" (literally "Why I Stay in England"), he describes how, during the course of his morning walks in Oxford, he was brought back every day to the remembered landscape of the small country town where he was born:

> In a short distance from my previous house [in Oxford], there was a large park.... Remarkably enough there began a cornfield from the edges of this park. I used to get out of the park and take to the footpaths within the cornfields, walking down for three or four miles. At the end of the road there was Cherwell river and climbing a bridge on top of it I would see, just like in Kishorganj, a river with clusters of reeds along its banks and ducks floating along.
>
> (107)

Conclusion

Such attempts to recover India in England, which complements Nirad Chaudhuri's efforts to combine his identity as an Indian with his desire to become English, make his anglicised self-fashioning very different from

Cornelia Sorabji's self-fashioning that sought to denounce all traces of Indianness. However, in spite of this fundamental difference, both Sorabji and Chaudhuri encountered the same difficulty in asserting their English identity within the metropolis because none of them was accepted as an equal member of the white English community. As I have argued in the introduction, this failure to be accepted as an equal undermined all Indian efforts at anglicisation right from the early decades of the nineteenth century. Every anglicised Indian that I discuss in this book had to deal with the disappointment of being shunned or even worse, patronised, by the English. However, it is Nirad Chaudhuri who most vocally protested against this refusal to be regarded as an equal of the coloniser and even pointed it out as the major failing of the British colonial project. Nirad Chaudhuri thus represents that unique figure who is both an anglicised Indian enamoured with the cultural wealth that the British Raj brought with it and a staunch critic of British colonialism in India. In the next chapter, I focus on this criticism that Chaudhuri levies against England and its colonial rule and explore the unique links that such a criticism of the metropolis has with the Indian self-fashioning as English.

Notes

1 This phenomenon of prominent politicians writing their lives as national history was not unique to India. It was equally manifest in other parts of the formerly colonised world that gained independence during the second half of the twentieth century (see Boehmer *Colonial* 192). Also see Boehmer "The Hero's Story" for an elaboration of the gender dimension that underlined these texts which were almost invariably written by male nationalist leaders.
2 Javed Majeed in his *Autobiography, Travel and Postcolonial Identity* makes a distinction between the autobiographies of the likes of Surendranath Banerjea and M.R. Jayakar, in which the self "is subsumed within a totalising nationalism"(3), and the autobiographies of the likes of Gandhi and Nehru which are underlined "by tensions between concepts of nationality and autobiographical concepts of selfhood" (2). However, as Majeed himself points out, despite these tensions, both for Gandhi and Nehru their nationalist projects were integrally associated with their autobiographical project of self-fashioning.
3 For an argument contesting the truth value of Chaudhuri's *Autobiography*, see Sudesh Mishra.
4 The original title of the book is *The Autobiography of an Unknown Indian*. However, when Jaico published the first Indian edition of the book in 1964, the definite article was dropped from the title and it was changed to *Autobiography of an Unknown Indian*. In my book, all quotations are from this Indian edition.
5 These words, which literally mean "India, that is me", is a play on the phrase "l'état, c'est moi" or "I am the state" which is usually attributed to King Louis XIV of France to illustrate his egotism as well as his absolute grasp over his kingdom.
6 It is significant to note here that Gandhi in his autobiography insists that his life narrative should not be read as history. However, as Holden convincingly argues, the narrative actually contradicts this assertion. Holden points out how,

after returning to India and joining the Indian National Congress, Gandhi tells that his life "merged with the history of the nationalist struggle" (74). Similarly, Holden also notes how Nehru's autobiography, after depicting his return to India and his subsequent participation in the peasant movement in the United Provinces, "becomes the unfolding story of the quest for Indian independence, in which Nehru's personal life merges with a national narrative" (90).

7 For an analysis of the novel along this line, see Nandy's *An Ambiguous Journey* (19).
8 For a more elaborate analysis of how the colonial imposition of the disciplinary clock time changed the character of labour, especially male labour, in the Indian urban spaces, see Dipesh Chakrabarty's "Difference-Deferral of (A) Colonial Modernity".
9 The city of Calcutta as founded by the British was originally bordered on the west by the river Hooghly and on the east by a semicircular moat that ran from north to south. This moat or ditch was dug up as a means to protect the city from the Maratha raiders and thus earned the name of Mahratta Ditch.
10 Sudhir Kakar in his book *The Indians* describes the ideal "joint family" as a family structure "in which brothers remain together after marriage and bring their wives into the parental household" (4).
11 This association that Chaudhuri makes between joint family and village is not quite accurate. As Kakar points out, "[i]t is ... untrue that the large joint family is found more often in villages than in cities; studies tell us that it is more common in urban areas, as also among the upper landholding castes, than in the lower castes of rural India" (9). Chaudhuri's seamless association of the joint family with the village thus stems from his personal experience as an individual belonging to the landholding castes.
12 Interestingly, though Chaudhuri evaluates his position in his ancestral village in Banagram and the sub-urban Kishorganj through Maine's theoretical framework, he uses Maine's theory against its grain. Maine's "status to contract" theory was originally used to forge a conservative post-1857 British imperialist discourse that sought to resist the attempt to transform India from a society based on kinship to one based on contract and not to augment the process. In other words, within the context of India, Maine's theory would have prioritised the life led in Banagram rather than the life of Kishorganj. (see Koditschek 226–232, and Mantena).
13 In Chaudhuri's autobiographical works, this idealisation of England is underlined by a deep contradiction. While he depicts the England of his imagination as entirely amiable, he portrays the British community in India who provided the flesh and blood correlative to this imagined England as almost wholly repulsive, exerting "an evil influence on Indo-British political and social relations" (*Thy Hand* 60). This reveals the very problematic relation that exists in Chaudhuri's texts between his conceptualisation of England and the British Empire centred on it, and the coercive reality of the colonial order that he experienced in India through his encounter with the local British community. I discuss this point in more detail in the next chapter.
14 Dipesh Chakrabarty in his essay "Remembered Villages" refers to this passage from *Thy Hand* to show how the rural landscape of East Bengal was romanticized during the nineteenth century to produce the image of "Mother Bengal" as a land of pastoral bounty. Chakrabarty writes, "Indeed, one could argue, nationalist perceptions of the Bengal landscape owed much to the labour of cultural workers such as [Nirad] Chaudhuri himself" (2148).
15 This ethnological aspect of William Jones' philology is elaborated in Majeed's *Ungoverned Imaginings* and Trautman's *Aryans and British India*.

4
ANGLICISATION, CITIZENSHIP, AND NIRAD CHAUDHURI'S CRITIQUE OF THE COLONIAL METROPOLIS

In this chapter, I discuss the role of an anglicised Indian as a critic of the metropolis and the colonial rule. From the evidence that I have presented in this book so far, it might appear that the anglicised section of the Indian middle class actively supported the British colonial rule in India and was unequivocal in their appreciation of the colonial metropolis. However, I argue here that the attitude of the anglicised Indians towards the British Empire as well as towards the colonial metropolis was much more nuanced than mere slavish admiration. Indeed, any amount of respect felt by anglicised Indians towards the colonial rule was always inevitably shot through by the frustration of being treated as an inferior by the ruling population. Similarly, their desire to journey to the much longed for metropolis and be part of its national life was always soured by the racist discrimination that they faced there. Interestingly, the late twentieth-century political attempts to counter this discrimination towards coloured immigrants from the colonies by turning the metropolitan society into a multicultural "community of communities" was also equally problematic for the anglicised Indians and their relationship with England. In what follows, I explore these grievances that informed the English self-fashioning of the middle-class Indians by focusing on Nirad Chaudhuri's largely neglected text, *Why I Mourn for England*, which is perhaps the most comprehensive as well as the most idiosyncratic document produced by an anglophile Indian critiquing England and its colonial rule.

Mourning for England as an anglophile

Why I Mourn for England was the last English text to be published under Chaudhuri's name during his lifetime and collects together the newspaper articles and lectures that he wrote lamenting the political, cultural, and moral decline of England from after the Second World War. Dhruva Chaudhuri, Nirad Chaudhuri's eldest son and the editor of this volume, observes in Preface that the pieces collected in the book express the "strong sense of resentment" (5) that his father felt towards the direction in which England had started moving since the general election of 1945 that brought Clement Atlee's Labour Party in government. Dhruva Chaudhuri writes that the "political event [of 1945] made my father really angry, and he correctly predicted the decline of the British Empire" (5). By the winter of 1946–1947, Nirad Chaudhuri had published three articles in Britain's *New England Review*, sharply criticising what he saw as the decadence of the English people and their national character, exemplified by their renunciation of the overseas empire. Referring to these three articles, Dhruva Chaudhuri points out that his father assumed the role of a critic of the colonial metropolis even before he started writing *Autobiography of an Unknown Indian*, which is usually held up as "proof of his partisanship towards the British people and their Empire" (5). As the other pieces in this collection prove, Chaudhuri continued being a vocal critic of England throughout his career as an author and a public intellectual. Indeed, as Dhruva Chaudhuri perceptively argues, these critical pieces marked an important trend in Nirad Chaudhuri's entire oeuvre. But how does one reconcile such persistent criticism of the metropolis with Chaudhuri's well-known and equally persistent expressions of anglophilia?

One way of disentangling Nirad Chaudhuri's apparently contradictory love–hate relationship with the colonial metropolis might be by reading it chronologically. In other words, by reading Chaudhuri's admiration for England as being directed towards the land which was still the beating heart of a large empire and by reading his criticism as directed towards the post-war England which had given up on its colonial project and its civilising mission. Such a reading can indeed be substantiated by the opening paragraph of the essay which gives its title to the collection under discussion. In this 1968 article, Chaudhuri writes:

> My earliest premonition of a decline of English greatness was provoked by the news of the general election of that year [1945]. Until then my confidence in a greater future for the English people after their victory in the [Second World] war remained unshaken. It was shattered on that day: Britain had voted for Labour's soft option. I felt that the English spirit was broken, and a demolition squad would begin its work on the external greatness of the English people.
>
> (14)

According to Chaudhuri, the formal retreat of the British government from India marked the culmination of the work of this demolition squad on English greatness. Interestingly, in Chaudhuri's book *A Passage to England*, which documents his experiences on his first visit to England in 1955, we do not find any trace of this disillusionment about post-war Britain. But in a later essay, compiled in *Why I Mourn for England* under the title "Britain through an Indian's Eyes", Chaudhuri clarifies that this was because during his first visit he was overwhelmed by encountering whatever traces he could find of the England that had excited his imagination as a child. This England of Chaudhuri's childhood imagination was Victorian. So in a way his *A Passage to England* was not about the modern realities of Britain at all but rather a paean to the old England that had inspired in him the desire for anglicisation and the unswerving belief "that if we died in England what would become for ever England would be a little foreign flesh" (*Autobiography* 126–127). It was this England of his childhood dreams that Chaudhuri felt he had lost after 1945, and he had little more than bile for the new England that had gradually shaped itself during the second half of the twentieth century. Comparing that bygone colonial metropolis with the England that he found himself in at the end of his life, Chaudhuri writes:

> The days when a Bengali boy of 10, barebodied as well as barefooted, could share in English greatness are gone forever. Today, at the age of 90 I see Bengalis ignorant of English arriving in jumbo jets from that same East Bengal to turn England into a multi-racial, multi-lingual and multi-cultural country.

There is an obvious contradiction here in Chaudhuri's criticism of post-war Britain and its efforts to promote multiculturalism. Wasn't Chaudhuri himself a part of this migration of people from the periphery to the metropolis who were making England socially diverse? How does one explain a brown Indian anglophile's objection to a post-war multicultural England that was becoming more accommodative of other coloured migrants like him? We will need to come back to these questions later. But I would first like to point out that the apparently neat distinction between a pre-war "good England" and a post-war "bad England" that emerges from the above discussion is a rather simplistic understanding of Chaudhuri's attitude towards the metropolis. In his 100th year, Chaudhuri, while writing an essay titled "Apologia Pro Scripta Sua" that forms the introductory piece of *Why I Mourn for England*, points out that the much-cited dedication of his *Autobiography of an Unknown Indian* was actually a criticism of the British Empire rather than an unconditional celebration of the colonial rule:

> The dedication to the "memory of the British Empire in India" was really a condemnation of the British rulers for not treating us equals. It was imitation of what Cicero said about the conduct of Vewes [sic],[1] a Roman proconsul of Sicily who oppressed the Sicilian Citizens, although in their desperation they cried out: "Civis Romannus Sum".

(12)

Chaudhuri in crying out "Civis Britannicus Sum" was claiming his rights to be considered as an equal citizen of the British Empire and at the same time criticising Britain's reluctance to accept him entirely as one of its own despite his meticulous efforts to anglicise himself. Chaudhuri was thus anguished not only by the political turn that the metropolis had taken after 1945 but also by how it treated anglicised Indians during the colonial period. In what follows, I would first discuss the pieces in *Why I Mourn for England* in which Chaudhuri elaborates on this criticism of the colonial rule and the lack of citizenship that defined his position as an anglicised Indian within it and then move on to his critique of post-war England and its politics of multiculturalism.

Metropolitan Englishness and the denial of equality

As a preamble to a discussion of Chaudhuri's criticism of the British Empire and his sense of marginalisation within it, it is important to explore how colonialism complicated the relationship between a person's affiliation to the English state and his claim to an English identity. As discussed in the introductory chapter, one of the significant ways in which English identity or Englishness has been construed within the metropolis is by relating it to the expanding English state and its legal institutions. Thus, as Robert Colls suggests, the English national identity has as its fountainhead the seat of the English monarch in London and stretches across all the territories over which the monarch's "axes of law and law-enforcement" (3) have sway. However, simply understanding England's identity in terms of political authority and military-juridical institutions leads us to a theoretical problem. If merely being ruled by English laws made one part of England, then there should not have been any distinction between a Welsh, for instance, and a colonised India. The very fact that even an ardent anglophile like Nirad Chaudhuri had to throw the words "Civis Britannicus Sum" as a "challenge" to the colonial metropolis means that in spite of his desire to be English, he felt himself to be inadequately integrated within the English state. One way of understanding this difference between the sense of belongingness that a Welsh or a Scot or an Irish enjoyed within the British Empire and the lack of citizenship that an Indian suffered from as a British subject is to read the history of England's expansion as marked by two separate phases and forms of empire building, one "internal" and the other "external". Building on John Seeley's 1883 treatise *The Expansion of England*, Krishan Kumar argues that the English created a double empire, the first being a land empire or an internal empire constituting the different kingdoms that were clubbed together to form "Great Britain or the United Kingdom"[2] (35) and the second an overseas empire or external empire which again had two phases, the first marked by the conquest of North America and the Caribbean and the second marked by the conquest of India and South-East Asia. Kumar makes the interesting claim that within the formation of this land empire, which is colloquially referred to as Britain, the English did not consciously create a strong and distinct sense of a national identity. Rather, they stressed on the idea of Britishness within which the non-English members of the internal empire could participate as equals. Kumar writes:

> The English—along with the Scots, the Welsh and the Irish—were urged to see themselves as part of a large enterprise, a political project, that was catapulting Britain into a leading position among world powers.
>
> In all this the English could not but be aware of their leading role; by the same token, they were equally aware of the need not to trumpet this as an English achievement, but to see it as a joint effort of all the British nations. To do so would be in fact to threaten the very basis of their commanding position. When you are securely in charge it is best not to remind others of this fact too often or too insistently.
>
> (36–37)

If we compare this relationship between an English identity and the internal empire to the relationship between English identity and the external empire, we notice a complex pattern of similarities and differences.

India gradually became a formal part of the English state over a period of 85 years starting with the passage of the 1773 Regulating Act which brought the workings of the East India Company under the supervision of the British Parliament[3] and culminating in the 1858 proclamation by Queen Victoria which brought the subcontinent under the direct governance of the monarch in London. This gradual introduction of India within the folds of the English state was reflected in the integrationist cultural policies that marked the British colonialism of India for a very long time and found its most vocal advocate in T.B. Macaulay.[4] As Uday Singh Mehta notes, to make India truly politically integrated into Britain, it was assumed by the votaries of liberalism that it first had to be brought to a level of civilisational adulthood through education and social reforms because

> political institutions such as representative democracy are dependent on societies having reached a particular historical maturation or level of civilization. Hence, those societies in which the higher accomplishments of civilization have not occurred plainly do not satisfy the conditions for representative government. Under such conditions liberalism in the form of the empire services the deficiencies of the past for societies that have been stunted through history.[5]
>
> (81)

This integrationist approach, characterised by attempts to rectify the "deficiencies" of the colonised societies in order to make their inhabitants the equals of the metropolitan citizens was, however, countered by a strong exclusionary tendency that operated within the British Empire. An interesting but controversial text with which to start understanding the exclusionary tendency inherent within the hegemonic notion of English identity that was at the core of British imperialism is George Orwell's 1944 essay "The English People". In this essay, Orwell argues that being suspicious of foreigners was one of the eight main characteristic features that defined the English national identity. According to Linda Colley, in the two centuries following the 1707 Act of Union, this sense of who the foreigner was got primarily determined by two facts—the incessant wars with France and the spread of colonies in the global South. In the wars against France, the English, Welsh, and the Scots could all participate together as a culturally homogenous body of Protestants who were united against the foremost Catholic power of Europe. This gave rise to a British national identity but, as discussed earlier, it was really an expanded form of the English national identity with the English juridico-legal system at its core. This English/British national identity was further bolstered by the overseas colonial project where again the members of the United Kingdom could realise themselves as a homogenous community who were trying to gain control over a horde of brutish foreigners. As Colley writes:

> They defined themselves against the French as they imagined them to be, superstitious, militarist, decadent and unfree. And, increasingly, they defined themselves in contrast to colonial peoples they conquered, peoples who were manifestly alien in terms of culture, religion and colour.
>
> (5)

Thus, in spite of the attempts to culturally integrate the overseas empire with the metropolis, there was also a desire to construct the colonised subjects as the alien other so as to bolster the English/British national identity. Hence, for the overseas colonies, being under the sway of the English monarch's "axes of law and law-enforcement" did not automatically translate into being part of the English national identity as it was understood in the metropolis.

Such exclusion of colonies like India from being part of the English identity was largely centred on the idea of whiteness which, as Radhika Mohanram has pointed out, increasingly became a conscious part of the metropolitan identity from around the middle of the nineteenth century. This stress on whiteness as the marker of national identity served two different purposes. Firstly, it allowed to unify the internal empire and make it part of a homogenous sociocultural community. Thus, even the Irish, who as Catholics had remained out of the pale of the British solidarity forged through the shared values of Protestantism, could now be folded within the metropolitan national identity because of their white skin.[6] Secondly, it allowed the colonial administration to stop short of acknowledging the colonised subjects as their absolute equals, thereby constantly maintaining an upper hand over them, including those who sought to culturally transform themselves into English. As Radhika Mohanram points out:

> The Indian's inability to assimilate himself completely [was] because of the residue left behind by his darkened body. In fact, his visible difference would prevent him from ever being conferred with a liberal subjectivity. He was a British man who could never be fully realized.
>
> (12)

This equivocation regarding the overseas colonies which were simultaneously included within the purview of the English state and excluded from the metropolitan understanding of Englishness and English identity got reflected in the complicated relationship that a colonised subject had with metropolitan citizenship. The understanding of English identity as coterminous with the reach of the English laws enacted in the name of the monarch residing in London assumes *ius soli* as the basis of English/British citizenship. As Colls writes:

> The historic view of British nationality was that it involved some sort of personal bonding between subject and monarch. This bonding happened either "naturally" or ius soli, that is, by being born in the monarch's dominions, whether at home or abroad. Or for those in foreign countries, it could be declared to have happened by oath of allegiance in a process of legal naturalization. For all British subjects, including those of Ireland and the colonies, the difference between being "nationals" and being "citizens" was blurred. Anyway, the question rarely arose.
>
> (159)

However, within the overseas colonial empire, there was hardly any blurring of the lines between subjecthood, citizenship, and national identity. Niraja Gopal Jayal elaborates on this strong demarcation between the status of being an imperial subject and that of being a British citizen which, as we have seen, haunted Nirad Chaudhuri's anglicised self-fashioning. Jayal argues that though all the individuals residing within the British monarch's domain were equally considered to be subjects of the crown who were expected to show allegiance to the sovereign and were guaranteed equal protection under the British common law, "[i]n point of fact, of course, such rights as subjects enjoyed lay in the custody of Parliament, rather than the monarch, and varied enormously" (30). In the context of colonial India, this meant that the non-white colonised subjects who were designated either as "non-European, natural-born British subjects" or "British Protected Persons"[7] did not enjoy the same rights that were given to the citizens of the metropolis or even to the various categories of Europeans and Eurasians living in India. As Jayal writes:

> Neither non-European British subjects nor British Protected Persons (BPPs) could become fully naturalized members of the British Empire, and political equality with other white subjects of the empire was by definition precluded.
> (31).

This lack of equality was brought to the fore in India through a whole series of controversies that erupted at regular intervals between the late nineteenth and early twentieth centuries. One such major controversy was associated with the efforts of Lord Lytton, who was the viceroy of India from 1876 to 1880, to reduce the already miniscule population of Indians who could apply for the Indian Civil Service examinations by bringing down the age bar from 21 to 19. Another controversy was about the passage of the Ilbert Bill, which was first drafted in 1883 and originally proposed to allow Indian judges to try Europeans. The stiff resistance that this bill faced from the white population in India meant that it could only be passed in a thoroughly diluted form which compromised the notion of equality that had originally underlined the intention of this judicial reform.

If the right to vote can be considered as the core feature of citizenship, then Indians remained unenfranchised till the last decades of the nineteenth century. Indeed, it was not before the 1909 Morley-Minto reform that a substantial section of Indians could vote to elect members to the Imperial Legislative Council, the apex body which oversaw the administration of British India, and thereby gain a semblance of de jure citizenship.[8] However, even this restricted form of citizenship was extended to an extremely small section of Indians, primarily men of substantial wealth and land ownership who, as late as 1919, amounted to no more than 3 percent of the adult Indians (Jayal 44). Indeed, during the entire period of British rule in India, the number of people with voting rights never expanded beyond one-fifth of the adult population (Jayal 44). For most Indians, including Nirad Chaudhuri, what provided a counterweight to such widespread denial of political agency was the assurance of equal treatment contained in the 1858 proclamation by Queen Victoria which asserted that the monarch was going to be bound by the same obligation towards the natives of India that bound her to all her subjects everywhere. Thus, as Jayal points out:

> Indian political liberalism clung to the ideal of the greater achievement of citizenship *within* the framework of British rule and, even when it aspired to Swaraj, *within* the empire.
>
> (42)

Hence, the desire of individuals like Chaudhuri to fashion themselves as English and be a part of the national life of the metropolis unfolded within a peculiar sociopolitical context that was marked simultaneously by the promise of equality, which was being continuously reiterated by the liberal ideologues of colonialism and indeed by the English monarch herself, and an evident lack of equality that was part of the lived reality of all the colonised Indians.[9] This explains the note of criticism against the British Empire contained in the dedicatory lines of *Autobiography of an Unknown Indian*. But the note of criticism that was only cryptically included in Chaudhuri's first autobiography was elaborated by him much more extensively in the three articles that he wrote for *The New English Review* between November 1946 and January 1947. It is to these articles that I turn next.

Distorting the ideals of imperialism

In the first article in this series of three, titled "The Future of Imperialism" and published in the November of 1946, one already encounters the arguments that would later go on to brand Nirad Chaudhuri as an anti-Indian author with a "perverse intent" of glorifying the imperialism from whose shackles India had managed to break free. Yet, like the dedicatory lines of *Autobiography of an Unknown Indian*, the arguments in this essay are complex and can appear to be deceptively celebratory of the British Raj. What the article does in fact is glorify the ideals of imperialism to provide a critique of the shortfalls of the British Empire. Hence, just as the dedicatory passage of Chaudhuri's autobiography, this article too plays on the gap between what was expected of British imperialism and what was actually delivered. In discussing the future of imperialism, Chaudhuri argues that imperialism is an inevitable force underlying the evolutionary impulse that defines not only human history but indeed also the history of the biological world in its entirety. In fact, in Chaudhuri's view, empire building is the most fundamental process through which "anything good, great, wise, abiding, or new" (72) is brought into this world. Chaudhuri explains this by arguing that the emergence of new classes and orders of animals have always meant the establishment of new imperial hierarchies within the animal world. This is how a piscean imperialism had apparently given way to a reptilian imperialism which in turn had given way to a mammalian imperialism, and this finally had given way to the imperialism of the human beings (72). Chaudhuri traces this same pattern of imperialism and evolution in human history as well:

[H]uman history is only the continuation of biological evolution. Rather, there is no longer any biological evolution but only social, intellectual, and moral evolution. I risk the dogmatic assertion that zoological speciation has ceased and only mental and moral speciation is now going on.

(75)

According to this theory offered by Chaudhuri, it is this continuing process of evolution, now registered only in the form of mental and moral speciation, that manifests itself in human history through the rise of new orders of civilisation which is spread through a series of empires, one following the other and each new empire being more expansive than its predecessor: "It is in the fulfilment of this process that Sumeria, Egypt, Greece, Rome and Islam, to name only a few, created new civilizations and empires in ever expanding circles" (71). Chaudhuri argues that as one empire exhausts its capacity for mental and moral leadership, it gives way to another one so that in the whole of human history, though individual empires keep rising and declining, the fact of imperialism remains constant. The British Empire for Chaudhuri is only the most recent in this series of empires providing intellectual and moral leadership, and consequently its reach has also been the largest: "The creation of the British Empire is only the latest phase of this process, in which the Europeans are creating a world empire and a new world civilization" (71). Such a view of world history leads Chaudhuri to argue that the overseas empire possessed by Britain is not an alien appendage to the British nation which can be simply done away with without causing any fundamental damage to the national character of the metropolis. Rather, the empire is the fulfilment of the British national character and its historical role in the course of human evolution. In Chaudhuri's words, "They could not disinterest themselves in it without abrogating their historical mission and eliminating themselves from one of the primary strands of human evolution" (71). Thus, for Chaudhuri, the relation of colonial subjugation that brought India under the sway of an imperial Britain was a natural fulfilment of a well-entrenched evolutionary process which operates as an inevitable force within the biological world.[10]

Importantly, Chaudhuri adds a moral nuance to this argument about the inevitability of imperialism. He draws on Aquinas's distinction between just and legitimate authority and the authority exercised by a tyrant. In the first case, the authority is marked by a desire to serve the common good of all citizens and in the next, the authority is directed by a concern for the personal gains of the ruler who treats his or her subjects like a master would treat a slave.[11] Chaudhuri sums up Aquinas's position on just and unjust authority thus: "man cannot bear over man the domination which a master has over his slave, but one who excels in knowledge and justice might govern another for his good" (74). Chaudhuri argues that the British rule over

India represented such a force of knowledge and justice which entitled them to rule over India. He even refers to a conversation between Rammohun Roy and Victor Jacquemont to substantiate this argument (74). As we have seen earlier, similar assertions about the British being more knowledgeable or more civilisationally advanced than the Indians and hence having the right to rule over Indians were an integral part of the Indian middle-class discourse during the late nineteenth century. But such an argument only represents the moral obligation of the British to rule others to help them evolve civilisationally. It does not establish whether British imperialism fulfilled this moral obligation or not. This distinction is important because Chaudhuri's criticism about the British only bestowing subjecthood and not citizenship on anglicised Indian stems from this gap between what the British imperialism was morally obliged to do and what they ended up doing.

Chaudhuri admits that any imperial force trying to pioneer new civilisational values "swims with a millstone round his neck" (76), and in spite of all its efforts to spread the impact of social, intellectual, and moral evolution, "those who go forward constitute only a fraction of those who lag behind" (75). This large fraction of laggards, according to Chaudhuri, regards the civilising imperial power with unabated malevolence. Consequently, he states that "the urgent function of imperialism [is] to defend civilization against this vile revolt and protect it against the rancour of the futureless" (76). However, this protection of civilisation from those who refuse to learn its mores and thereby remain "futureless" is only one aspect of the moral obligation. The other aspect, which Chaudhuri describes as the more "humane *rôle*" (76) of an imperialism spreading an evolved mode of civilisation, is to "reclaim large numbers of that great mass of men who are simply inert, having either exhausted their promise or still to show it" (76). To this, Chaudhuri adds the role of "receiv[ing] as equals those who came forward to join the civilized order" (76). Did Britain accept those within her empire who came forward to join its civilised order by anglicising themselves? In other words, did Britain fulfil the humane side of its moral obligation as an imperial power? In this 1946 essay, Chaudhuri does not directly answer this moot question. Yet, at the very end of this piece, he does hint at the fact that Britain might not have lived up to that moral ideal and fulfilled its obligations of accepting as equals those who had responded to its civilising influence and fashioned themselves in the model provided by the coloniser. In fact, Chaudhuri regards this moral failure as one of the main reasons why imperialism as an idea had ultimately fallen from grace in the metropolis. In Chaudhuri's own words:

> No nation is so poor in spirit as to think well of an ideal which it has not the strength to follow. Therefore, imperialism is tarred and feathered today. But that by itself settles nothing. In its own conscience imperialism is only sad, not degraded.
>
> (77)

For Chaudhuri, the moral lapse of not accepting as equal those who anglicised themselves was only deepened by Britain's decision to altogether abandon the imperial project and renounce its historical role of civilising the world population. This final degradation of the ideals of imperialism in Britain happened with the coming to power of the Labour Party under Clement Atlee in 1945 which initiated the process of dismantling Britain's overseas empire. In the essay "'Stasis' in England", published in January 1947, Chaudhuri argues that between the tenure of Prime Minister William Pitt the Younger in the late eighteenth century and the tenure of Prime Minister H.H. Asquith in the beginning of the twentieth century, political power had regularly shifted between the Conservatives and the Liberals. However, Chaudhuri argues that whether the pendulum of power was tilted to the right or to the left

> h[ad] not made the slightest difference to the national career of Great Britain. Her growth as a world Power, the growth of her dominions and commerce, and the growth and expansion of English culture, h[ad] gone on uninterrupted by the party vicissitudes.
>
> (88)

For Chaudhuri, the Labour Party's more recent jettisoning of the project of imperialism was a revolt against this "national career of Great Britain" which had enjoyed cross-party support for more than a century. Chaudhuri presents this attitude of the contemporary left towards imperialism that had given the English, and by extension the British, a sense of national purpose as akin to the behaviour of a problem child who "rebels against the family tradition, which means the same thing as the Nomos of the community" (93). Thus, in Chaudhuri's view, the denunciation of the imperialism by the Labour Government under Atlee precipitated a crisis of national identity in the metropolis resulting in an "attenuation of that condition—regarded by Plato as the mark of the best-ordered state—in which the greatest number of persons apply the terms 'mine' and 'not mine', 'his' and 'not his' in the same way to the same thing" (94). For Chaudhuri, such confusion resulting from the folly of giving up the empire, rather than undoing the shortcomings of the British imperial project, only compounded them and ensured a premature decline of England from its glorious position of the civilisational leader of the world.

Calibans of the British Raj

Chaudhuri's criticism against the moral failure of British imperialism in not accepting anglicised Indians as the equals of English colonisers would grow sharper with years. As discussed earlier, a jibe against British imperialism was already incorporated by Chaudhuri in the dedicatory lines of his

Autobiography of an Unknown Indian. This note of criticism is sounded again and even more clearly in the second instalment of his autobiography, *Thy Hand, Great Anarch!*, published in 1987. We find it repeated yet once more a year later in a lecture delivered at the London School of Economics which is printed in *Why I Mourn for England* under the title "My Views of the Real East-West Conflict". In this essay, Chaudhuri claims that the general attitude of the British community in India towards Indians was almost uniformly that of animosity, and this animosity was especially virulent against the English-educated middle-class Indians who could match the colonisers in their own domain of intellectual and cultural accomplishments. Chaudhuri substantiates this argument by referring to the completely unwarranted spite that Rudyard Kipling directed against Rabindranath Tagore after he had received the Nobel Prize for his English version of *Gitanjali*: "Rudyard Kipling wrote: 'Well, whose fault is it that the Babu is what he is .... We have worked without intermission to make this Caliban'" (35). Chaudhuri adds that he too is one such "Caliban" of the British Raj who have benefitted from the cultural influences that the colonisers had brought with them but who, just like Tagore before him, has remained unacknowledged as a civilised equal of the English.

The conflict that Chaudhuri points out between British imperialism's historical mission of promoting a new order of civilisation and its reluctance to accept as equals those who adopted that civilised order reflects an exclusionary tendency that was at the heart of the liberal philosophy which informed much of Britain's imperialist ideology. Uday Singh Mehta in his analysis of the connection between liberalism and British imperialism elaborates on this by noting how liberalism's universalistic claim of political inclusion of all human beings was hedged to demarcate an exclusive category of people who could be treated as citizens:

> The universalistic reach of liberalism derives from the capacities that it identifies with human nature and from the presumption, which it encourages, that these capacities are sufficient and not merely necessary for an individual's political inclusion.
>
> However, concealed behind the endorsement of these universal capacities are the specific cultural and psychological conditions that are woven in as preconditions for the actualization of these capacities. Liberal exclusion works by modulating the distance between the interstices of human capacities and the conditions for their political effectivity. It is the content between these interstices that settles boundaries between who is included and who is not.
>
> (49)

It is important to note here that what Chaudhuri criticises is not this exclusionary strategy that informed the liberal ideology of British imperialism. In fact, his own argument about British imperialism having to defend the civilisational values against the "rancour of the futureless" suggests a similar faith in excluding from citizenship large sections of the society which do not come forward to adopt the new civilised order. Chaudhuri's criticism is levied against British imperialism using racial prejudice to deny equality to those who have fashioned themselves as English. This explains why, in spite of being critical of British imperialism for not granting him equality as a citizen, Chaudhuri was even more critical of Britain's multicultural agenda which moved away from the hierarchical model of civilisation and abandoned the condition of adopting the cultural mores of the most "evolved" nation in the world to enter the civilised order. This is why, while mourning for England that was being swamped by "Bengalis ignorant of English arriving in jumbo jets", Chaudhuri finds succour in a notice posted outside the Christ Church Meadow at Oxford restricting the entry of several different categories of people who were presumed to be unfit for civilised society. Writing about this notice in a piece incorporated in *Why I Mourn for England* under the title "Diary", Chaudhuri mentions how it barred the entry of "all beggars, all persons in ragged or very dirty clothes, persons of improper character or who are not decent in appearance and behaviour" (115). For Chaudhuri, such a notice was an affirmation of the exclusionary idea of a civilised order that he was witnessing crumbling around him in the metropolis. He writes, "upon seeing that notice I did say to myself that even if only by a notice Oxford still proclaims her loyalty to lost causes" (115). Thus, while Chaudhuri's complaint against imperial Britain was that it did not include as equals those who were worthy to be brought within the pale of its civilisational order, his complaint against post-war Britain was that it did not rigorously exclude from its society those who had not come forward to join Britain's civilised order. To deny this framework of exclusion that would separate his anglicised self from the crowd of colonised subjects arriving in England without even knowing the fundamentals of the English language was to deny Chaudhuri's lifelong effort to adopt the cultural code of the British coloniser and transform himself into an Englishman. Unsurprisingly, therefore, Chaudhuri felt his English identity to be rudely undermined in a multicultural Britain that was engaged in an effort to break free from the hegemony of Englishness and the colonial hierarchies that it has historically informed. In the next section, I situate this idea of multiculturalism as it emerged within the context of post-war Britain before moving on to analyse Chaudhuri's critique of the multicultural Britain from the perspective of an anglicised Indian.

Multiculturalism in post-war Britain and the denunciation of Englishness

Though the term multiculturalism gained widespread currency within Britain only during the last few decades of the twentieth century, the roots of a multicultural Britain can be traced as far back as the passage of the British Nationality Act in 1948. It was through this act that all the subjects of the British monarch residing either within the British isle or in its colonies and the Commonwealth were legally formalised as British citizens. The basis for British subjecthood before this law was simply allegiance to the monarch. Within this feudal concept, anyone born within the territory where the British monarch was a sovereign enjoyed the status of British subjecthood and, at least in theory, enjoyed the same rights, privileges, and protection. However, this notion of an overarching homogenous British subjecthood radiating from the seat of the British monarch in London to the farthest reaches of its colonies was undermined when, in 1945, the British dominion of Canada unilaterally decided to create the category of Canadian citizenship over and above the category of British subjecthood. Such introduction of citizenship laws that were specific to one dominion complicated the status of British subjecthood that was so far shared uniformly across the empire. This precipitated a unique constitutional crisis which forced Britain to formulate its own citizenship laws that would reinterpret the relationship between the British state and all its imperial subjects. This was the imperative behind the formulation of the British Nationality Act in 1948 (Hansen 77). There is of course irony involved in the fact that three years before Nirad Chaudhuri published *Autobiography of an Unknown Indian*, where he complained about being denied citizenship within the British Empire, the mother country had formalised through its nationality act the status of all its subjects as citizens, thereby reasserting[12] their equality under British law. In fact, the discussion on this bill in the British Parliament was accompanied by some of the most emphatic declarations of the metropolis's uniform responsibility towards all of its imperial subjects. Explaining why the bill was about granting British citizenship not merely to those subjects residing within the United Kingdom but also to those residing within the colonies and the member states of the Commonwealth, the Lord Chancellor stated:

> It may be asked why do you add and Colonies? Why not let the Colonies have their own species of citizenship? [But] is it right that we should differentiate our own people and the people for whom we are trustees? We think that is not right.
> (quoted in Deakin 79)

Indeed, such emphasis on equality of the British subject had to be reiterated by the Lord Chancellor more than once to reassure the Parliament that no discriminatory practice would be introduced within the metropolis as a consequence of this bill. Thus, when Lord Altrincham, the former governor of Kenya, expressed his concern that the bill might undermine the "proud boast that all British subjects have equal rights in the United Kingdom" (quoted in Hansen 83), Lord Chancellor had to assuage him by confirming that all the British subjects would have the same right to enter the United Kingdom and claim citizenship:

> The Bill does not differentiate between British subjects. . We can say that people who come from one part of the British Empire should not be allowed in and people from another part shall be allowed in, but in this great metropolitan centre of the Empire I hope we never shall say such a thing.
> (quoted in Hansen 83)

One of the consequences of this open-door immigration policy that the act introduced was that in just 14 years of its introduction, the number of coloured immigrants from the overseas colonies in the metropolis increased from 20,000/30,000 to 500,000 (Hansen 95).

However, it is to be noted here that this legislative effort to formally grant equal citizenship and rights to enter the metropolis to all its subjects by the post-war British government was framed by the same kinds of equivocation and racist bias that had informed all of Britain's colonial policies before. Indeed, an exploration of the subsequent amendments to the citizenship and immigration rules by Britain makes it evident that Chaudhuri's complaint about being denied citizenship was not rendered superfluous by the passage of the 1948 British Nationality Act. Thus, within two years of the passage of the act, the British home secretary was already chairing a committee of ministers "to explore the means that might be adopted to check 'coloured immigration' into the country" (Hansen 91). By 1962, the government implemented the first Commonwealth Immigrants Act which accepted only those people as belonging to the metropolis who were either "indigenous Britons [or] who had passports issued by the UK Government" (Hampshire 30). The act effectively denounced the rights of all its erstwhile imperial subjects to claim themselves as British citizens and indeed marked the formalisation and legalisation of the racist objections towards the inflow of coloured immigrants in the metropolis which had resulted in incidents like the Notting Hill race riots of 1958. Efforts to exclude erstwhile imperial subjects of colour from entering the metropolis and claiming it as their home continued unabated throughout the next decade. It was a period marked by such explicitly racist discourses like Enoch Powell's "rivers of blood" speech and such equally racist legislations like the Commonwealth Immigrants Act of 1968 and the Immigration Act of 1971 which were created to stop the entry of people from the Commonwealth to the United Kingdom (Karatani 144–178). All of this culminated in the overhauling of the British Nationality Act in 1981 which finally ended Britain's pretensions of being the mother country of an overseas colonial empire by "shift[ing] away from a system in which citizenship was rooted in territory, to a system based on lineage" (Hampshire 43). The window that was briefly opened after

1948 for the colonised subjects to move to the metropolis and be accepted as an equal citizen was comprehensively closed. However, even as Britain progressively sought to reduce the immigration of coloured people from its overseas empire, it was also seeking ways to ensure that those who had already migrated from the colonies and were inside the metropolis should be better accepted within the British society. One such effort was the framing of a series of anti-racism laws in 1965, 1968, and 1976. But the major attempt to socially accept the coloured immigrants was characterised by officially embracing the philosophy of multiculturalism as a counterweight to Britain's colonial past. The multicultural Britain of the late twentieth century has thus been described as "'Janus-faced', with tough restrictions on outsiders cast primarily in racial terms, but substantial protections for internal cultural pluralism" (Ashcroft and Bevir 5).

Within this growing trend of multiculturalism in Britain, the empire increasingly came to be regarded as at best irrelevant to Britain's self-interest and at worst a moral crime. Dismantling the empire was seen as necessary for diplomatic reasons as well as to make resources available to transform metropolitan Britain into a welfare state (Holland 200–210). This political and economic self-interest was coupled with what Nicholas White has described as an "ethical revolution" because of which many Britons came to regard the colonial enterprise as morally dubious and inimical to the progressive ideals of the day (41–42). By the 1970s, however, the moral opprobrium had given way to a widespread apathy. To quote Bernard Porter:

> People ceased to relate to the empire, and then to remember it: in schools and universities, for example, where it was squeezed out of most history curricula. It was done, past, finished; a chapter of Britain's history that had now—surely—definitely come to an end.
> (*The Lion's* 296)

In between these years, when the empire first became a superfluous entity and then a forgotten chapter in the history of Britain, the nineteenth-century project of the British liberals to culturally educate the colonised subjects into coloured Englishmen was thoroughly abandoned. The sea change in Britain's approach to cultural identity can best be gauged by placing Macaulay's 1835 Minute on Indian education against this speech delivered in 1966 by the then British home secretary Roy Jenkins when immigration from the colonial periphery to the metropolis was at its peak:

> I do not think that we need in this country a 'melting-pot', which will turn everybody out into a common mould, as one of a series of carbon copies of someone's misplaced vision of the stereotyped Englishman.

> I define integration, therefore, not as a flattening process, but as equal opportunity accompanied by cultural diversity in an atmosphere of mutual tolerance. This is the goal.
>
> (quoted in Cantle 65)

What Jenkins presents here is the vision of a multicultural Britain whose main thrust would be to value and preserve cultural difference. This turn to multiculturalism came to be coded in its most comprehensive as well as controversial form in the report produced by the Commission on the Future of Multi-Ethnic Britain in 2000 and published under the aegis of the Runnymede Trust. Also popularly referred to as the "Parekh report", it builds on the liberal idea of citizenship based on universal equality and human rights, but then goes on to state that

> citizens are not only individuals but also members of particular religious, ethnic, cultural and regional communities, which are comparatively stable as well as open and fluid. Britain is both a community of citizens and a community of communities, both a liberal and a multicultural society, and needs to reconcile their sometimes conflicting requirements.
>
> (ix)

The conflict mentioned here arises from the ways in which multiculturalism tries to modify the liberal assumptions about citizenship. The basic argument of liberalism is that a state should protect the rights of its citizens as human beings of equal worth irrespective of their affiliations to specific groups or communities. The differences that such affiliations might create are matters of private life and need not concern how a state relates to its individual citizens as equals. As Will Kymlicka points out, when liberals make exception to this rule of equal treatment by arguing for special rights for any section of population disadvantaged or discriminated against by the majority population on the grounds of race, for instance, then the intention is to use the "affirmative action as a temporary measure to move more rapidly towards a 'colour-blind' society" (4). In other words, irrespective of these "special cases" entertained by a liberal state, the advocates of liberalism "reject the claim that group-specific rights are needed to accommodate enduring cultural differences, rather than remedy historical discrimination" (Kymlicka 4). In contrast, as is evident from the earlier quotation from the Parekh report, the multicultural argument is that a state should recognise a citizen's belongingness to cultural communities which makes him share a distinct group identity that differentiates him from members of other cultural communities. The multicultural thrust is therefore to recognise these cultural differences as part of the public sphere and build the idea of citizenship on this acknowledgement of group rights over and above the human rights that are acknowledged based on the notion of commonality of all human beings. Tariq Modood, one of the most vocal supporters of multiculturalism in Britain and an adviser to the committee that produced the Parekh report, writes:

> Multiculturalism is clearly beyond toleration and state neutrality, for it involves active support for cultural difference, active discouragement against hostility and disapproval and the remaking of the public sphere in order to fully include marginalized identities.
> (59)

It is important to note here that since British multiculturalism developed as a response to the arrival in the metropolis of the "visible minorities" from the colonies, cultural communities came to be defined primarily in terms of race, ethnicity, and religion and not in terms of gender or sexuality or even class for instance. As Modood notes:

> The object of our concern is a very specific set of realities, namely, the dynamic outcome of social and political struggles and negotiations surrounding racial, ethnic and religious differences in relation to non-white migration into white countries.
> (114)

This specific set of realities informed by the migration from colonies has also meant that multiculturalism has been inextricably associated with the assertion of the cultural identity of the coloured minority against the dominance of the majority culture which exerts its hegemony under the name of nationalism. Consequently, the same Parekh report which talks about Britain being a community of culturally different communities finds cultural markers like Englishness or Britishness that are associated with the white majority problematic. The report argues that Englishness/Britishness is marred by its racist undertones and its association with colonialism, which makes it unpalatable to the Asian, African-Caribbean, and African immigrants who themselves or whose forefathers had once been colonised subjects:

> For them Britishness is a reminder of colonisation and empire, and to that extent is not attractive. [T]he concept of Englishness often seems inappropriate, since to be English, as the term is in practice used, is to be white. Britishness, as much as Englishness, has systematic, largely unspoken, racial connotations. Whiteness nowhere features as an explicit condition of being British, but it is widely understood that Englishness, and therefore by extension Britishness, is racially coded.
> (38)

The report also argues that for the coloured immigrants to be forced to get assimilated within this white majority culture of Britishness/Englishness would involve losing their own distinct cultural identity which they had brought with them from the colonies and have not lost touch with even after their migration:

> [A]ssimilation really meant the absorption of so-called minority differences into the so-called majority—people were expected to give up everything in order to belong. But since racism has continued, assimilation has come to be seen as an impossible price to pay—blackness and Asianness are non-tradable. Cultural difference has come to matter more.
>
> (37)

These complaints against Britishness and Englishness make two basic assumptions, both of which are relevant for our understanding of Chaudhuri's critique of the multicultural Britain from his position as an anglicised Indian. The first assumption is that the migrants from the colonies possess certain unique cultural traits which give them their distinct identity that is very different from the majority identity of Britishness or Englishness. Indeed, it is assumed that the cultural identities of the immigrants are so fundamentally different from the cultural identity of the majority inhabitants of the metropolis that any attempt at assimilation would inevitably mean the former having to pay the "impossible price" of trading off crucial aspects of who they are. The second assumption is that Britishness or Englishness is "unacceptable" to the coloured immigrants from the colonies because all of them share anticolonial sentiments and regard these cultural categories as tainted by their association with a colonial regime and its oppressive cultural policies. In the previous section, I have already discussed how Nirad Chaudhuri regarded it to be the historical role of Britain to spread their culture in the colonies and help the colonised subjects evolve civilisationally. This gives the lie to the argument that all immigrants were against colonialism and its integrationist cultural policies. In the concluding section that follows, I build upon this argument by unpacking the ways in which Nirad Chaudhuri critiques the essentialisation of the cultural identity of the coloured immigrants and the devaluation of Englishness in the metropolis to show how multiculturalism was as inimical to the anglicised self-fashioning of an Indian immigrant like him in the metropolis as racism was under the colonial rule.

Critiquing multicultural equality

To understand Chaudhuri's critique of multicultural Britain, it is important to understand how the philosophy of multiculturalism misreads the conception of cultural assimilation which is at the heart of an Indian's self-fashioning as English. Brian Barry, in his influential attack on multiculturalism from the vantage point of liberalism, argues that cultural assimilation may not necessarily mean the forcible destruction of the cultural practices of a particular community and absorbing those members within the cultural community of the aggressor. Indeed, assimilation might also happen as a voluntary process. As Barry writes, "Much assimilation has always occurred as a result of groups or individual members of groups acting on the judgement that they will have better life prospects if they can shed their present identity and acquire another" (75). However, trying to acquire the identity of one cultural community may not always result in becoming a member of that community since such membership can only be obtained through a process of ratification. To elaborate this situation, Barry refers to the distinction offered by Rainer Bauböck between the two terms, "assimilation" and "acculturation". In Bauböck's words:

> We may use the term acculturation for a process by which an individual comes to acquire cultural practices belonging to the tradition of another group. Assimilation would then indicate a change of membership which makes an individual similar to a receiving community in a sense that its members recognize her as one of their kind.
>
> (40)

As is evident from the discussion of Chaudhuri's critique of British imperialism above, such recognition as "one of their kind" might not be forthcoming from the community whose culture is being emulated. Indeed, as we have already seen, the story of the Indian desire for anglicisation can be constructed as a tragic narrative of voluntary acculturation and denied assimilation. The philosophy of multiculturalism doesn't address this lack of equality resulting from a refusal to provide cultural membership to an accultured individual. Rather, as Barry points out, multiculturalism approaches assimilation as invariably coercive and therefore invariably evil. Acknowledging that coercive attempts to assimilate people culturally do happen, Barry goes on to note that

> we should not conflate it with assimilation that occurs in the absence of coercion. The thesis of "difference-blind" liberalism is that it would be an improper interference with individual liberty to design public policies aimed at frustrating the wishes of those who would like to assimilate under those conditions.
>
> (76)

For an anglicised Indian like Chaudhuri who is desirous to be recognised as English, the problem with British imperialism was that it was inadequately "difference blind" since its universalist doctrine was routinely trumped by racial prejudices against the colonised subjects. However, a multicultural metropolis presented someone like Chaudhuri with precisely the opposite problem, that of "improper interference" which frustrated his desire for assimilation as much as the earlier doctrine of racist liberalism. With its excessive concern for preserving cultural difference, multicultural policies in Britain not only delegitimised the idea of a coloured migrant's quest to mould himself as an Englishman but also forced him to identify with a cultural label that announced his ethnicity, country of origin, or ancestral religion.

Such a multicultural approach which, in order to safeguard the communal identity of coloured immigrants from coercive cultural assimilation, ended up undermining a colonised subject's efforts to integrate as equal was the mainstay of British political ideology for much of the post-war period. In Ted Cantle's words:

> A defensive and protective policy based upon multicultural separateness gained support from both sides of the political divide. The Right opposed integration and racial mixing in principle and the left feared that it would precipitate further hostility and that the cultural heritage of minorities would be undermined in a wave of assimilation.
>
> (56)

As Cantle points out, such a policy meant that the right to be equal was overshadowed by the right to be different, thereby creating ghettoised cultural identities for the erstwhile colonised subjects within the metropolis. The response of the multicultural Britain to the discrimination that haunted its colonial past was to dismantle the hierarchical scale that had earlier informed its imperialist thinking by destigmatising the unique cultural legacies of its coloured migrants. However, at the same time, it trapped the coloured immigrant within the cultural specificities of his community of origin based on his religion or his country of birth which apparently marked him as different from the mainstream white English population of the metropolis. Such an attitude made it injudicious if not impossible for the coloured migrant from the colony to voluntarily assimilate.

As early as 1951, when the publication of *Autobiography of an Unknown Indian* earned him a reputation in the metropolis, Chaudhuri was particularly conscious of not being presented as a "niche interest" author for readers looking for oriental exotica. Rather, he wanted this English autobiography to be read as an equal of any other mainstream English literature that was being produced and consumed in the metropolis. In his own words:

> I did not wish my book to be regarded as one of special Indian interest, but to be read by ordinary English readers of serious books. I

actually said that "it has not been conceived or executed as a contribution to what may be called Orientalia".

(*Thy Hand* 899)

Consequently, when Macmillan accepted his autobiography for publication, Chaudhuri was ecstatic primarily because "that time Macmillan did not publish books about India" (*Thy Hand* 900). In 1951, this assured Chaudhuri that he had managed to escape being categorised as an "Indian" writer of English literature and was now to be regarded as a peer of such canonical English authors like Thomas Hardy and Rudyard Kipling who were also published by Macmillan (*Thy Hand* 900). However, by the time Chaudhuri moved to Britain, he could acutely feel the refusal of the metropolitan audience to accept him as an "English" author. Thus, when in 1986, he was invited to the Ilkley Literature Festival of 1986 as a representative "Indian" author of English literature, it came as an anti-climax to Chaudhuri's lifelong effort to anglicise himself. Consequently, in his speech there, which is compiled in *Why I Mourn for England* under the title "The English Language and Indian Life", Chaudhuri took great pains to counter this cultural ghettoisation. In fact, he started that speech by categorically dissociating himself from the label of being an "Indian writer in English":

> I was both surprised and gratified when the organizers of this unique festival asked me to participate in it. However, I was also made uneasy by the thought that, in view of the new feature they had included in this year's celebrations, they must have given me a status which I do not have. I would therefore begin by telling you that you should not take me as a representative of Indian writing in English, nor am I going to offer you a specimen of it.
>
> (49)

In an English studies seminar held in Cambridge in 1983, Salman Rushdie had experienced a similar kind of uneasiness when confronted with the label of Commonwealth literature. In his essay "'Commonwealth literature' Does Not Exist" which built upon this sense of uneasiness, Rushdie argues that such qualifiers are used to divide the category of English literature and recreate the colonial hierarchy. It draws a boundary around the English literature produced in the metropolis and allows the academic institutions, publishers, critics, and readers to club together literature in English produced by erstwhile non-white colonised subjects "and then more or less ignore it" (66). Like Chaudhuri, Rushdie too advocates against the use of qualifiers that marginalise certain groups of writers writing in English and proclaims the right of the non-metropolitan non-white writer in English to be read as an equal of his British counterpart. However, their claim for equality rests on two different arguments. Rushdie asserts equality on the ground that in a postcolonial world, the English language is no longer the language of the English and has been appropriated and domesticated by the colonised subjects ("Commonwealth" 64). In other words, Rushdie claims that the English language has been transformed, and literature produced in each of these transformed versions of the language should be weighed equally. Chaudhuri in his speech delivered at the Ilkley festival, on the other hand, argued that it was the English language and English literature that had transformed the life of colonised subjects like him who were born during the heydays of the British rule in India:

> That life was created by the impact of the English language and English literature on us in India in the nineteenth century. ... It is this, and not the political legacy, which I regard as the greatest achievement of British rule in India, for it was nothing less than renovation of the *life* of a people who had fallen into a state of stagnancy and stupor.
> (49, emphasis in original)

According to Chaudhuri, this transformation from stupor to a new life made individuals like him the cultural equivalents of the colonising population. He therefore seeks equal treatment not simply because he is a writer in the English language but also, and more importantly, because he is an Englishman writing in English.

Interestingly, in such later writings like his address to the Ilkley Literature Festival, Chaudhuri turns his earlier complaint of being denied equality and assimilation by the colonial society on its head. He does that by tracing the post-1945 history of Britain as a history of deepening decadence. Thus, whereas in the 1946 pieces written for *The New English Review* Chaudhuri is merely apprehensive of the ways in which the national life of the metropolis would be affected by the dissolution of its overseas empire, by the 1980s he is convinced that with the denouncing of the colonial project the vitality of English civilisation was gone. As Chaudhuri declares in a lecture delivered in 1988, included in *Why I Mourn for England* under the title "Decadence of English Life and Civilization", "The decadence I feared is in full swing" (42). Elaborating on this decadence, Chaudhuri argues that like all ancient civilisations, the destruction of England's glory was not merely the handiwork of "imported barbarians" (42) but also of the homegrown ones: "Just as there are in England today young savages who mug and even kill helpless old women, so there are also the same kind of savages who perpetrate the same type of crimes on an old civilization" (42). For Chaudhuri, unsurprisingly, the imported hordes of "barbarians" were the inadequately anglicised colonised subjects who had arrived in the metropolis in ever growing numbers throughout the first few decades following the Second World War. The homegrown "barbarians", on the other hand, were those who were reversing what Chaudhuri regarded as the order of civilisational progress. Thus, while addressing his English audience at Ilkley, Chaudhuri complains: "You are Hinduizing yourselves not only by taking to Yoga, but also by becoming vegetarian" (50). The reason why such cultural adaptation by the English is regarded by Chaudhuri as sacrilegious even while advertising his own anglicisation as an Indian and a Hindu as a cherished achievement is because the latter for him represents a "natural" desire to progress beyond the confines of a civilisation that has exhausted its life force to a new civilisational order which represented the avant-garde. The former, in contrast, is perceived as an "unnatural" desire to renounce one's affiliation to what should have been the dominant civilisation of the day and atavistically returning to an earlier mode of civilisation. In the face of such "barbarism", Chaudhuri puts himself forward before his audience as the sole representative of that earlier glory of an English life, English language, and English culture that was engaged in the grand project of leading the evolution of human civilisation:

> I have been able to give you only flitting glimpses into the world of English in which I was born and brought up. It was a hidden garden even then, and now it has disappeared. Perhaps only I remain of those who saw it and can describe it from personal knowledge.
> (67)

In the piece titled "Diary", Chaudhuri elaborates on this point by mentioning a "flippant joke" (110) that he was wont to share with his guests and acquaintances about his life in England. The joke constituted of him answering whenever he was asked as to why he had decided to stay in England in spite of facing economic hardship there by stating: "In order to show Englishmen how their fathers dressed, how their fathers ate and drank, and how their fathers wrote English" (110). The humour in this joke, of course, derives from the irony that Chaudhuri, who as a colonised subject was denied the status of an English citizen in spite of his English self-fashioning, went on to survive as the only Englishman in a multicultural metropolis that was trying to distance itself from the legacies of cultural colonialism and the stereotyped image of an Englishman.

Conclusion

At this point, however, we are confronted with a crucial question. Does Chaudhuri's assertion of being the iconic Englishman to the modern-day metropolitan society and his assertion of living an "Indian" life in Oxford amidst a pastoral setting that was reminiscent of the East Bengal of his childhood make him a figure of cultural in-betweenness? I would argue that just as in the case of Cornelia Sorabji, reading Chaudhuri too through the lens of cultural in-betweenness would be to miss the complexity of his self-fashioning. Firstly, for Chaudhuri, to be English was to be culturally an Indian in a more refined and, indeed, in a more authentic way. This is clearly evident from the way he uses the Aryan migration theory as well as the liberal theory of human civilisational progress in his works. In fact, within the framework of Chaudhuri's argument, being an authentic Indian Aryan was to be quintessentially English both racially and culturally. Furthermore, resisting anglicisation amounted to keeping oneself confined to the ossified condition which the once vibrant Aryan civilisation had come to acquire in India with the passage of time. Thus, whereas Sorabji tried to avoid the position of cultural in-betweenness by carefully removing from her identity any traces of "Indian womanhood", Chaudhuri sought to avoid the position by constructing Indianness and Englishness not as separate cultural codes that can only be brought together as a hyphenated entity but rather as poles of the same cultural continuum. From this perspective, labelling Chaudhuri as an "Indian" English writer does not make much sense. For Chaudhuri, such a label would either be a tautology, or, worse, it would be an undermining of his English self-fashioning that would amount to a Kiplingesque accusation of his being an inadequately civilised Caliban who was merely trying to ape the English.

Notes

1 This is probably a misprint of the name Gaius Verres.
2 Such synonymous use of the terms Great Britain and the United Kingdom, of course. presents its own problem as it erases the distinction between the union of the three kingdoms of Wales, Scotland, and England that was formally achieved by the beginning of the eighteenth century and the formal inclusion of the Kingdom of Ireland that happened about a century later.
3 The supervision of East India Company's rule over India by the British Parliament was increased even further by the 1784 Pitt's India Act.
4 Interestingly, Macaulay in his 1835 Minute speaks of educating Indians as inhabitants of the "British territories" so that they can become "English in tastes, in opinions, in morals and in intellect". This desire to turn Indians into "English" rather than merely "British" betrays the hegemonic role that the English cultural and political identity exercised within the project of British imperialism.
5 As noted in the chapter on Cornelia Sorabji, the Indian rebellion of 1857 led to a rethink about the ideology of liberalism and the reformist agenda within the British colonial administration. However, among the metropolitan public in general, the potential of western cultural values bringing about good in the colonies enjoyed approval even among those who were against these values being forced down the throats of the colonised subjects. See Porter (*The Absent-Minded* 244) and Matikkala (4).
6 See Chapter 6 in Mohanram.
7 This category referred to the inhabitants of the Indian principalities which were vassal states of the British Raj.
8 Before 1909, a miniscule section of Indians had enjoyed voting rights in municipal councils and rural boards since 1882. See Chiriyankandath.

9 Chaudhuri was, of course, not the only Indian trying to negotiate this gap between the promise of equality and its denial within the colonial context. Sukanya Banerjee in her book, *Becoming Imperial Citizens*, explores how others like Dadabhai Naoroji, M.K. Gandhi, Cornelia Sorabji, and Surendranath Banerjea too sought to bridge the gap between subjecthood and citizenship in colonial India.
10 As Shruti Kapila has argued, such theories of evolutionism, inspired primarily by the works of Herbert Spencer but also of Charles Darwin, were well entrenched within the late nineteenth-century Indian intellectual milieu to which Nirad Chaudhuri was ideologically rooted. See Kapila's "Self, Spencer, and Swaraj" and "The Enchantment of Science".
11 For an analysis of Aquinas's views on authority and the distinction between the ruler who rules for the common good and the tyrant who rules for personal benefit, see Finnis.
12 I use the term "reasserted" because the fundamental equality of the colonised Indians with all the other British subjects anywhere within the Empire was already stated in Queen Victoria's proclamation of 1858.

5

DOM MORAES'S ANGLICISATION AND THE AMBIGUITY OF RETURN

In our discussion on Nirad Chaudhuri's English self-fashioning, we have seen how he reverses the poles of exile and home by travelling from his native East Bengal to England and finally settling down in Oxford. In this chapter, which focuses on the English self-fashioning of Dom Moraes, I explore the narrative of a return journey from England to India in which the poles of exile and home are yet again renegotiated. As I have already discussed in Introduction, such return journeys are often regarded by critics as the quintessential pattern that underlies the life trajectories of the colonial Indian middle class that emerged during the nineteenth century.[1] Whereas the nationalist narrative dealing with the life stories of individuals like M.K. Gandhi or Jawaharlal Nehru presents these return journeys as a coming back not only to one's roots but also to a more purposeful life, for many anglicised Indians the prospect of having to relocate to India was filled with a sense of dread. This distinction can be clearly observed by comparing the return journeys of the two brothers, Manmohan Ghose and Aurobindo Ghose. Both had a thoroughly anglicised upbringing, and both were sent to England by their father for higher studies. Aurobindo Ghose, who later styled himself as Sri Aurobindo, returned to India in 1893 and immediately felt a sense of relief which he later described in the following words:

> [A] vast calm ... descended upon him[2] at the moment when he stepped first on Indian soil after his long absence, in fact with his first step on the Apollo Bunder in Bombay; (this calm surrounded him and remained for long months afterwards).
>
> (110)

Tracing a graph similar to Gandhi and Nehru, Sri Aurobindo found India conducive to his project of self-actualisation and went on to become first a significant leader of the Swadeshi movement and then a major Hindu mystic of the twentieth century. In contrast, Manmohan Ghose, who kept himself out of active politics throughout his life and only reluctantly returned to India in 1894,[3] felt himself to be "denationalised" (Naik 45) in his country of origin. In what follows, I explore this sense of denationalisation that a significant section of anglicised Indian suffered from in their country of birth, especially after their return from the metropolis. I do this with reference to the writings of Moraes who not only made a similar reluctant journey back to India almost a hundred years after Manmohan Ghose but also devised interesting literary strategies to deal with the sense of alienation.

Though a sense of being alienated from India pervades all of Moraes's writings, it is especially evident in his prose works. In them, Moraes obsessively returns to the theme of his disconnection from his native country and the fear and anxiety that accompanied his return from England. However, since Moraes's reputation has rested primarily on his early fame as a poet, these prose texts that elaborate on the theme of his anxiety-ridden return have remained almost completely neglected by critics. In this chapter, I focus on these forgotten prose writings of Moraes and place them within the larger framework of what I call the "literature of return" through which postcolonial authors have articulated their physical journey back to their country of origin and which, in the context of Indian English literature, is represented by a rich corpus of works produced by authors as diverse as Jawaharlal Nehru and V.S. Naipaul.

Exiled at home

Though born in the Indian city of Bombay, Moraes spent his childhood in an environment that produced the illusion of being British. Moraes would later recall the Bombay of the 1940s where he grew up as "still a British city in many obvious ways" (*Bombay* 37). There was a British governor running the city and young Moraes could see from his parent's apartment, located "in one of the more British parts of the city" (*Bombay* 37), protective barrage balloons gyrating over the Arabian Sea as "symbols of the British war in which Bombay had become embroiled" (*Bombay* 37). But he notes that it was "[n]ot only the appearance and feel of the city but the life we led [which] made me think that Bombay was British" (*Bombay* 38). Much like Sorabji, Moraes belonged to a thoroughly Westernised Indian Christian family. Within it, life was oriented more around England than around anything Indian. Moraes's father, like his grandfather before, had been educated in Oxford and, although the former had returned to India as a young man with nationalist views, they had not connected him or his family very deeply with the subcontinent. Thus, to Moraes, it was self-evident from his very early years that

> [m]y mother and my father had nothing to do with India itself: they were simply themselves, as I was myself, and our relationship had to be worked out independent of where we were.
> (*My Son's Father* 163–164)

For Moraes, this inherited sense of detachment from the lived reality of India crystallised around the use of language. His family was entirely English-speaking and the only Indian vernacular that he was familiar with was "the pidgin Hindi in which I spoke to the servants" (*My Son's* 9). Thus, English was effectively the only language available to Moraes through which to access the world around him. This meant that he was excluded from the vernacular Indian life that was beyond his immediate family and its small group of English-speaking friends:

> In the streets of India I felt uneasy, knowing neither the language, nor, because of not having come in contact with many Indians who were not from an English background, the people.
> (*Gone Away* 9)

Moraes's traumatic childhood made this feeling of being alienated from India more acute. He had lost his mother as a caring presence early in his life when she gradually became insane and started having violent fits of rage during which she once attacked Moraes with a knife. Consequently, the estrangement that he felt in the streets of India became coupled in his mind with the sense of estrangement and danger that was evoked by his mother. As Moraes describes: "Ever since then, I had connected my mother to India in all its aspects. One of them was language" (*Out of* 21). He goes on to write that when, after being briefly and happily away from India with his father, he was suddenly sent back to India to his mother, his hatred for the country and for its vernacular language had taken hold of him even more deeply:

> [E]ver since my forced return to India, I had increasingly disliked and feared the country and the Hindi language that I was expected to speak that was not, and never had been, mine.
> I sheltered in my own language. I read and wrote English poetry.
> (*Out of* 21)

English thus provided both a barrier and a bulwark for Moraes, which, while it alienated him from the India in the streets, also simultaneously allowed him to fashion for himself the identity of an outsider separated from his mother(land) that plagued him with the emotions of incomprehension, despair, and danger. Hence, from very early on in his life, through his readings of English literature and his own efforts to produce English poetry in imitation of Dylan Thomas and W.H. Auden, Moraes constructed for himself a mental world that was distinct from the India that physically surrounded him. As a friend of Moraes's father observed:

> [Y]ou yourself are a very English person. Your reactions aren't Indian .... You seem quite naturally to live in a world of English poetry and English painting, and you are an English poet.
> (*My Son's* 164)

What problematised this self-fashioning as an English person who inhabited a space imagined through English poetry was, however, Moraes's body. It uneasily jutted out of this imagined reality, marking an ambiguous threshold that both separated and dissolved the English inner life of his language and mental images on the one hand and the Indian world outside in which his body was spatially situated on the other:

> The brown-skinned people of whom I was one swirled past me like the sea outside the window. I had separated myself, to stand on the unknown mournful rocks left when the tide had passed.
> (*My Son's* 106)

This ambivalent relationship with his brown-skinned body and the bodily reality that surrounded him in India would go on to underline almost all of his writings, but most prominently his prose works on India like *Gone Away*, *Out of God's Oven*, and *The Long Strider*. However, to locate these works of Moraes that are informed by the uniqueness of his crisis as an anglicised Indian within the genre of the literature of return, I would first need to recast Moraes's personal alienation in more general terms.

Forever in combat with his own image

To explore the wider resonances of this singular relationship between the consciousness of the self and its encompassing bodily reality that Moraes's life story opens up, I would like to mobilise Kaja Silverman's theorisation of the process of identity formation. Silverman builds her theory of identity upon Jacques Lacan's formulation of the Mirror Stage, which she summarises in the following words:

> [T]he ego comes into existence at the moment when the infant subject first apprehends the image of its body within a reflective surface, and is itself a mental refraction of that image.
> (10)

In this proposition of Lacan, the sense of the self is bound up with the body because the individual finds, or rather misrecognises, in the reflection of the body the desired unity of an integrated identity. Silverman proposes an alternative model connecting the self and the body in which she suggests that the ego comes into existence not only through an encounter with the reflection of the body but also through the bodily sensations experienced by an individual by the virtue of being located within a particular point in space. Thus, in this model, the sense of the self is associated with the body in two different ways. It is connected to the mirror image of the body, but it is also connected non-visually to the body through "proprioceptivity"—a concept which Silverman explains in these terms:

> Proprioceptivity can best be understood as that egoic component to which concepts like "here", "there", and "my" are keyed. It encompasses the muscular system "in its totality", including those muscles which effect the "shifting of the body and its members in space".... Indeed, proprioceptivity would seem to be intimately bound up with the body's sensation of occupying a point of space, and with the terms with which it does so.
>
> (16)

Silverman further proposes that a sense of identity is arrived at when this proprioceptive component of the self, embedded within the body, gets fitted to the reflected image of the body. As she writes: "The experience which each of us at times has of being 'ourselves' ... depends on the smooth integration of the visual imago with the proprioceptive or sensational ego" (17).

Importantly, Silverman argues that the postural deployment of the body through which an individual is fitted into the surrounding spatial envelope and which constitutes the essence of proprioceptivity is not a biological given. Rather, the bodily posture is culturally constructed, and to prove this Silverman refers to Michel Foucault's theory "about the postural coercions induced on behalf of work and education" (16), as elaborated in *Discipline and Punish*. However, this cultural constructedness of the postural body is perhaps more concretely understood through Pierre Bourdieu's concept of "hexis", which deals with how the body of the individual is socialised so that it becomes embedded within a particular framework of cultural codification. Elaborating on this concept, Bourdieu writes:

> One could endlessly enumerate the values given body, *made* body, by the hidden persuasion of an implicit pedagogy which can instil a whole cosmology, through injunctions as insignificant as "sit up straight" or "don't hold your knife in your left hand", and inscribe the most fundamental principles of the arbitrary content of a culture in seemingly innocuous details of bearing or physical and verbal manners, so putting them beyond the reach of consciousness and explicit statement.
>
> (69, emphasis in original)

Thus, the body here is perceived to be the site in which a particular sense of the self, oriented along the lines of a particular cultural code, is inscribed through pedagogy.

Within the colonial system, this pedagogic construction of the postural body creates a singular result. As Frantz Fanon notes in his *Black Skin,*

White Masks, in the colonial periphery the cultural self that gets inscribed within the body of a native is often that of a white European. He writes:

> The black schoolboy in the Antilles, who in his lessons is forever talking about "our ancestors, the Gauls", identifies himself with the explorer, the bringer of civilization, the white man who carries truth to the savages—an all-white truth.
> (147)

This identification with the white man mapped on to the corporeal schema of the Antillean schoolboy makes him react "like real little Parisians and produce ... such things as 'I like vacation because then I can run through the fields, breathe fresh air, and come home with *rosy* cheeks'" (162n, emphasis in original). This is precisely the case with all the anglicised Indians discussed in this book, including Moraes whose self-fashioning constituted of culturally training themselves through their Western education to "feel" English from within. However, when the proprioceptive consciousness of the Antillean schoolboy who parallels the self-fashioning of anglicised Indians encounters its corresponding visual image in a coloured body, there is, as Fanon puts it, a sense of "betrayal" (193). To understand the nature of this betrayal, which also crucially informs Moraes's relation to his own image as a brown-skinned Indian, I again turn to Silverman.

In explaining the dynamic process of integrating the non-visual consciousness of the self that is culturally embedded within the body and its visual image, Silverman argues that an individual can identify only with those bodily images which are culturally ratified and idealised. Hence, within a culture that idealises whiteness, the visual image that deviates from the white body is difficult to be identified with. As Silverman states:

> It is not possible, ... to be completely "inside" any other kind of image [than the idealised one], even momentarily. When held by the cultural gaze to an identification with a deidealizing image, the subject often experiences it as an external imposition. At the very least, he or she refuses to invest narcissistically in the image ..., and attempts in all kinds of ways to maintain his or her distance from it.
> (20)

This explains why, according to Fanon, a Westernised individual like that Antillean schoolboy with a coloured body situated outside the metropolis is "forever in combat with his own image" (194). He finds the image of his body as being scripted by "thousand details, stories, anecdotes" (111) of "tom-toms, cannibalism, intellectual deficiency, fetishism, racial defects [and] slave-ships" (112) associated with the colonised space of his origin. Similarly, for the anglicised Indians, their brown bodies located them in a space that is informed by what Dipesh Chakrabarty refers to as the "history of lack". Writing within the context of India, Chakrabarty notes:

> The tendency to read Indian history in terms of a lack, an absence, or an incompleteness that translates into "inadequacy" ... is ancient, going back to the beginnings of colonial rule in India. The British conquered and represented the diversity of Indian pasts through a homogenizing narrative of transition from a medieval period to modernity.
>
> (32)

The transition to modernity is, however, never completed in this narrative and within this story of deferred modernity "the 'Indian' [i]s always a figure of lack" (32) locked up in the "waiting room of history" (8) with his coloured body never becoming adequate enough to house an English subjectivity inside it.

As we have already seen, one very powerful response displayed by the anglicised Indians to this sense of being trapped within a narrative of lack is to try and remove oneself from the bodily reality that surrounds him or her within India. Thus, for Moraes, the desire to distance himself from the inadequacy of his coloured body and to stand separated from the brown-skinned people who "swirled past me like the sea" resulted in the solipsistic poems of his early youth in which the consciousness of the immediate physical reality surrounding his body is almost completely missing. Moraes himself would later note that "in these poems I had created a world of pure imagination" (*Never at Home* 38), which did not have "anything to do with the world" (*Never at Home* 38).[4]

This world of pure imagination is, of course, the familiar world of a dream England gleaned from the pages of English literature that we have seen being repeatedly created by anglicised Indians starting with Madhusudan Dutt. We have also seen how this imagined world had regularly propelled anglicised Indians to journey towards the colonial metropolis in search of a "homeland" since the nineteenth century. Thus, in the mid-twentieth century, when young Moraes would speak of his alienation from the Indian reality within which he was bodily located and his sense of a more natural affiliation to the England that he had encountered during his study of English literature, he would be echoing a host of individuals that we have already encountered before. Consequently, the voice in which he articulates the following lines appear to be thoroughly familiar:

> For years I had read English poetry and novels that bore no relation to my life in India. In London, all the fiction that I had read became reality. People here behaved and spoke as my reading told me they

> were supposed to. There were real poets here, artists whose work I only knew from books.
>
> (Moraes and Srivatsa, *Out of* 25)

Similarly, when young Moraes would confess to the poet Stephen Spender his desire to make England his home, the sentiment would reveal not only his individual sense of alienation from India that developed out of his unique personal history but also his location within the familiar trajectory of "homeward" journeys to the metropolis:

> I said I wanted to settle in England. ... England for me was where the poets were. The poets were my people. I had no real consciousness of a nationality, for I did not speak the language of my countrymen, and therefore had no soil or roots.
>
> (*My Son's* 100)

However, as we have seen in the preceding chapters, the physical journey to England does not lead the anglicised Indian to a "home" with which s/he can unproblematically associate. Nor does it rescue the anglicised Indian from his location within the history of lack and grants him entry as an equal within the metropolitan English community. Rather, it enhances the disjunction between the self and the surrounding bodily reality. The coloured body of the anglicised Indian, which uneasily protrudes out of his imagined reality in the colonial periphery, becomes even more irreconcilable within the metropolitan social space informed by the normativity of whiteness. This in turn deepens the loathing towards the coloured body and the burden of inadequacy to which it keeps the anglicised Indian tied to even after s/he has escaped India and successfully journeyed to England.

For Moraes, the discomfort that his brown body created for him within the metropolis resulted in an attempt to state even more emphatically his separation from his mother(land) and the traces of Indianness that it had left on him at the most physical level. This attitude is best expressed in a poem titled "Letter to my Mother" that Moraes composed in the 1960s before he "knew that [he] would ever live in any other place except England" (*Never at Home* 1):

> Your eyes are like mine.
> When I last looked in them
> I saw my whole country,
> A defeated dream
> Hiding itself in prayers
> A population of corpses,
> Of burnt bodies that cluttered
> The slow, deep rivers, of
> Bodies stowed into earth
> Quickly before they stank

> Or cooked by the sun for vultures
> On a marble tower.
> You pray, you do not notice
> The corpses around you
> Sorrow has stopped your eye.
> Your dream is desolate
> It calls me every day
> But I cannot enter it.
> You know I will not return.
> Forgive me my trespasses.
>
> *(In Cinnamon Shade* 52)

The hated figure of Moraes's mother whose presence was unique to Moraes's own history of trauma and loss becomes in this poem the embodiment of the more general history of lack within which all the coloured bodies are trapped. Moraes's childhood desire to escape from his mother merges here with the desire to tear himself away from this history, which finds its spatial coordinates in the colonial periphery of India—a land whose inadequacy is conveyed through images of death, decay, and superstition. It culminates in the strongly worded denunciation of the penultimate line: "I will not return". Yet, the lines at the beginning and at the end of the quoted section, which frame the repulsive image of the mother(land), also indicate the impossibility of such an attempt to sever connections with it. Thus, the eyes of Moraes's mother reflect not just the putrefaction and moral depravity of his native land from which he tries to escape, but also juxtapose onto it the image of Moraes's own body, because it is he who "last looked into them" and saw himself reflected there. The physical movement away from the mother(land) thus dissolves into a physical identification with it.

This complex to-and-fro motion that keeps turning between identification and disavowal is again played out in the last two lines of the poem. The statement "I will not return" is thus balanced in the very next line by Moraes asking for forgiveness for his trespasses. The word "trespass" here is identical to the word "return" in so far as it suggests the same movement back to India. The crucial difference, of course, lies in the fact that whereas "return" signifies a coming back to the point of origin, and carries, within the context of this poem, the sense of homecoming, "trespass" signifies the entry of a stranger into another's land with which he is in no way connected. This distinction that Moraes draws between "return" and "trespass"—between coming back to India as a native and entering India as a stranger—is at the core of all his later writings that deal with his country of birth. They are all concerned primarily with the question of how to come back without being sucked into the sea of brown-skinned people, how to maintain the line of demarcation between his English self and his native surrounding which to Moraes signified lack, inadequacy, death, and decay. In other words, how to return as a stranger.

Outsider looking in: narrative grammar of the literature of return

In our discussion of Nirad Chaudhuri, we have observed how the conflict between holding on to one's English identity within a hostile metropolitan environment while reconciling it to one's Indian roots is tentatively resolved through a "metaphoric" return to the country of origin. While never physically returning to India after he finally moved to England in 1970, Chaudhuri nevertheless diligently created the illusion of living in the pastoral setting of his childhood East Bengal while being located in Oxford. Such creations of an imagined homeland to cope with the sense of maladjustment faced in the metropolis are, however, not specific to the writings of anglicised Indians. Indeed, this is one of the most identifiable traits of postcolonial diasporic literature in general. As Zoë Wicomb, the diasporic South African novelist, observes, the displaced author, conspicuous by the visual salience of her skin and unable to easily fit her coloured body within the metropolitan space, uses fictions of memory to build around herself another spatial envelope to inhabit—"'another land of counterpane' ... with which to keep at bay the Northern chill" (Wicomb 152). Within the context of Indian English literature, it is this particular form of return through memory that has attracted the most amount of critical attention, especially since the publication of Rushdie's *Midnight's Children*—"a novel of memory and about memory" ("Imaginary Homelands" 10)—in which India is reconstructed by the author from his childhood reminiscences cast in "CinemaScope and glorious Technicolor" ("Imaginary Homelands" 10) while sitting in a room in North London.

However, in weaving this counterpane of memory gathered from childhood, the conflict with the native land that had initially propelled the postcolonial author towards the metropolis is not altogether resolved. On the contrary, this attempt by the displaced author to inhabit an imagined homeland constructed out of the memories of the past is often accompanied by an inhibition to make a physical return back to the country of origin. As Bharati Mukherjee, the America-based author of Indian origin, writes:

> I have joined imaginative forces with an anonymous driven underclass of semi-assimilated Indians with sentimental attachment to a distant homeland, *but no real desire for permanent return*.... Instead of seeing my Indianness as a fragile identity to be preserved against obliteration (or worse, a "visible" disfigurement to be hidden) I see it now as a set of fluid identities to be celebrated.... Indianness is now a metaphor, a particular way of comprehending the world.
> (quoted in Meenakshi Mukherjee "The Anxiety" 2610, emphasis added)

Contra Mukherjee, Wicomb argues that the strain of having to imagine through fiction a decontextualised homeland in the metropolis ultimately proves to be unsustainable for the author:

> [R]eading Salman Rushdie's last book, *The Ground Beneath Her Feet*, something struck me that was really frightening for me. ... [I]t seemed to me clear that he has mined his Indian childhood and he had come to a point where that mine was exhausted. ... I suddenly realized I can't be a writer and keep on living in Scotland. ... You can't go on writing if you're not living close to the place that you're writing about.
>
> (150–151)

At one level, the instance of Nirad Chaudhuri gives a lie to this assertion that one can't go on imaginatively recreating one's native country in the metropolis for a very long time. He went on "mining" his life in India for almost three decades after he had shifted to England. Interestingly, Wicomb herself has continued living in Scotland and not returned to South Africa. But, on the other hand, the life story of Cornelia Sorabji alerts us to the dangers inherent in a continuous attempt to recreate the life of one's country of origin without being physically in touch with its ground realities. In Moraes, we encounter an alternative trajectory of return presenting a different possibility of resolving the conflict between one's self-identity and the physical space that surrounds it. He provides us with an example of an anglicised Indian and a postcolonial diasporic author who decided to reengage with his country of origin by physically returning to it after a long stay in the metropolis. In what follows, I explore how Moraes sought to reconcile his English identity to his being physically located in India, and how this reconciliation took the form of writings that can be categorised as "literature of return".

However, before moving on to Moraes, I would like to clarify my use of the phrase "literature of return". I use it to signify the body of texts produced by individuals who write about their country of origin after physically returning to it either as a traveller or as a return migrant subsequent to their spending a considerable duration of time abroad. Thus, I understand the literature of return in opposition to the diasporic literature where the native homeland is imaginatively constructed from abroad by weaving together strands of memories along with family history. Among the texts discussed in this book, Cornelia Sorabji's *India Calling*, where India is portrayed by the author from within the country, provides a typical example of what I mean by the literature of return. On the other hand, Nirad Chaudhuri's *Thy Hand, Great Anarch!*, in which the author describes the social, political, and cultural history of India while settled in Oxford, would provide an example of diasporic literature about a homeland imagined through the aid of memory. As we shall see in the discussion below, this difference in location plays a crucial role in how the author situates himself or herself within a life writing or even a travelogue because the social gaze that is directed at the author's body in each particular location is different. In other words,

I argue that writing about the physical realities of India as a brown sahib while being submerged in a sea of similar-looking brown people and writing about India from memory while being located in the white normative space of the metropolis as a "not quite/not white" anglicised Indian shape the authorial position in two uniquely different ways.

Moraes's first account of his physically journeying back to India was also his first major prose work. Titled *Gone Away*, this text deals with one of Moraes's extended visits to India at the age of 22, some years after he had moved to England as a student. Moraes states in one of his autobiographies how, when he had gone to his father to consult about the book, the latter had observed:

> I imagine you want to write this book as an outsider looking in. I couldn't do that myself, about India. The only way I can help is imagining that *you* are an outsider.
> (*Never at Home* 8, emphasis in original).

This authorial position of an "outsider looking in" was, however, not unique to Moraes. Rather, as we have seen with Sorabji's text, it is a common characteristic feature found underlying many instances of the literature of return.[5] A similar outsider's perspective is also found in Jawaharlal Nehru's *The Discovery of India*, which is another iconic example of this literary genre. While referring to the disconnect that he experienced from his native country as someone who had spent many of his early years in England and who owed his intellectual affiliation to the West, Nehru writes:

> India was in my blood and there was much in her that instinctively thrilled me. And yet I approached her almost as an alien critic, full of dislike for the present as well for many of the relics of the past that I saw. To some extent I came to her via the West, and looked at her as a friendly Westerner might have done.
> (50)

This passage articulates the same conflict that also plagues Moraes's writings on India—a conflict between a sense of filial belongingness to the land and the desire to speak from the position of a detached observer who approaches India "via the West". The conflict is reflected in Nehru's major writings, *Toward Freedom* and *The Discovery of India*, through a mingling of the forms of travel narrative and autobiography. This is worth exploring in greater detail because a similar mingling of form also characterises Moraes's writings on India.

Javed Majeed has observed that Nehru's autobiographical writings (along with Gandhi's and Iqbal's) are also simultaneously travelogues as they interlace the distant and non-participant traveller's perspective with the autobiographical perspective of an involved protagonist. Thus, Nehru's autobiographical writings, in spite of being appropriated as instances of "symbolic autobiographies" (Boehmer *Colonial* 183) where the personal life is read as being representative of the national community, are texts where "there is no attempt to simply subsume [the] individual autobiographical voice within a group identity" (Majeed 3).[6] Yet, to what degree is it possible to maintain this isolated stance of being a detached Western observer segregated from a group identity while travelling through the native country? Nehru in *Toward Freedom* states that in spite of his detached Westerner's perspective, he felt a growing sense of responsibility towards the "vast multitude of semi-naked sons and daughters of India" (57) amidst whom he journeyed. His "travel autobiographies", as Majeed calls them, are thus agonistic in their essence, where the desire to become a part of the greater collectivity and become their representative voice contests the desire to maintain the detached voice of an individual observer who is acutely aware of his isolation and apartness.

This conflict-ridden mixture of the narrative forms of travelogue and autobiography is also evident in V.S. Naipaul's writings on India, which are closer to Moraes's writings in time. In his study *London Calling*, Rob Nixon notes how Naipaul's books on his ancestral land of India are situated at the generic crossroads of travel writings and autobiographies which lead Naipaul to constantly shift between being a detached metropolitan traveller who merely observes and being a subject whose family roots are deeply embedded within this country. Thus, like Nehru's travel autobiographies, Naipaul's texts on India too are sites of a contestation where the author's identity as an uninvolved traveller, whose vision and value system are detached from the subcontinent and aligned to the metropolis, clashes with his sense of belonging to India. As Nixon notes with regard to Naipaul's first book on India, *An Area of Darkness*:

> Naipaul's ... dual fantasies of immersion and elevation ultimately subvert each other; indeed, both the flair and the confusion of the book are intimately connected to the unsettling effects of his efforts to harmonize such discordant voices.
>
> (80)

Moraes's texts on India sway between a similar duality of "immersion and elevation" and use the same narrative grammar as in the works of Nehru and Naipaul that blends together the autobiographical form with the form of the travelogue. Hence, *Gone Away* begins with a short autobiographical introduction that describes how, growing up in Bombay as part of a thoroughly anglicised family, he had always felt alienated from India and how this had led him to come to England and try and make

London his home. This is followed by the description of his journey to India starting from his departure from London so that the poles of home and exile are reversed. London becomes the point of reference from which India is approached and written about, making the native country appear as the exotic overseas destination that is viewed from the perspective of a metropolitan tourist who passively observes and passes by. But this careful distinction between home and exile, and the reversal of the poles of homeland and foreign country, which was to frame each of Moraes's subsequent journeys to his country of birth, become confused as soon as he arrives in India. Moraes vividly describes this effect that coming to India has on him in his autobiography, *My Son's Father*, which was his second prose publication. A book written while Moraes was still living in England, this autobiography narrates how the moment of arrival in his city of birth from London seems at first to reinforce his consciousness of being an alien in India:

> When I landed in Bombay, I was suddenly aware that I was a foreigner. The gestures and intonations of the people around me were strange. The quality of the dust, the trees, and the air were different from what I was used to.
>
> (224)

But in the days that follow, what starts troubling this sense of alienation is his memories that evoke a latent sense of belonging. As the various memories that associate Moraes with the people, the sounds, the scents, and the landmarks of India gradually resurface, it makes his identity as a foreign traveller more and more complicated:

> My eyes were those of a tourist: the beggars, the palm trees, and the teeming whiteclad crowds were reflected in them, but did not penetrate. It was all very strange. Yet, naggingly, behind it all, there were echoes and scents which awoke some memory in me. Like a dream, the city was a new experience, which I knew that I had before.
>
> (224)

His traumatic past, which had pushed Moraes into exile, also draws him back through echoes of his memory into the native land, making his guise of foreignness unsustainable in India. In the following sections of this chapter, I explore how Moraes grapples with these echoes of memory and the processes through which they identify him with his native country, by reading his two last texts on India, *Out of God's Oven* and *The Long Strider*, both of which he co-authored with Sarayu Srivatsa.

Out of God's Oven and the echoes of personal memory

In 1980, Moraes was advised by his literary agent to permanently shift to India because, as he said: "The publishers connect you with India now" (*Out of* 26). Moraes writes:

> In 1980, it had sounded like a prison sentence. Peter Grose [Moraes's literary agent] could not have known the disgust I felt for life in India. I sympathized with the poor, but too many of them existed. India had the most brutally stupid middle class in the world[7]. I wanted London and my friends.
>
> (*Out of* 27)

Two decades later, this disgust for India was to become the most palpable emotion underlining the introduction of *Out of God's Oven*—a book which records through two interconnected narratives what Moraes and his co-author Sarayu Srivatsa saw, heard, and experienced during their extensive journeys through India spanning more than five years. The template on which these experiences are recorded is the familiar narrative of the history of lack that had also informed Moraes's "Letter to my Mother". Published in 2002, the year of the infamous Godhra incident and the Gujarat riots that left thousands dead in its wake,[8] *Out of God's Oven* is announced by Moraes as a document recording the beginning of the end of India which had always been for him the site of "inadequacy", stowed with dying and decaying brown bodies. Thus, Moraes writes in the introduction:

> All that we experienced and described led up to the Gujarat riots, a terrible landmark in Indian history. Now the frightening name of Ayodhya is once more frequently heard. It may well be that the events that have been enacted on the stage of Gujarat are not the climax to the drama of contemporary India; only the first act.
>
> (xv)

Interestingly, a year after *Out of God's Oven* was published, Srivatsa clarified in an article that "the book was my idea in the first place" ("Out of the Oven"). Such a clarification was needed because the book had come to be associated primarily with Moraes. A somewhat exasperated Srivatsa notes in her article that during the book's launch, Moraes had himself encouraged the reporters to think that *Out of God's Oven* was his own project and that it was he who had chosen Srivatsa, the lesser known author, to be his collaborator. When confronted by Srivatsa, Moraes had merely stated that this "would be good for the sales of our book" ("Out of the Oven"). Yet, on reading the text, it becomes evident how, by the time it was published, it had clearly become Moraes's book in a far more significant way than he himself was ready to admit or his co-author ready to acknowledge. The introduction and the prologue of *Out of God's Oven*, through which the reader is led into the text, both are written by Moraes. Even within the text proper, where the narratives of the two authors interlace, the first and the last segment are those of Moraes's. Hence, much before the reader encounters Srivatsa's narrative, heavily bracketed within sections written by Moraes, the agenda and the tone of the book have already been established. Srivatsa's inputs thus appear more as a foil to Moraes's narrative than it being the other way round. More importantly, the text of *Out of God's Oven* both in its form and in its content echoes very closely the conflict between the psychological positions of an insider and an outsider, and between the narrative strategies of the autobiography and the travelogue that had animated Moraes's earlier works on India. In fact, as I show below, *Out of God's Oven* can be read fruitfully as an attempt to resolve this conflict in a new way where the duality of being an involved native insider and a detached objective outsider that had characterised Moraes's previous writings splits into the separate narratives of the two authors.

As Srivatsa herself states in the same article in which she accuses Moraes of stealing her thunder, such a narrative design informed the book from its very inception: "we took our positions and adopted roles. He became the outsider. I became the insider" ("Out of the Oven"). Creating this insider–outsider distinction allowed Moraes to extricate himself from India, even while writing from within it, by distancing himself from the echoes of memories and personal associations that it evoked. This attempt to erase his memories and personal associations that identify him with the country is made evident through the two contrasting ways in which the elements of autobiography and travelogue are intertwined in the sections of Moraes and Srivatsa. Hence, Srivatsa, when she travels across India, almost never leaves her "home", both literally and metaphorically. Her journey through India takes her to places where her relatives live, and her part of the story is thus largely contained within this autobiographical web of extended family spread across the country and their shared memories of the family history. This unquestioned sense of belonging to India, not only spatially but also temporally through memories of the family, is opposed to Moraes's sense of alienation. As Srivatsa writes:

> Dom was both bewildered and exhausted by the things that Indians believed, did or chose to do. As for me, I never really questioned any of them because my country was there for me, shining-free, when I was born.
>
> (73)

The autobiographical involvement of Srivatsa with India is best highlighted during the last leg of the journey that ends in Ayodhya. This city, which is evoked in the introduction as one of the terrible landmarks in contemporary Indian history and which embodies for Moraes its essence of lack and its impending disintegration, becomes for Srivatsa a site that firmly connects her to her Indian roots and reaffirms her sense of being an integral part of India. She finds by the city of Ayodhya the river Sarayu and, dipping her feet into these waters that carry her name, she proceeds to immerse the ashes of her father that she had carried with her during the journey. This tableau with which the book ends, and which underlines Srivatsa's sense of belonging to her native land, also includes the sharply contrasting image of Moraes's disconnection from India. Thus, during the deeply personal ritual that Srivatsa performs in the waters of the river Sarayu that harmoniously connects her with the history of her ancestors as well as the surrounding landscape, Moraes sits at a distance on the river bank as a detached outsider somewhat mystified by the scene unfolding before him: "It seems like an ancient ceremony, connected with time and the river, but I do not know what it is" (387). This contrast between the involved insider and the detached outsider, so clearly pictured in this last scene of the book, is sustained throughout the text. Hence, unlike Srivatsa's narrative, the sections that Moraes writes are almost entirely bereft of autobiographical elements. What little personal details Moraes shares with the readers are wholly contained within the first chapter and are woven around London, highlighting his sense of detachment from India. In contrast to the familiar/familial India of Srivatsa's narrative, Moraes travels through an India that is uncannily exotic in its myriad manifestations of brutalities—from the streets of Gujarat ravaged by communal riots where "the charred ruins [of] a few houses remain, like teeth left in a skull" (6) to the villages of Bihar where men who have been blinded by acid while in police custody wait in vain to be compensated by the state. Moraes's uninvolved gaze travels across this nightmarish landscape while, to quote from one of his poems tellingly named "Exile", "his attire, quartz armour,/Acquired in winter courts,/Shelter[ed] him from our summer" (96).

However, the contradiction that underscores this position of Moraes as an outsider in his own native land soon begins to unravel in the text. His body that had uneasily kept merging with the sea of brown-skinned people that surrounded him as an adolescent in Bombay now again problematises his position as a detached stranger. During his travels in India, whenever Moraes becomes the object of a reciprocal gaze, his British cultural mooring is found to be in contradiction with his insufficiently "English" body. This makes him in the eyes of other Indians at best pretentious and at worst an imposter. Thus, when there is a police raid in the hotel in Ahmedabad where Moraes and Srivatsa were staying during their journey, his ambiguous identity as an English outsider in a coloured Indian body becomes difficult to interpret, immediately marking him as a suspect. Snatching Moraes's British passport from him, the police officer exclaims:

"Ah! I knew there was something wrong. British. You are British?" He inspected Dom from head to toe. "Real English British? No-no-no. It can't be. To me you look very Indian. From Mumbai. Maybe Goa. ... Yes-yes. Your skin, dark like Indian-skin. ... So how you get this British passport, eh?"

(224)

Apart from the body, what also dissolves the barrier that separates Moraes as an English foreigner and reclaims him as a native insider in *Out of God's Oven* is his poetry. This is particularly ironic given the fact that in his early years, his sense of estrangement from his native land had taken shape around the poetry that he read and wrote. Moreover, it was his poetry that had ultimately driven him to seek a distant homeland in England where "real poets" lived. However, as Moraes travels across India, more than three decades after his quest for the dream England had led him away from it, he finds that his own poems have made their way into the lives of others just like his personal life was shaped by the poems of Dylan Thomas, W.H. Auden, and their likes. While visiting Kerala, Moraes meets a Malayali poet, running a rehabilitation centre for destitute children and mentally disabled women, who presents herself as one of his most ardent admirers. When, at her request, Moraes recites some of his poems, she becomes visibly overwhelmed:

> His poetry, she said in a choking voice, "It has tranquillized my mind and spirit".
> Dom raised her hands to his eyes. "You are not returning to London", she asked searching his eyes.
> Dom didn't reply.
> "Don't go back", she said urgently, clinging to his hands, "you belong here. In this country. It is yours".

(352)

The beseeching glance of his admirer not only compels Moraes to "belong here" but also revives the echoes of memory that Moraes tries to suppress throughout the text of *Out of God's Oven*. Srivatsa mentions that one of the poems that Moraes recites to the Malayali lady is "about his mother who turned mad" (352). Though it is not specified in the text, the poem in all probability is his "Letter to My Mother". Moraes had repeatedly evoked this poem in many of his writings since the 1960s, when it was first composed, to convey his visceral disgust for his mother and his motherland and his attempt to physically distance himself from the narrative of lack that they represented for him. But now, sitting in a mental asylum in Kerala amidst the presence of destitute children and abandoned women, this poem and the memory of his mad mother contained in it become the bridge that connects

Moraes to the piece of India that bodily surrounds him. The disturbing memory of alienation ceases to be a personal nightmare and becomes a shared feeling, locating Moraes within a greater collectivity and countering his "I will not return" with the refrain, "you belong here".

It is interesting to note that both these encounters, the one with the police and the other with the supervisor of the mental asylum, which breaks through Moraes's "quartz armour" of an uninvolved English outsider and identifies him with his native country, are narrated in Srivatsa's section of the book. Moraes's own part of the text remains almost wholly devoid of any such accounts of personal memories and associations that connect him to India, thereby preserving the binary of the insider/outsider subject positions that patterns *Out of God's Oven*. But this pattern is disrupted within Moraes's narrative at least once, when he speaks of how, while he was staying in Calcutta during the course of his journey to write *Out of God's Oven*, the son of an old acquaintance, Monodeep, came to visit him in his hotel. Moraes had been first acquainted with Monodeep while accompanying a BBC team to do a feature on Naxalism that had gathered momentum in and around Calcutta during the late 1960s and early 1970s. Though from a rich business family, Monodeep was actively involved in this militant leftist movement and when Moraes met him he was being hounded by the police. When the Naxal movement died down, Monodeep became reluctant to speak about his past, about the ideals that animated him as a young graduate, and his subsequent failure to stay true to those ideals in his personal life. Moraes had written about him in his reportages during the 1960s, and when the erstwhile Naxalite had come to know that Moraes was in Calcutta, he had sent his son to meet him. Moraes, Monodeep felt, was one of the few persons who had witnessed him in his past role and who could now connect his son with that clandestine but heroic past. As Moraes writes, "In sending his son to me, he had been brave. He had thrown himself upon my goodwill. ... He deserved any kindness I could show him" (149). Thus, here again, as in the mental asylum of Kerala, Moraes is compelled to relive his personal memory of a past association with India and once more his own memory and his own associations get plugged into a pool of shared sentiments and shared memories incorporating him within the web of a greater collectivity.

These moments of identifications, when Moraes's dark-skinned body and his personal memories merge him with his native land, make *Out of God's Oven* a deeply aporetic text. The feeling of disgust that frames the narrative is repeatedly undercut by moments of assimilation and empathy, and the essence of India as a site of lack proves to be too elusive to be pinned down and properly hated. As Moraes journeys across his native land and physically situates himself within its terrain, the "truth" about India becomes infinitely complicated to be encoded within the reified vision of Indianness contrived in the distant "winter courts" of the metropolis through metaphors of death, decay, and inadequacy:

> In the end, what was truth? Pilate would never have found the answer in India. Here events took on diffused shapes that overlapped and faded into each other. Sometimes the truth could be glimpsed briefly, from the corner of an eye, like a rat that streaks across the floor and disappears. It was glimpsed, it has gone; nobody can tell where it may hide now.
>
> (68)

Thus, *Out of God's Oven* in many ways marks a culmination of all of Moraes's earlier literature on India. Its indecisive tone, its conflicting juxtaposition of the desire to be an outsider and the simultaneous sense of belonging, and its tussle with personal memories, all are continuations from his previous narratives. But this later text also marks a point of departure in revealing inadvertently, and almost in spite of its insider/outsider binarism, how deeply imbricated Moraes's personal memories and emotions are within the field of shared memories and desires. *Out of God's Oven* marks not only Moraes's physical return to his native country but also a psychological return to a sense of community. This becomes further evident in the way Moraes constructs the idea of India in his last book *The Long Strider*, which is both very different and more complex than the repulsive images of a disintegrating and putrefying India that had previously been at the core of his writings.

The Long Strider and the return to a community of longing

The Long Strider, which was the last book that Moraes wrote, is about the seventeenth-century traveller, Thomas Coryate, who, as the subtitle of the book announces, "Walked from England to India in the Year 1613". Originally from a little village named Odcombe in Somerset, Coryate had decided to go to India at a time when the Mughal emperor Jehangir was on the throne of Delhi, and English traders were just starting to arrive on the subcontinent. It was also the time that Sir Thomas Roe was preparing to forge the alliance with Jehangir that would give the British a stronger foothold in India and pave the way towards their colonial future. However, Coryate's own intention in going to India was not to engage in trade. It was informed by something rather more unique, considering the time to which he belonged. In the first chapter of the book, Coryate is seen explaining to the dramatist Ben Jonson in the famous Mermaid bar why he intends to visit the Indies: "Master Ben, I wish to write of places none of us know" (6), "I shall be the first man to write of those places Master Ben. It is by what I do there that Odcombe shall be remembered" (7). What has ultimately survived to this day of Coryate's ambitious project to write about the exotic land of India is only five letters that he wrote from there. Thus, apart from the meagre information provided by these letters, the story of Coryate in

The Long Strider is an imaginative reconstruction of how that intrepid traveller came to visit India, how he perceived it, and how he was ultimately drawn into it.

Like *Out of God's Oven*, *The Long Strider* too is co-authored by Moraes and Srivatsa, but it bears the stamp of Moraes even more strongly than the previous book. *The Long Strider* was, in fact, the fulfilment of a project that Moraes had dreamt of since his very childhood:

> I have always had an obsessive desire since I first, as a schoolboy, read about Coryate half a century ago, to know much more about him and to write a book on him.
>
> (xi)

Indeed, when the book finally came to be written, it became as much a narrative about Coryate as about Moraes. Thus, in *The Long Strider*, Moraes's account of Coryate's journey from England to India is interlaced with Srivatsa's account of how Moraes retraced Coryate's footsteps and travelled from the English village of Odcombe to India. In both these narratives, Moraes is at the centre, either as the author or as the subject. Moraes's role, however, pervades the text also in a more subtle way. In *Out of God's Oven*, he had taken up the role of the outsider in India, whereas Srivatsa had represented the position of an insider. In *The Long Strider*, on the other hand, the insider–outsider division no longer informs the two strands of narrative. The burden of being an outsider in India, which Moraes had carried on his shoulders whenever he was in his native land, now comes to be shared not only by Coryate but also by all the inhabitants of the subcontinent.

Thus, Moraes makes Coryate learn even in his first experience of India that it is a place of exile not only for him as an Englishman but indeed for everyone living there who had originally arrived as successive waves of invaders and immigrants and then settled in. Each new group of people in turn reconstructed India spatially to fit it into a different image of homeland, and with every one of those attempts, previously constructed ideas of homeland had been laid to ruins. As Marco, one of the first people whom Coryate meets in India, tells him:

> In this country ... all are foreigners except the heathens who first lived in the forests. Some of us who have come after have built temples and some have built mosques. But, Tommaso, you whites will be the next conquerors. Where our mosques were, your people will build churches.... And then, believe me, those will fall also.
>
> (115)

These ruins of temples, mosques, and churches mark the India of *The Long Strider* as a similar site of lack and disintegration through which Moraes had journeyed himself while writing *Out of God's Oven*. However, the crucial difference between the two texts is that whereas in *Out of God's Oven* the fractured land of India as a site of lack remains unredeemed, in *The Long Strider*, the ruins of the fractured present are shown to trigger nostalgic dreams of the past in which India is reconstructed as a site of wholeness and fulfilment. Moraes constructs his Coryate narrative through dwelling upon this constant switching between the ruins of the fragmented present and redeeming visions of nostalgic pasts and lost homelands. But, before I go on to show how Moraes achieves this in *The Long Strider*, I would like to focus more closely on the concept of nostalgia because it crucially brings together two of the ideas that I have been elaborating through this essay—memory and homecoming.

Nostalgia, which denotes a rose-tinted memory of the past and a longing to return to it, is also literally translated as a longing to return home (*nostos* = return home; *algia* = longing). Svetlana Boym in her study of this phenomenon identifies two different ways in which nostalgia seeks to reconnect the present that signifies lack with a past that is imagined as whole and complete. The first form of nostalgia is what Boym refers to as "restorative" because it seeks to "restore" the present by reconstructing it in the model of a prelapsarian past within which it locates the idea of a lost home. It is a project that is inextricably associated with the national myth-making and therefore, as Boym observes, the restorative nostalgia "characterizes national and nationalist revivals all over the world" (41) that "manifests itself in total reconstructions of the monuments of the past" (41). Individuals connect with this restorative nostalgia and its project of "a transhistorical reconstruction of the lost home" (Boym xviii) by participating in the single teleological plot of what Boym calls the "national memory", which presents "a coherent and inspiring tale of recovered identity" (53). The demolition of the Babri Masjid in Ayodhya and the attempt to "restore" in its place the *Ramjanmabhoomi*,[9] an event that forms the historical backdrop of *Out of God's Oven*, is a perfect example of this restorative nostalgia. It attempts to restore spatially the Hindu national memory of a mythic past, thereby transforming India from a site of lack and inadequacy to the site of a revivified glorious Hindu past.

The Coryate narrative, however, exhibits a nostalgic transformation of India through a different route, which, following Boym's typology of nostalgia, can be classified as "reflective". What distinguishes reflective nostalgia from restorative nostalgia is that unlike the latter, "[r]eflective nostalgia does not pretend to rebuild the mythical place called home; it is 'enamoured of distance, not of the referent itself'" (Boym 50). Thus, in reflective nostalgia, the transformation from a site of lack to a site of wholeness does not take place through a total reconstruction of space. Rather, this transformation is achieved in dreams of "another place and another time"—dreams in which the ruins of the present are reconstructed into a wholeness and completeness through fictions of past. As Boym writes: "reflective nostalgia lingers on ruins, the patina of time and history, in the dreams of another place and another time" (41). Moreover, unlike the restorative nostalgia which is guided by the single plot of the national memory and which conceives its reconstructed version of the past as inviolable truth (Boym xviii), a reflective nostalgic is aware of the fictionality of his reconstructed past and is therefore indulgent towards multiple versions of individual nostalgic fictions. These are fictions which are informed by the diversities of individual memories and desires. Hence, unlike the national communities that form around the restorative nostalgia, reflective nostalgics are not connected through a shared concept of home. What connects them, however, is their shared sense of longing to reach their differently imagined homelands of desire. As Boym succinctly puts it: "*Algia*—longing is what we share, yet *nostos*—the return home—is what divides us" (xv–xvi).

The Coryate narrative is a typical example of this reflective nostalgia and its multiple versions of imagined pasts. It becomes evident from the way Moraes constructs the seventeenth-century India experienced by Coryate by bringing together memories of the twentieth-century individuals that Moraes and Srivatsa met during their journey across India. These memories are not homogenous and do not present a single story like the restorative national memory. Rather, these memories are shot through with different stories of lost homelands and varied nostalgic dreams. Thus, for instance, while researching on Jehangir to whose court Coryate arrived in 1613, the authors enter a bookshop run by a Sikh. The mere mention of the name of the seventeenth-century Mughal emperor immediately leads the shop owner into a fit of pique because Jehangir reminds him of the terrible anti-Sikh riots of 1984 and the series of violence directed against the Sikh community throughout its long history, which had turned them into aliens in their own country:

> Many years ago, the Muslims under Jehangir started to persecute the Sikhs. Under Aurangzeb, it became worse. Even our gurus were killed. This has become a tradition in India. When the Muslims are not following it, the Hindus do. Look at 1984 and everything that happened after that year.
>
> (135)

Later in the narrative, the reader meets one Sultan Ahmed of Agra, the caretaker of one of the Babri Masjids. For Ahmed too, the present is an alienated homeland ruined by the political rise of radical Hinduism as a consequence of which, "[t]he old localities, the bazaars, the old havelis have all been destroyed" (196)—a ruination most symbolically represented by the 1992 demolition of the Babri Masjid in Ayodhya. Again, near the end of the text, we encounter Sheila and Ila, two eunuchs, who fantasise how the eunuchs of the past held important places in the king's court and how nothing auspicious happened without their blessings, while all the time bitterly aware of the present situation when, in their own words, "[n]o one respects us. We live like beggars. We have become outcasts" (320).

Like the Sikh bookseller, the caretaker of the mosque and the eunuchs, almost all modern Indian characters the reader encounters in the book regard themselves as outcasts who are exiled in their own homeland. Their nostalgic longing for "another place and another time" where they are not merely passive victims of persecution, where their communities are valued, and where they can feel at home, finds direct reflection in the construction of the Coryate narrative. The chapter that tells of the grievances of the Sikh bookseller is thus followed immediately by Coryate's meeting a Sikh carpenter about to return from Agra to Punjab to join the forces that would avenge the killing of Guru Arjun Singh by Jehangir. Similarly, Sultan Ahmed's longing for the time when Muslims were the rightful owners of the country and ruled over the Hindus who now persecute them is also answered in the Coryate narrative when the Englishman, on entering India for the first time, perceives the country as essentially a Muslim land, where the Hindus are "a slave race, allowed by its masters to practice its own forms of worship unhindered" (111).

The figure of Coryate who stands at the centre of these narratives of nostalgia, woven out of the multiple dreams of individual memories and desires, is himself a figure of nostalgia. If the modern Indian characters are temporally displaced from their ideas of home, Coryate finds himself displaced from it in space, and throughout the narrative he is presented as dreaming of a glorious return to his home in England—a return that will earn him fame and social stature. Thus, even in the last chapter of the Coryate narrative, where the reader meets him after he has gone through prolonged physical suffering and unmitigated pain, the slightest sign of recovery assures him that he will be able to return to England and helps him dream about his home:

> He became certain that he would finish his book on India and be knighted for it; come home to Somerset once more; and at last die and be buried in Odcombe, in a tomb magnificent in marble, the showplace of the county. There he would lie in splendour, peace and fame, his travels and travails done.
>
> (324)

However, Coryate is a figure of nostalgia not only because he is portrayed as a nostalgic himself but also because he reflects the nostalgia of Moraes. If the India that he traverses is a collage of the desires and longings of modern-day Indians, the England that he comes from is a patchwork of Moraes's own childhood memories. It is the same England that Moraes had conjured up early in his life from his readings of English literature while living in Bombay. Coryate's home is the very image of the England as a land of poets that Moraes had always longed to inhabit. The last vision that Coryate has of his home while travelling in India is thus infused with this vision of Moraes's dream world of England as a land of poets. As he lies dying in the Indian port city of Surat waiting for a ship that will take him back home, Coryate imagines himself sitting in the tavern frequented by some of the greatest seventeenth-century English dramatists and poets, including William Shakespeare and Ben Jonson:

> Clearly as in a picture, Coryate saw himself in the Mermaid, fire burning in the hearth, orange flames tinctured with blue. He sat by Jonson's side, a mug of sack in his hand.
> (337–338)

Coryate is also a projection of Moraes's longing to become English not only in mind but also in body. Hence, during the course of the text, it soon becomes evident that whatever happens to Moraes in his journey to retrace the travel of Thomas Coryate also befalls Coryate himself. The chapter in which Coryate is warned by dramatist Ben Jonson that his journey to India will ultimately be "a journey that will lead him to his death" (36) is intertwined with the chapter in which Moraes, before undertaking the project of retracing Coryate's footsteps, is informed by the doctor that he has cancer and will not live much longer. In the journeys that follow, the deterioration in Moraes's health, punctuated by periods of convalescence, is also reflected in Coryate's body as he moves through India. Indeed, Moraes and Coryate share the same body not only in terms of physical ailment but also more generally in terms of physical consciousness. They both fuse together proprioceptively as Moraes tries to feel through his own skin Coryate's "bod[ily] sensation of occupying a point of space" (Silverman16). Moraes makes it clear to his co-author that "in absence of much material about Coryate, what I want … is to be in the same place as Coryate may have been. I want to feel him with me. I want to shut my eyes and imagine Coryate there" (168). Through the rest of the narrative, whenever the reader meets Moraes, s/he sees him less as a modern-day writer and traveller and more as a man looking through the eyes of the seventeenth-century figure, seeing what he saw, feeling what he felt, and even touching what he touched. Srivatsa mentions Moraes touching the wall of a mosque during their journey to try and feel in his fingertips the exact sensations that Coryate might have felt while touching it four centuries ago:

> Had Coryate touched this wall? I knew this was what he was thinking. As if to unravel a hidden code, Dom ran his fingertips over the

mortar grooves. He looked at the particles of mud on his fingertips; each grain containing a speck of the past.

(195)

This attempt to physically become Coryate serves an interesting purpose. While trying to look at India as it might have appeared to an Englishman, Moraes finds a justified ground to view and, indeed, to bodily locate himself in India not as an insider who strives to maintain his alienation, but as a genuine outsider. Looking through the eyes of Coryate, Moraes finally comes to occupy a subject position that he had craved to establish throughout his life—a subject position that aligns him with England and affords him to look at India solely as a land of exile. Yet, this sense of exile also connects Moraes with other Indians like the Sikh bookseller, Sultan Ahmed, Sheila, and Ila in a community of shared longing. The home that Moraes/Coryate dreams of is distinctly different from the homelands of their dreams. But each of their dreams is evoked by the common perception of present-day India as a site of lack. More importantly, each of their nostalgic longings to return to those dream homelands, located in the fictions of "another place and another time", is contained within a shared framework of memories. It is this network of shared memories and the sense of community that it implies which the Coryate narrative vividly brings together.

Conclusion

Associated with this book is the story of yet another intriguing return. Nearly 400 years after Coryate died in the Indian city of Surat with the dream of returning to England and earning a magnificent marble tomb in his native village in Odcombe still unrealised, Moraes dies in his native city of Bombay. Shankarlal Bhattacharya who had been one of the last people to interview Moraes ends his essay reminiscing his last meeting with him by providing this piece of information:

> It is now known that on the night before he died, [Moraes] had talked of returning to the Somerset village of Odcombe and even settling there. On July 19, 2004, on Moraes's 66th birthday, 26 of his friends attended a simple ceremony in which a tablet was placed near the entrance to the Church of St. Peter and St. Paul in Odcombe. The 18-inch by 2-ft tablet of Jaisalmer stone read: "Dom Moraes who followed Thomas Coryate's footsteps and returned home".

(Bhattacharya 190)

This stone memorial supplements and even completes in a unique way the narrative of *The Long Strider* and indeed all of Moraes's writings on his native land. It reinforces the ambiguity of Moraes's coming back to India as also the ambiguity of his sense of belonging to England. Both these places were at worst lands of exile and at best ambivalent homelands to which the anglicised self of Moraes could only return as a stranger and settle in as an outsider.

Notes

1 For a discussion on the crucial role that this circular journey between India and England played in shaping the colonial middle class in India, see Sumita Mukherjee.
2 In *Autobiographical Notes*, Sri Aurobindo refers to himself in third person.
3 Lotika Ghose writes that Manmohan Ghose had originally intended to settle down in England but failed to get a job that could sustain him there. When his father died in 1893, Ghose had no choice but to return to India and look for work. See Lotika Ghose (26–27).
4 Interestingly, V.S. Naipaul in his essay "Jasmine" also writes about experiencing a similar sense of "unreality" in his native Trinidad, which, according to him, resulted from the hollowness of Trinidad's literary tradition.
5 It is, however, important to note here that not all literature of return is produced by authors trying to fashion themselves as outsiders in their country of origin. Ved Mehta is a case in point here. Mehta, who knew Moraes in Oxford, accompanied him in his first major visit to India from England. Like Moraes, he then went on to write a memoir, *Walking the Indian Streets*, based on that visit. Yet, unlike Moraes, the authorial position that Mehta adopts in his book is very much that of an Indian "insider" who has come to visit his home and family. For a detailed discussion of Mehta's memoir and how it presents a different kind of literature of return than what is represented by Moraes's work, see Mukherjee and Chattopadhyay.
6 I have already noted in the chapter on Nirad Chaudhuri the subtle distinction that Majeed makes between the autobiographies of the likes of Surendranath Banerjea and M.R. Jayakar, in which the self is completely incorporated within a totalising nationalism, and the autobiographies of the likes of Gandhi and Nehru which exhibit a tension between the self and the nation.
7 This is an interesting commentary by a representative of the old colonial middle class on the new middle class which emerged in India during the late twentieth century following economic liberalisation.
8 For a more in-depth study of this tragedy, see Siddharth Varadarajan's *Gujarat: The Making of a Tragedy*.
9 An interesting book that recounts the history of the events that finally led to the demolition of the Babri Masjid is P.V. Narasimha Rao's *Ayodhya: 6 December 1992*. Rao, who was the prime minister of India when the mosque was demolished, uses this book to explain his apparent inaction and inability to prevent the horrific turn of events.

CODA
Anglicisation and aporia

Has the phenomenon of Indian self-fashioning as English come to an end? For someone like Bankimchandra Chattopadhyay, who was one of the first middle-class intellectuals to articulate the "need" for such a self-fashioning, it was important to emulate the colonisers to regain political agency. According to Chattopadhyay, learning from the colonisers and becoming like them was necessary to retrieve the glorious Indian/Hindu identity of the past so as to be reinstated as the rightful rulers of the country after more than 700 years of subjugation. In such a scheme of things, should the phenomenon of Indian self-fashioning as English not have died its natural death after 1947, when India became independent? Or indeed, should it not have died out much earlier when Gandhi picked apart the whole project of trying to become like the colonisers by pointing out the folly inherent in the idea of a home-grown "English rule without the Englishman"? The promptness with which Cornelia Sorabji was forgotten after independence, or Nirad Chaudhuri dubbed as "the last Englishman"[1] in India, seems to answer the above questions in the affirmative. The case of Dom Moraes, who was born more than three decades after Chaudhuri and yet fashioned himself as English, does somewhat problematise the epithet of "the last Englishman" ascribed to the latter just as Chaudhuri being called "the last Englishman" problematise Jawaharlal Nehru's use of that label to describe himself. But this problem has been largely contained by framing Moraes as an isolated freak, who is even more anachronistic than Chaudhuri in his perverse xenolatry and his desire to "find favour in England and America" (De Souza quoted in Pandey 72) by doing the "white man's dirty work" (De Souza quoted in Pandey 72) of presenting India as "a country peopled by grotesques and morons" (De Souza quoted in Pandey 72).

However, though political subjugation might have triggered the phenomenon of Indian self-fashioning as English, it became effective, as I have shown earlier, through the internalisation by the colonised Indians of certain sets of prioritised values that constitute the image of "the West". This image of the West that forms the kernel of the phenomenon of Indian anglicisation has most definitely not become redundant with India's attainment of independence. Hence, though the disappearance of the English colonisers as the reference group for the Indian middle class has meant that instances of Indian self-fashioning as English have waned, it has not died down entirely. This is evident from the fact that in the last few decades, the figure of the anglicised Indian has repeatedly appeared in the works of contemporary Indian English novelists. We meet this figure, for instance, as Saladin Chamcha in Salman Rushdie's *The Satanic Verses* (1988), as Arjun in Amitav Ghosh's *The Glass Palace* (2000), and more recently as Jemubhai Patel in Kiran Desai's *The Inheritance of Loss* (2006). The presence of these characters in contemporary Indian English fiction reveals that their authors are still grappling with the Indian desire to become English. However, a study of these characters also reveals that for these more recent authors who are born after the independence (or just a couple of months before it in case of Rushdie), the project of becoming English represents less a viable mode of self-fashioning and more a problematic inheritance from the colonial past which must ultimately be superseded and a new identity formed beyond it. In this concluding chapter, I would like to focus on this desire to transcend the phenomenon of Indian self-fashioning as English and the possibility of a new identity that such a transcendence might make available.

Colonial decay and the impossibility of becoming English

A reading of Amitav Ghosh's portrayal of Arjun in *The Glass Palace* reveals the sense of uneasiness that is typical of the more recent depictions of Indians trying to become English. In the novel, Arjun, who is born into a Bengali middle-class family in Calcutta near the beginning of the twentieth century, finds himself suddenly inducted into the privileged circle of the English colonisers when he passes a public examination that qualifies him to train as a commissioned army officer. The historical backdrop is the period between the two World Wars when there was a conscious effort undertaken by the colonial administration to "Indianise" the British Indian army by recruiting officers from the subcontinent. Arjun is presented in *The Glass Palace* as one of these new recruits who feels pleasantly overwhelmed by the illusion that he has been elevated from the status of the colonised subject to that of the coloniser. He thus tries his best to fit into what he considers to be his new "superior" role in life by learning how to dance tango and how to eat "English" food served in the officers' canteen with a knife and a fork, and before long emerges as "the most English" (297) among all the Indians in his battalion.

In the novel, this attempt of Arjun to become English is, however, evoked only to bring out the sheer futility of such attempts within the colonial context. As Ghosh observes in an e-mail conversation with Dipesh Chakravarty shortly after the publication of *The Glass Palace*, the path that appeared to connect the "inferior" state of being an Indian to the "superior" state of being an English within the colonial order was, in effect, always blocked to the colonised subject by the insurmountable barrier of putative racial difference ("A Correspondence" 148). In the novel, therefore, Arjun finds his English identity undone when during the course of the Second World War, he accompanies his battalion to the war front of South-East Asia and finds that in spite of being an officer, his racial status as an inferior "Asiatic" debars him from being an equal of an English in social spaces. In the battlefields of Malay, this disintegration of his English identity is compounded by yet another crisis—the disintegration of the British Empire. When his battalion suffers a devastating loss in the battle of Jitra, Arjun's sense of losing his Englishness is exacerbated by a sense that the whole world order as he knew it was collapsing around him. Sorabji, Chaudhuri, and Moraes all found themselves facing this same predicament when confronted with signs that the empire was breaking down. As I have discussed in the previous chapters, they responded to it through laborious attempts to shore up the British Raj by articulating their loyalties towards it. These attempts ranged from outright denial of the anticolonial movements by Sorabji to nostalgic fictional evocations of the *ancien régime* by Chaudhuri and Moraes. However, for an author like Amitav Ghosh, looking at history from the vantage point of the last years of the twentieth century, these responses prove to be too self-delusional to be admitted as possibilities. Thus, in the novel, Arjun is depicted as becoming completely unable to respond when faced with the double crises affecting his English self and the British Empire. He ends up in an existential aporia where he becomes a stranger to himself. The notion of an unwavering loyalty that had been central to Arjun's career and his identity as an army officer gives way to an impasse of thought:

> The old loyalties of India, the ancient ones—they'd been destroyed long ago; the British had built their Empire by effacing them. But the Empire was dead now—he [Arjun] knew this because he had felt it die within himself, where it had held its strongest dominion—and with whom was he now to keep faith?
>
> (441)

In the end, Arjun joins the army of rebel soldiers who, during the Second World War, rallied under the flag of the Indian National Army to end the British rule in the subcontinent. However, he does so without finding any new object on which he can rest his faith. For him, the consciousness that "the Empire is dead now" is too stark a revelation to allow any attempt to cling on to the old world order. On the other hand, it is also not a revelation that leads to an easy embrace of nationalist ideals. Hence, even while joining the national army, Arjun remains thoroughly convinced of his "un-Indianness". Whereas his Indian body had initially prevented him from becoming English, everything but his body now resists his identifying himself as an

Indian. Articulating a double bind that is distinctly reminiscent of Moraes' precarious position in India, Arjun points out to one of his fellow army officers, "except for the colour of our skin, most people in India wouldn't even recognise us as Indians" (439).

The intertwined themes of colonial decay and existential aporia, which Ghosh elaborates through the character of Arjun, are also echoed in *The Inheritance of Loss*, in Kiran Desai's portrayal of Justice Jemubhai Patel. However, whereas in Ghosh's novel Arjun's English identity is shattered with a rude suddenness, in the novel of Desai the English identity that Jemubhai cultivates for himself fades gradually into meaninglessness. The judge, as Jemubhai is referred to in Desai's narrative, travels to England in the late 1930s to qualify for the Indian Civil Service examination. He is propelled by a dream, which is as much his father's as his own, to rise up the social ladder and be inducted into the exalted companionship of the English administrators who ran the country:

> He might be a district commissioner or a high court judge. He might wear a silly white wig atop a dark face in the burning heat of summer and bring down his hammer on ... phony rigged cases. ... So fantastic was their dreaming, it thrilled them like a fairytale, and perhaps because this dream sailed too high to be tackled by logic, it took form, began to exert palpable pressure.
>
> (59)

This is the same fantastic dream that is also dreamt by Arjun in Ghosh's novel, the dream of becoming transformed from a colonised subject to a coloniser. But, like the dream of Arjun, the judge's dream too founders against the barrier of his skin colour. Faced with racism in England, the dream becomes laced with an intense hatred that the judge directs towards aspects of his own identity that connect him with India. He begins loathing his accent, his skin colour, the companionship of other Indians, and everything else that exposes his filiation to his native country and stops him from becoming "truly" English:

> [H]e grew stranger to himself than he was to those around him, found his own skin odd-coloured, his own accent peculiar. ... He could barely let any of himself peep out of his clothes for giving offence. ... To the end of his life, he would never be seen without socks and shoes and would prefer shadow to light, faded days to sunny, for he was suspicious that sunlight might reveal him, in his hideousness, all too clearly.
>
> (40)

Back in India, the judge finds in Cho Oyu a perfect envelope to this "non-hideous" English identity, which he fashions in England by painstakingly separating himself from anything humiliatingly Indian. Cho Oyu is described as a house built in the hills of Kalimpong to fit the colonial fantasies of a Scotsman. An avid reader of Orientalist adventure fictions, the Scotsman had commissioned Cho Oyu so that he could relive those adventures in person in the slopes of the Himalayas. When the judge buys the house from the Scotsman, he wishes to relive this colonial romance. Like Moraes, who tries to belong to India by stepping into the shoes of Thomas Coryate so as to remain an outsider in his land of birth even while returning to it, the judge too can think of belonging to India only by living out a white man's dream that provides him "with the solace of being a foreigner in his own country" (29). But ironically, by moving into Cho Oyu, what the judge steps into is not a place vacated by a white colonial officer but rather the empty shell of a colonial fantasy that is already outmoded. With the disappearance of the British Raj, the Scotsman, who originally owned Cho Oyu, retires to his native Aberdeen and the house that he leaves behind as the legacy of the colonial past represents, as the title of the novel suggests, the inheritance of a loss—an uninhabitable pile whose crumbling structure symbolises the putrefaction of the old colonial order. The judge adamantly tries to cling on to this empty inheritance by staying on in Cho Oyu, but his efforts prove futile as with each passing year the house becomes less and less usable. Microscopic jaws of woodlice ceaselessly turn the house into a pile of sawdust (34) and this constant gnawing cuts through the English life that the judge had hoped to live in India, reducing his meticulously fashioned English identity into nothingness.

Caught within this ruination is Sai, the judge's orphaned granddaughter who comes to live with him. Educated in a convent in Dehra Dun, Sai, like her grandfather, is "a westernized Indian ..., an estranged Indian living in India" (210). Yet, unlike the judge, Sai can see that to remain in India as an English foreigner is to be lost in a blind alley. She is thus convinced that she needs to escape from the house, and the cloistered and outdated existence of being an English in India that it symbolises: "She'd have to propel herself into the future by whatever means possible or she'd be trapped forever in a place whose time had already passed" (74). Yet, this future that lies beyond being an English outsider in India remains elusive. The novel ends with the reiteration of Sai's conviction that "[s]he must leave" (323), but the narrative does not show her actually leaving. Like Arjun in *The Glass Palace*, Sai too seems to be stuck within her English identity even while realising that this identity is riddled with contradictions that are impossible to sustain. In each of the two novels, these contradictions are laid bare, but they are not resolved. Rather, they are presented as aporias that cannot be thought through. Salman Rushdie's *The Satanic Verses*, however, is one of the few Indian English fictions which depicts a character who successfully transcends the aporia of his English self-fashioning. It is to this novel that I now turn.

CODA

The absent cause of an implacable rage

The narrative strand dealing with the life and career of Saladin Chamcha, born Salahuddin Chamchawala, in Rushdie's *The Satanic Verses* retraces the already familiar outline of the phenomenon of Indian self-fashioning as English, but gives it a parodic slant. Thus, the pleasure of becoming acquainted with English literary texts, which set most of the authors discussed in this book on their quest to become English, is replaced in the Saladin Chamcha story with the pleasure of chancing upon a wallet full of "[p]ounds sterling, from proper London in the fabled country of Vilayet" (35). However, the "crisp promises of pounds sterling" (37) that Chamcha finds inside the wallet is essentially the same promise that authors like Michael Madhusudan Dutt or Nirad Chaudhuri or Dom Moraes found inside the covers of their books of English verses—the promise of a utopic England laden with the possibility of removing oneself from the sordid Indian reality and becoming transformed into a superior and more civilised species of human beings. Hence, Chamcha's determination after finding the wad of "magic billfold" (37) to "escape Bombay, or die" (38) almost exactly reiterates the sentiment that informed Michael Madhusudan Dutt's letter in which he wrote to his friend Gourdas Basak in the mid-nineteenth century that he "must either be in England or cease 'to be' at all" (quoted in Murshid, *Heart* 33). It also reflects the kind of sentiment that Rushdie himself grew up with as a child in an anglicised middle-class family in Bombay. As Rushdie notes:

> In common with many Bombay-raised middle-class children of my generation, I grew up with an intimate knowledge of, and even sense of friendship with, a certain kind of England: a dream-England composed of Test Matches at Lord's ...; of Enid Blyton and Billy Bunter, in which we were even prepared to smile indulgently at portraits such as "Hurree Jamset Ram Singh", "the dusky nabob of Bhanipur". I wanted to come to England. I couldn't wait.
> ("Imaginary Homelands" 18)

The problem that the brown Indian body poses to such a passion to belong to the "dream England" or "the fabled country of Vilayet" and the fantasy that it generates of being able to transform oneself physically is also presented in *The Satanic Verses* with a parodic twist. Chamcha's professional identity in England shuttles between being a faceless voice artist and the hero of a television series who has the protean body of an alien which can apparently change shape and colour, but which in effect is achieved by spending hours to hide his own brown-skinned body under "the latest in prosthetic make-up" (63). The uneasy relationship that Indian authors trying to be English establish with the white members of the English community is also reflected in Rushdie's novel through the failed marriage between Chamcha and his wife Pamela Lovelace. As I have noted before, the process of transforming oneself into an English crucially hinges on being accepted within the white English community, whether that community is conceived in terms of personally known English friends or in the more abstract terms of a metropolitan readership. For Chamcha, this entire question of being accepted by the English community comes to rest on his being acknowledged by Pamela, who with her "hearty, rubicund voice of ye olde dream-England" (180) comes to personify for him the utopic metropolis to which he wants to belong. Chamcha in his desire to transform himself into an Englishman thus believes "that if she d[oes] not relent then his entire attempt at metamorphosis would fail" (49–50). The irony in Chamcha's relationship with Pamela is that her acceptance of Chamcha is predicated on the very Indian identity that he seeks to deny. Indeed, as Jumpy Joshi, one of Chamcha's friends and Pamela's lover, observes, Chamcha's whole appeal to English women rests on the fact that he can appear as "everybody's goddamn cartoon of the mysteries of the East" (174). This is again a familiar paradox that I have already discussed in some detail, where an Indian author trying to fashion himself or herself as English invariably finds his or her attempt buffeted by an implicit injunction to remain "Indian" so as to be acceptable in the metropolis.

However, as noted earlier, Chamcha's story is significant here not because of the way it retraces the recognisable script of Indian authors trying to anglicise themselves but because of the way it attempts to go beyond this well-worn script and open up the possibility of a new kind of identity. To see how it does this, I begin by focusing on the motive that Rushdie ascribes to Chamcha for trying to become English. Chamcha starts realising his dream of belonging to England when his father, Changez Chamchawala, "out of the blue, offered him an English education" (39) and accompanied him in his journey to London—his journey "from Indianness to Englishness" (41). Once in London, Changez insists that everything on the trip be paid with the money that Saladin had found in the wallet in Bombay. Forced to be thrifty, the latter tries to smuggle in his hotel room a roast chicken, bought from a cheap food joint, by hiding it inside his mackintosh:

> When he brought the chicken into the hotel lobby he became embarrassed, not wanting the staff to see, so he stuffed it inside double-breasted serge and went up in the lift reeking of spit-roast, his mackintosh bulging, his face turning red. Chicken-breasted beneath the gaze of dowagers and liftwallahs he felt the birth of an implacable rage which would burn within him, undiminished for over a quarter of a century; which would boil away his childhood father-worship and make him a secular man ...; which would fuel, perhaps, his determination to become the thing his father was-not-could-never-be, that is, goodandproper Englishman.
>
> (43)

This important scene presents a *mise en abyme* of the Saladin Chamcha narrative, which portrays in a miniature the conflict that structures Chamcha's self-fashioning: his desire to be English (reflected in his attire of double-breasted serge mackintosh) being undermined by the metropolitan gaze (of dowagers and liftwallahs), making him acutely embarrassed at the "inappropriateness" of what he is carrying inside his clothes—a cheap roast chicken, a brown-skinned Indian body, both fused together by the term "chicken-breasted".

Central to this scene and indeed to the whole life story of Saladin Chamcha is "the birth of an implacable rage" which gives Chamcha the determination to "boil away" his filial connections that tie him to India and be a "goodandproper Englishman". We have encountered this implacable rage before, in Desai's *The Inheritance of Loss*, where the judge Jemubhai Patel's anger at not being accepted as an equal by the English transforms into a seething hatred with which he tries to distance himself from everything Indian, including his own Indian body. If we try to work out the relation between this rage and hatred, and the attempt to become English that these fictions bring out, then we will see that the relation has a long history. Thus, Chamcha's rage and hatred towards a parental figure, which provides an alibi for staying back in England and assuming an English identity that "was-not-could-never-be" his father's, mirrors the rage and hatred that Dom Moraes felt towards his mother and towards India, both of which merged for him in an unredeemable picture of death, decay, and putrefaction. In the autobiographical writings of Cornelia Sorabji and Nirad Chaudhuri, a similar rage and contempt underline the project of becoming English with the only difference that in these texts, the rage and hatred are seen directed not at a definite parental figure but more vaguely (though not less intensely) towards the faceless masses of India. Crossing over to the nineteenth century, we find this rage again in Bankimchandra Chattopadhyay's writings informing his portrayal of the contemporary Hindus/Indians and providing the motivation to create a distance from this "childish", "unicivilised", and "uneducated" lot by emulating the English colonisers. Going even further back, we find the echo of this rage and contempt in Michael Madhusudan Dutt's attempt to separate himself from the Hindus and the "despise[d] Ram and his rabble" (quoted in Murshid *Lured* 147) that they worship even while using their epic, *The Ramayana*, to mould his magnum opus, *Meghnad-badh-kabya*.

As this brief survey makes evident, an implacable rage and hatred put a specific version of India—an India that is impotent, inferior, degenerate, and uncivilised—at the very heart of the phenomenon of Indian self-fashioning as English (even when this self-fashioning is garbed in the form of a quest for true Indianness). It is this hateful image of India that acts as the pivot supporting the attempt to become English because the attempt is informed as much by the desire to approximate oneself to a mental image of an idealised West as by the desire to separate oneself from a mental image of a dystopic India. But, this hate-filled core around which the attempt to become anglicised crystallises, when explored, reveals an abyss in which the idea of India that evokes rage and that needs to be properly hated in order to make the English self-fashioning possible regresses eternally. As noted in the chapter on Dom Moraes, this perpetual regression of the idea of India is briefly referred to in *Out of God's Oven*, where Moraes compares the "truth" about India to a rat that streaks across the floor and disappears. In *The Satanic Verses*, this infinite regress is more consciously foregrounded as part of the textual strategy. Thus, the *mise en abyme* described above opens up into a bottomless abyss where the birth of Chamcha's implacable rage, his desire to be separated from India, and his determination to become English are caught in an endless series of reflection and reiteration. Hence, on going back to a few pages from the one that describes the incident at the lift as Chamcha's life-changing moment, we read of the incident of Chamcha's father confiscating the wallet full of pounds sterling from him evoking exactly the same set of emotions and the same steely determination to transform himself into an Englishman:

> Changez Chamchwala had stolen the crock of gold. After that the son became convinced that his father would smother all his hopes unless he got away, and from that moment he became desperate to leave, to escape, to place oceans between the great man and himself.
> ... The mutation of Salahuddin Chamchawala into Saladin Chamcha began, it will be seen, in old Bombay, long before he got close enough to hear the lions of Trafalgar roar.[2]
>
> (36–37)

Almost as soon as this incident is narrated, the text leads to another event in Chamcha's life which proffers yet another cause of his rage and yet another different reason for his removing himself from his native land. This time the father who bullies and humiliates the son is replaced by a bony stranger who molests Chamcha on the beach outside his house. Nevertheless, the structure of the scene remains the same: Chamcha feeling degraded because of an adult male, and his helplessness and embarrassment giving rise to an intense loathing for his country of origin and his desire to remove himself to England:

> It seemed to him that everything loathsome, everything he had come to revile about his home town, had come together in the stranger's bony embrace, and now that he had escaped that skeleton, he must also escape Bombay, or die. He began to concentrate fiercely upon this idea .... He dreamed of flying out of his bedroom window to discover that there, before him, was—not Bombay—but Proper London itself.
>
> (38)

This continually differing reinscription of the reason why Chamcha is outraged and why he decides to escape to England does not reveal any core cause that might explain his trying to turn himself into an Englishman with such a vengeance. In fact, in the narrative, each of these incidents operates as mutually replaceable pegs on which Chamcha hangs his resentment towards his father, his hometown, and his native country. But since they are replaceable, with each incident of humiliation and embarrassment immediately and incessantly giving way to another, they neither reveal the origin of Chamcha's resentment nor justify his English self-fashioning that is apparently based on this elusive but unflinching anger. This lack of justification becomes evident when the middle-aged Chamcha, after a long absence from India, once again confronts his father Changez and tries to blame the latter for what he has been "compelled" to become:

> He came to accuse .... He came to avenge his youth .... Of what did the son accuse the father? Of everything: espionage on child-self, rainbow-pot-stealing, exile. Of turning him into what he might not have become.
>
> (69)

The seriousness of these allegations is, however, made trivial by the causes that sustain them—a wallet of pounds confiscated by his father when he was 13 and a roast chicken he was made to carry inside his mackintosh as an adolescent (68). Whatever significance these stories of deprivation might have had in the distant past, they have long become insignificant anecdotes which can no longer be used to validate either Chamcha's self-imposed exile from India or his turning himself into English. Changez Chamchawala points this out to his son in no uncertain terms: "Face it, mister: I don't explain you anymore" (69).

Chamcha's failure to convincingly pin the cause for his Indophobia on his father, and his inability to explain the rage and hatred that apparently "turn[ed] him into what he might not have become", ultimately dismantles his English identity by revealing its empty core. But this dismantling, though it finally culminates in Chamcha's return to India and his rapprochement with his father, does not immediately follow the encounter between the father and the son. As Changez observes, his son still goes on "carrying [his] take-away chicken" (71) and refuses to stop being "th[e] pretender, ... [the] imitator of non-existing men" (71). Here we come across the shadow of the impasse that haunts the lives of Arjun and Sai who, like Chamcha, cannot let go of their English identities even after realising that these identities are based on illusions. But whereas the other two fail, Chamcha succeeds in going beyond these illusions that sustain his English self-fashioning by working through the issues of rage, hatred, and forgiveness. The resolution of these issues is, however, presented in the novel through the changing contours of another male bonding—that between Saladin Chamcha and Gibreel Farishta, the worst of adversaries and the best of friends.

The (im)possibility of forgiveness

Chamcha's fate gets inextricably intertwined with Farishta's when they both fall from mid-air into London "embracing head-to-tail and ... performing ... geminate cartwheels all the way down" (6). Following their conjoined fall and miraculous survival, the lives of Chamcha and Farishta take different courses. Chamcha, who during his fall had become transformed into a devil with goat-legs and a pair of horns, is promptly detained by the police as an illegal immigrant and brutally tortured in custody. As he becomes an outcast, alienated both from his wife and the life he led before his fall and transformation, Chamcha starts hating Farishta with the same obsession with which he hates his father. Farishta, whom the fall had turned into an angel and who escapes arrest, does not intervene while the police take Chamcha in their custody. Consequently, just as Chamcha insists on blaming his father for "everything" that happened after his 13th year because of the confiscated wallet and the roasted chicken, he also insists on blaming Farishta for the way his life and career get messed up following his arrest: "*to hell with mitigations and what-could-he-have-dones; what's beyond forgiveness is beyond. You can't judge an internal injury by the size of the hole*" (426, emphasis in original).

Chamcha's refusal to forgive Farishta leads us back to the larger question of reconciliation and forgiveness that was opened up during Chamcha's encounter with Changez but was left unresolved. It is a question that persistently lurks beneath the tortured relationship of the father and the son, but it is only made explicit in this parallel context of Chamcha's relationship with Farishta. The question is: "What is unforgivable?" (426). What is that "Inexcusable Thing" (426) for which Farishta, like Changez, must be "declared guilty, for all perpetuity" (426) and be incessantly hated and raged against? Chamcha's impatience with the mitigating circumstances, with the "what-could-he-have-dones", suggests that what he regards as Farishta's "treason" (427) is yet another "roasted chicken" which he carries about but which offers only a flimsy ground on which to base the notion of an inexpiable offence and an interminable rage. Chamcha is seen clearly suffering from a persecution complex. But this gives rise to another question which has a wider significance with regard to the phenomenon of Indian self-fashioning as English. Does Chamcha hate others like Farishta and Changez because he has transformed himself into English? In more general terms, does the process of English self-fashioning pervert the "true" self of Indians, thereby making them morally corrupt—a corruption which then breeds the evil of rage and hatred that embitters their relationship with their native country and their countrymen? This is one of the possible explanations for Chamcha's implacable rage that is considered in the text:

> Saladin Chamcha is a creature of *selected* discontinuities, a *willing* reinvention; his *preferred* revolt against history being what makes him, in our chosen idiom, "false"? And might we then not go on to say that it is this falsity of the self that makes possible in Chamcha a worse and deeper falsity—call this "evil"—and that this is the truth, the door, that was opened in him by his fall?
> (427, emphasis in original)

However, this proposition that Chamcha, by trying to fashion his own identity, wilfully deviates from his "real" self and consequently becomes false and evil—"unnatural, a blasphemer, an abomination of abomination" (49)—is repeatedly raised in the text, only to be repeatedly undermined: "Such distinctions [between 'true' and 'false' selves], resting as they must on an idea of the self as being (ideally) homogenous, non-hybrid, 'pure',—an utterly fantastic notion!—cannot, must not, suffice" (427). I will have to come back to this concept of a "pure" self later because one of the most significant ways in which *The Satanic Verses* undoes the confining hold of Indian self-fashioning as English and gestures towards the possibility of an identity beyond it is by dismantling this essentialist notion of a pure and true self. For now, however, I would like to focus on another explanation of Chamcha's hatred that is offered by the narrative, which is that he continues to be resentful and vindictive not because he is singularly evil but because evil is "natural". In other words, it is in human nature to hate and to remain unforgivingly resentful even with the knowledge that the others, at whom this resentment is directed, might actually be blameless: "evil may not be as far beneath our surfaces as we like to say it is.—That, in fact, we fall towards it *naturally*, that is, *not against our natures*" (427, emphasis in original).

Chamcha's persistence to take revenge on Farishta, even after knowing that the latter "is going off [his] ... wretched head at a rate of knots" (436), and the indifference with which he wrecks the life not only of Farishta but also of his partner Alleluia Cone who is entirely innocent as far as Chamcha is concerned, proves this thesis of the "naturalness" of evil. However, this proof is undermined by the subsequent actions of Farishta. In spite of having good reasons to be avenged on Chamcha for ruining his relationship with Cone, Farishta risks death to rescue him from the blaze of Shaandaar Cafe: "Gibreel Farishta steps quickly forward, bearing Saladin along the path of forgiveness into the hot night air" (468). What is important to note here is that Farishta's forgiveness is not premeditated. The narrative deliberately keeps the question—"Is he vengeance or forgiveness?" (457)—open-ended till the final moment. Farishta's saving Chamcha is thus revealed as a spontaneous act, which suggests that forgiveness can come as "naturally" as the evil of resentment and hatred, "that evil is never total, that its victory, no matter how overwhelming, is never absolute" (467). What Farishta proves by forgiving Chamcha is, however, the possibility, not the certainty, of forgiveness. Once forgiven himself, forgiveness becomes an available option to Chamcha—an option, which he was previously convinced, did not exist. However, the ethical imperative to tread the path of forgiveness and actively seek to dissolve the implacable rage and interminable hatred that he had so far used as his alibi for becoming English rests on Chamcha's personal choice. Thus, finally, it is on this individual ethical choice to forgive and to stop hating that the possibility of finding a way out of the cul-de-sac of English self-fashioning comes to rest. Interestingly, in an interview with W.L. Webb, Salman Rushdie states that in his first draft of the novel, Chamcha was denied the opportunity to forgive and be reconciled with his father. He was to return to India to find that Changez had already died, thereby leaving the question of whether Chamcha is capable of forgiving and moving beyond the hatred and rage that animate his English self-identity unresolved. However, as Rushdie observes:

> I just thought in the end that there was more in it, in that final moment [of forgiveness], than could be explored if they didn't meet. So I rewrote it so that they did meet, and I think for me it made a colossal difference in the novel, that I did it that way.
>
> (Webb 96)

It is unclear as to what exactly constituted this "colossal difference", but it is probable that without depicting Chamcha's forgiveness, the theme of rage and hatred would have remained unresolved and *The Satanic Verses* would have ended in the same kind of aporia with which the theme of anglicised self-fashioning ends in the novels of Desai and Ghosh. In the final version of *The Satanic Verses*, however, the act of forgiveness does take place, culminating in Chamcha's reconciliation with Changez. This allows Chamcha to ultimately let go of his "roasted chicken" and acquire a new sense of selfhood that is no longer predicated on being able to interminably bear a grudge. It is the contours of this new self-identity of Chamcha that I explore in the final section.

The promise and aporia of eclecticism

Chamcha suffers a heart attack in the Shaandaar Cafe while he is being rescued by Farishta. Following the thematic protocols of *The Satanic Verses*, where to die is to be born again, this near-death experience is followed by a new phase in Chamcha's life. On hearing the news that his father has been diagnosed with terminal cancer, Chamcha comes back to his native city of

Bombay to care for Changez in his deathbed and thus begins a new process of self-transformation:

> [a] process of renewal, of regeneration, that had been the most surprising and paradoxical product of his father's terminal illness. His old English life, its bizarreries, its evils, now seemed very remote, even irrelevant, like his stage-name. ... [He] return[ed] to *Salahuddin*.
> (534, emphasis in original)

This process of renewal and regeneration crucially involves an acceptance of his mother tongue. Previously, to escape his connections with the subcontinent and to fashion himself as English, Chamcha had not only given up Urdu but had also made diligent efforts to scrub off the Bombay lilt from his English. "Now Salahuddin found better words, his Urdu returning to him after long absence" (530). Here, we are again brought back to the archetypal trajectory of "return and recovery" that I had referred to at the beginning of this book—the trajectory traced by Michael Madhusudan Dutt in the mid-nineteenth century when he gave up English to start a literary career in Bengali. As noted before, Dutt's "return" was not a simple sloughing off of his English identity and a recovery of his "true" indigenous self. Similarly, Chamcha's return is also not effected by a simple rejection of his "old English life" as "false" and a recovery of a homogenous, non-hybrid, and "pure" self. In *The Satanic Verses*, this essentialist notion of a "pure" self, which apparently becomes "corrupted" and "false" when one tries to consciously fashion one's own identity, is most persistently argued by Changez Chamchawala. Thus, when Chamcha tries to make himself English in the metropolis, his father repeatedly writes to remind him that "[a] man untrue to himself becomes a two-legged lie" (48), while all the time urging him to return to his "true" nature by coming back home. Chamcha's final homecoming, though it results in his accepting his father, is, nevertheless, marked by a rejection of his philosophy regarding true selves and essential natures. Rather, Chamcha finds his guide in Zeeny Vakil, the art critic who has authored a book "on the confining myth of authenticity, that folkloric straightjacket which she sought to replace by an ethic of historically validated eclecticism" (52). This eclecticism, which Vakil describes as underlined by the tenet "take-the-best-and-leave-the-rest" (52), is not a synthesis of disparate cultural elements with an indigenous core. There is no "pure" or "true" Indian essence that can be reached behind these eclectic cultural choices. As Vakil puts it: "Why should there be a good, right way of being a wog? That's Hindu fundamentalism. Actually, we're all bad Indians. Some worse than others" (52). Thus, when Chamcha returns home, he does not return to his one "true" "Indian" self. Rather, "Saladin felt hourly closer to many old, rejected selves, split off from himself as he made his various life choices, but which had apparently continued to exist, perhaps in the parallel universes of quantum theory" (523). His English self is not altogether lost but becomes one of these many selves, which momentarily gets discarded because of the new choices he makes in his life. However, it continues to exist and remains available to him just like his old Indian selves had continued to exist even after he had shed them in the metropolis.

This anti-essentialist concept of cultural eclecticism effectively dismantles the central conflict that animates Indian self-fashioning as English—a conflict between the consciousness of being European "inside" and the fact of being located in an "outside" that is physically, geographically, and socially non-English and therefore incompatible with the inner reality. But in its turn, this eclecticism opens up a new set of problematics. I would like to conclude this chapter by briefly gesturing towards some of these new conflicts and contradictions that accompany the theory of multiple cultural selves. On closely examining Zeeny Vakil's mantra of "take-the-best-and-leave-the-rest", it is found that it does not open up an infinite choice of cultural identities to an individual. Rather, the choices are framed by a very specific set of spatio-temporal coordinates, a specificity that is suggested by Vakil's emphasis on the "ethic of historically validated eclecticism". What is this history that defines and delimits cultural eclecticism for an individual? For Zeeny Vakil, it is the history of India. Thus, she substantiates her thesis by invoking the "national culture based on the principle of borrowing whatever clothes seemed to fit; Aryan, Mughal, British" (52). Within this formulation, the kind of wardrobe of identities that an individual can access is defined by his or her emplacement within the history of a particular geographical location. Hence, in *The Satanic Verses*, Chamcha feels hourly closer to his many Indian selves only when he physically returns to India and once again becomes a participant in its national history.

This spatio-temporally bounded eclecticism, however, presents a sharp contrast to the kind of eclectic position that Rushdie championed as a migrant author in his 1982 essay "Imaginary Homelands":

> [T]he imagination works best when it is most free. Western writers have always felt free to be eclectic in their selection of theme, setting, form; Western visual artists have, in this century, been happily raiding the visual storehouses of Africa, Asia, the Philippines. ... [As migrants,] [w]e can quite legitimately claim as our ancestors Huguenots, the Irish, the Jews; the past to which we belong is an English past, the history of immigrant Britain. Swift, Conrad, Marx are as much our literary forebears as Tagore or Rammohun Roy.
> (20)

This flattening of cultural influences, where disparate figures like Jonathan Swift, Rabindranath Tagore, and the Huguenots become *equally* available as cultural influences to an individual as a migrant (and in his essay "In Good

Faith", Rushdie states that the migrant condition provides "a metaphor for all humanity") (394), is made possible by imagining a flattened world in which a postcolonial individual simultaneously belongs to all places and is consequently an heir to all histories. As Timothy Brennan notes in his study of Salman Rushdie, whom he regards to be iconic of a whole generation of "cosmopolitan" "Third World" writers:

> For these writers the cosmopolis is no longer just life in the capitals of Europe and North America, nor that place of refuge for the native intellectual seeking a break from the barbarousness of underdevelopment at home. It is rather (and simply) the *world*—polyglot and interracial.
>
> (39)

In *The Satanic Verses*, the unbounded eclecticism of the migrant as a world citizen is pitted against the spatio-temporally bound eclecticism that Zeeny Vakil preaches, and this produces one of the key tensions in the text. Thus, on the one hand the migrant's ability to draw from multiple cultural roots and potentially use it to transform the world is upheld again and again in the novel, on the other hand it is also simultaneously undermined by the doubt as to whether such decontextualised borrowings are at all possible. This is best evident in the Uhuru Simba section of *The Satanic Verses*. Simba, a prominent black activist in Britain, is arrested as a suspected serial killer and this arrest becomes a rallying point for the migrant community. A discourse of resistance is forged by the followers of Simba that perfectly exemplifies the unbounded cultural ancestry which a migrant as an inhabitant of "the world" can apparently lay claim to. It seamlessly merges together elements drawn from African-American civil rights movement with slogans of Camus and Enoch Sontonga's Nkosi Sikelel' iAfrika. Chamcha, however, remains sceptical about this attempt: "it sounded like an attempt to borrow the glamour of other, more dangerous struggles, ... [a]s if all causes were the same, all histories interchangeable" (415). As noted above, the eclecticism in which Chamcha ultimately participates is the one framed more concretely by national space and national history. Yet, one remains unsure whether this is the version of eclecticism that Rushdie actually wants to privilege. In an interview with Ameena Meer, Rushdie tells how he conceived the character of Saladin Chamcha as someone who acts out the possibilities and makes the choices that Rushdie himself as a migrant does not wish to make:

> [T]he decision I have made for the moment about my life is that I don't want to go and live there [in India]. However, then it's very interesting to have a fictional character who makes the opposite decision. You can see what happens. You send him off to do it and

you don't have to do it yourself. I think that certainly had a lot of interest for me, in the Chamcha character.

(121)

Read from this perspective, the conflict between the two different kinds of eclecticism, and the different kinds of identities that they make possible, does not get resolved in *The Satanic Verses*. Behind Chamcha's decision to return lurks the spectre of his author's decision not to make that return journey, and each of these decisions makes the other seem something like a compromise. Thus, when placed against the eclecticism of the migrant, the nationally bound eclecticism seems to present too limited a choice. Though it liberates an individual from the straight jacket of "authenticity", it ties him up with the straight jacket of national history. On the other hand, the migrant's universalist vision lacks the historical specificity that gives cultural identities their substance. Cultural elements within this framework become too decontextualised to mean anything. The displacement of the phenomenon of Indian self-fashioning as English in *The Satanic Verses* thus reveals not only new possibilities of identity formation but also this aporia that underlines and finally undermines these possibilities.

Notes

1 Pankaj Mishra uses this appellation in his essay "The Last Englishman" published on Nirad Chaudhuri's birth centenary in 1997.
2 Here we find another of the many autobiographical echoes that connect Rushdie with the character Saladin Chamcha. As Rushdie writes in his memoir, *Joseph Anton*, he too sought to travel to England to distance himself from his father, to "put oceans between them and keep them there" (21).

BIBLIOGRAPHY

Appadurai, Arjun. "Putting Hierarchy in its Place". *Cultural Anthropology* 3.1 (1988): 36–49.

Ashcroft, Bill, et al. *The Empire Writes Back: Theory and Practice in Post-colonial Literatures*. London: Routledge, 1989.

Ashcroft, Richard T., and Mark Bevir. "Multiculturalism in Contemporary Britain: Policy, law and Theory". *Critical Review of International Social and Political Philosophy* 21.1 (2018): 1–21.

Bagchi, A. K. "European and Indian Entrepreneurship in India, 1900–30". *Elites in South Asia*. Eds. E. Leach and S.N. Mukherjee. Cambridge: Cambridge University Press, 1970. 223–56.

Bagchi, Jasodhara. "Representing Nationalism: Ideology of Motherhood in Colonial Bengal". *Economic and Political Weekly* 25.42/43 (1990): WS 65–WS 71. Accessed 2 Dec. 2019.

———. "Secularism as Identity: The Case of Tagore's *Gora*". *The Nation, the State and Indian Identity*. Eds. Madhusree Dutta et al. Calcutta: Samya, 1996. 47–67.

———. ""May the Sindoor on the Lips Never Perish": The 'West' in Colonial Humour". *Writing the West: Representations from Indian Language*. Ed. C. Vijayasree. New Delhi: Sahitya Akademi, 2004. 39–58.

Bakhtin, M. M. "Discourse in the Novel". Trans. Caryl Emerson and Michael Holquist. *The Dialogic Imagination: Four Essays*. Ed. Michael Holquist. Austin: University of Texas Press, 1981. 259–422.

Bald, Suresht R. "The politics of Gandhi's "feminism": constructing "Sitas" for *Swaraj*". *Women, States and Nationalism: At home in the Nation?*. Ed. Sita Ranchod-Nilsson and Mary Ann Tétreault. London: Routledge, 2000. 83–100.

Banerjee, Sukanya. "Empire, Nation and the Professional Citizen: Reading Cornelia Sorabji's *India Calling*. *Prose Studies: History, Theory, Criticism* 28.3 (2006): 291–317.

———. *Becoming Imperial Citizens: Indians in the Late-Victorian Empire*. Durham: Duke University Press, 2010.

Barry, Brian. *Culture and Equality: An Egalitarian Critique of Multiculturalism*. Cambridge: Polity, 2001.

Bauböck, Rainer. "The Crossing and Blurring of Boundaries in International Migration: Challenges for Social and Political Theory". *Blurred Boundaries:*

Migration, Ethnicity, Citizenship. Eds. Rainer Bauböck and John Rundell. 1998. London and New York: Routledge, 2018.

Bhabha, Homi. *The Location of Culture*. London: Routledge, 1994.

Bhattacharya, Shankarlal. "Death and Departure: Meeting Dom Moraes". *Time, Space, Text: Mapping Cultural Paradigms*. Eds. Chinmoy Guha and Tirtha Prasad Mukhopadhyay. Kolkata: UGC Academic Staff College and Department of English, University of Calcutta, 2008.

Boehmer, Elleke. *Colonial and Postcolonial Literature: Migrant Metaphors*. Oxford and New York: Oxford University Press, 1995.

———. "The Hero's Story: The Male Leader's Autobiography and the Syntax of Postcolonial Nationalism". *Stories of Women: Gender and Narrative in the Postcolonial Nation*. Manchester: Manchester University Press, 2005. 66–87.

Bose, Sugata. "Nation as Mother: Representations and Contestations of 'India' in Bengali Literature and Culture". *Nationalism, Democracy and Development: State and Politics in India*. Eds. Sugata Bose and Ayesha Jalal. Delhi: Oxford University Press, 1997. 50–75.

Bourdieu, Pierre. *The Logic of Practice*. Trans. Richard Nice. Cambridge: Polity, 1990.

Boym, Svetlana. *The Future of Nostalgia*. New York: Basic Books, 2001.

Brennan, Timothy. *Salman Rushdie and the Third World: Myths of a Nation*. London: Macmillan.

Brinks, Ellen. *Anglophone Indian Women Writers, 1870–1920*. Farnham, Surrey and Burlington, VT: Ashgate, 2013.

Burton, Antoinette. "Cornelia Sorabji in Victorian Oxford". *At the Heart of the Empire: Indians and the Colonial Encounter in Late-Victorian Britain*. Berkeley, Los Angeles and London: University of California Press, 1998. 110–151.

———. "Tourism in the Archives: Colonial Modernity and the Zenana in Cornelia Sorabji's Memoirs". *Dwelling in the Archive: Women Writing House, Home and History in Late Colonial India*. Oxford: Oxford University Press, 2003. 65–100.

Cantle, Ted. *Interculturalism: The New Era of Cohesion and Diversity*. Basingstoke: Palgrave Macmillan, 2012.

Chakrabarty, Dipesh. "The Difference-Deferral of (A) Colonial Modernity: Domesticity in British Bengal". *History Workshop Journal* 36.1 (1993): 1–34. Accessed 21 Nov. 2018.

———. "Remembered Villages: Representation of Hindu-Bengali Memories in the Aftermath of the Partition". *Economic and Political Weekly* 31.32 (1996): 2143–2145+2147–2151. Accessed 16 Oct. 2018.

———. *Provincializing Europe: Postcolonial Thought and Historical Difference*. Princeton and Oxford: Princeton University Press, 2000.

Chakravarti, Uma. "Whatever Happened to the Vedic Dasi? Orientalism, Nationalism and a Script for the Past". *Recasting Women: Essays in Colonial India*. Eds. Kumkum Sangari and Sudesh Vaid. New Brunswick, NJ: Rutgers University Press, 1990. 27–87.

Chandra, Sudhir. *The Oppressive Present: Literature and Social Consciousness in Colonial India*. Delhi: Oxford University Press, 1992.

Chatterjee, Partha. *Nationalist Thought and the Colonial World: A Derivative Discourse*. London: Zed, 1986.

Chattopadhyay (Chatterji), Bankimchandra. "The Confession of a Young Bengal". *Bankim Rachanabali*. Ed. Jogesh Chandra Bagal. Vol. 3. Kolkata: Sahitya Samsad. 1969.
———. *Anandamath, or The Sacred Brotherhood*. Trans. Julius J. Lipner. Oxford: Oxford University Press, 2005.
Chaudhuri, Amit. "Poles of Recovery". *Clearing a Space: Reflections on India, Literature and Culture*. Oxford: Peter Lang, 2008.
Chaudhuri, Nirad C. *A Passage to England*. London: Macmillan, 1959.
———. *Autobiography of an Unknown Indian*. 1951. Mumbai: Jaico, 1964.
———. *The Continent of Circe: Being an Essay on the People of India*. London: Chatto and Windus, 1965.
———. *The Intellectual in India*. New Delhi: Vir Publishing House. 1967.
———. *To Live or Not to Live*. New Delhi: Orient Paperbacks, 1971.
———. *Scholar Extraordinary: The Life of Professor the Rt. Hon. Friedrich Max Müller*, P.C. London: Chatto and Windus, 1974.
———. *Thy Hand, Great Anarch!* London: Chatto and Windus, 1987.
———. *Amar Debottor Shampatti*. Kolkata: Ananda, 1994a. Print.
———. "Ami Keno Bilete Achi". *Amar Debottor Shampatti*. Kolkata: Ananda, 1994b.
———. *Why I Mourn for England*. Calcutta: Mitra and Ghosh, 1998.
———. *Aji Hote Shatobarsho Age*. Kolkata: Mitra and Ghosh, 1999.
Chaudhuri, Rosinka. "'Young India: A Bengal Eclogue': Or Meat-Eating, Race, and Reform in a Colonial Poem". *Interventions: International Journal of Postcolonial Studies* 2.3 (2000): 424–441. Accessed 14 December 2019.
———. *Gentlemen Poets in Colonial Bengal: Emergent Nationalism and the Orientalist Project*. Calcutta: Seagull Books, 2002.
———. "The Dutt Family Album and Toru Dutt". *A History of Indian Literature in English*. Ed. Arvind Krishna Mehrotra. New York: Columbia University Press, 2003. 53–69.
———. "An Ideology of Indianness: The Construction of Colonial/Communal Stereotypes in the Poems of Henry Derozio". *Studies in History* 20.2 (2004): 167–187. Accessed 14 December 2019.
Chaudhuri, Supriya. "The Nation and its Fictions: History and Allegory in Tagore's Gora". *South Asia: Journal of South Asian Studies* 35.1 (2012): 97–117. Accessed 16 May 2020.
Chiriyankandath, James. "'Democracy' Under the Raj: Elections and Separate Representation in British India". *The Journal of Commonwealth and Comparative Politics* 30.1 (1992): 39–63. Accessed 30 May 2020.
Cohn, Bernard S. "The Past in the Present: India as Museum of Mankind". *History and Anthropology* 11.1 (1998): 1–38.
Colley, Linda. *Britons: Forging the Nation 1707–1837*. 1992. London: Pimlico, 2003.
Colls, Robert. *Identity of England*. Oxford: Oxford University Press, 2002.
Constable, John. *The Hay Wain*. London: National Gallery, 1821.
Dalmia, Manju. "Derozio: English Teacher". *The Lie of the Land: English Literary Studies in India*. Ed. Rajeswari Sunder Rajan. Delhi: Oxford University Press, 1992. 42–62.

Daruwalla, Keki N. *Two Decades of Indian Poetry, 1960–1980*. Ghaziabad: Vikas, 1980.

Das, Sisir Kumar. *A History of Indian Literature: 1911–1956; Struggle for Freedom: Triumph and Tragedy*. New Delhi: Sahitya Akademi, 1995.

Deakin, Nicholas. "The British Nationality Act of 1948: A Brief Study in the Political Mythology of Race Relations". *Race* 11.1 (1969): 77–83.

Derozio, Henry Louis Vivian, "The Harp of India". *The Golden Treasury of Indo-Anglian Poetry*. Ed. Vinay Krishna Gokak. New Delhi: Sahitya Akademi, 1970. 53–54.

Derrida, Jacques. "Structure, Sign, and Play in the Discourse of the Human Sciences". Trans. Alan Bass. *Writing and Difference*. 1978. London and New York: Routledge, 2001. 351–370.

Desai, Kiran. *The Inheritance of Loss*. London: Hamish Hamilton, 2006.

Dufferin and Harriot Ava. "Introductory Notes". *Love and Life Behind the Purdah*. By Cornelia Sorabji. Ed. Chandani Lokugé. New Delhi: Oxford University Press, 2003. 7–8.

Dutta, Krishna and Andrew Robinson. *Rabindranath Tagore: The Myriad Minded Man*. London: Bloomsbury, 1995.

Dutt, Michael Madhusudan. *The Captive Ladie: An Indian Tale in Two Cantos*. Madras: The Advertiser, 1849.

———. *Meghnadbadh Kabya: Part 1*. Calcutta: Ishwarchandra Basu, 1861a (January).

———. *Meghnadbadh Kabya: Part 2*. Calcutta: Ishwarchandra Basu, 1861b (July/August).

———. "The Anglo-Saxon and the Hindu". *Madhusudan Rachanabali*. Ed. Kshetra Gupta. Kolkata: Sahitya Sangsad, 1965. 520–534.

———. Letter to Gourdas Basak. 26 Jan. 1865. *Madhusudan Kabya Granthabali*. Ed. Muhammad Maniruzzaman. Dhaka: Pakistan Book Corporation, 1970.

Fabian, Johannes. *Time and the Other: How Anthropology Makes its Object*. 1983. New York: Columbia University Press, 2002.

Fanon, Frantz. *Black Skin, White Masks*. Trans. Charles Lam Markmann. London: Pluto Press, 1986.

Fernandes, Leela. *India's New Middle Class: Democratic Politics in an Era of Economic Reform*. Durham: Duke University Press, 2006.

Finnis, John. *Aquinas: Moral, Political, and Legal Theory*. Oxford: Oxford University Press, 1998.

Fisher, Michael Herbert. *Counterflows to Colonialism: Indian Travellers and Settlers in Britain 1660-1857*. Delhi: Permanent Black, 2004.

Flemming, Leslie. "Between Two Worlds: Self-Construction and Self-Identity in the Writings of Three Nineteenth-Century Indian Christian Women". *Women as Subjects: South Asian Histories*. Ed. Nita Kumar. Calcutta: Stree, 1994. 81–107.

Forbes, Geraldine. *Women in Modern India*. Cambridge: Cambridge University Press, 1996.

———. *Women in Colonial India: Essays on Politics, Medicine and Historiography*. New Delhi: Chronicle Books, 2005.

Foucault, Michel. *Discipline and Punish: The Birth of the Prison*. Trans. Alan Sheridan. New York: Vintage Books, 1995.

BIBLIOGRAPHY

Galbraith, John Kenneth. *Name Dropping: From F.D.R On*. New York: Mariner Books, 1999.

Gandhi, Leela. "Novelists of the 1930s and 1940s". *A History of Indian Literature in English*. Ed. Arvind Krishna Mehrotra. New York: Columbia University Press, 2003. 168–192.

Gandhi, M. K. *Indian Home Rule or Hind Swaraj*. *'Hind Swaraj' and Other Writings*. Ed. Anthony J. Parel. Cambridge: Cambridge University Press, 2009a. 1–123.

———. "Letter to H. S. L. Polak". 14 Oct. 1909. *'Hind Swaraj' and Other Writings*. Ed. Anthony J. Parel. Cambridge: Cambridge University Press, 2009b. 127–131.

Ghose, Lotika. *Manmohan Ghose*. New Delhi: Sahitya Akademi, 1955.

Ghosh, Amitav. *The Glass Palace*. London: HarperCollins, 2000.

Ghosh, Amitav and Dipesh Charabarty. "A Correspondence on Provincializing Europe". *Radical History Review* 83 (2002): 146–172.

Gokak, V. K. *The Golden Treasury of Indo-Anglian Poetry, 1828–1965*. New Delhi: Sahitya Akademi, 1970.

Gooptu, Suparna. *Cornelia Sorabji: India's Pioneer Woman Lawyer*. New Delhi: Oxford University Press, 2006.

Greenblatt, Stephen. *Renaissance Self-fashioning: From More to Shakespeare*. Paperback ed. Chicago and London: University of Chicago Press, 1984.

Guha, Ranajit. *Dominance without Hegemony: History and Power in Colonial India*. Cambridge, MA and London: Harvard University Press, 1997.

Gupta, Charu. "The Icon of Mother in Late Colonial North India: 'Bharat Mata', 'Matri Bhasha' and 'Gau Mata'". *Economic and Political Weekly* 36.45 (2001): 4291–4299. Accessed 3 Jan. 2020.

Hampshire, James. *Citizenship and Belonging: Immigration and the Politics of Demographic Governance in Postwar Britain*. Basingstoke: Palgrave Macmillan, 2005.

Hansen, Randall. "The Politics of Citizenship in 1940s Britain: The British Nationality Act". *Twentieth-Century British History* 10.1 (1999): 67–95.

Hobhouse, Mary. "Letter to the Editor of *The Times*". 13 Apr. 1888. *An Indian Portia: Selected Writings of Cornelia Sorabji, 1866–1954*. Ed. Kusoom Vadgama. Groombridge: Blacker Limited, 2011a. 52–53.

———. "Letter to the Editor of *The Times*". 12 Jun. 1889. *An Indian Portia: Selected Writings of Cornelia Sorabji, 1866–1954*. Ed. Kusoom Vadgama. Groombridge: Blacker Limited, 2011b. 55.

Holden, Philip. *Autobiography and Decolonization: Modernity, Masculinity and the Nation-State*. Madison, WI: University of Wisconsin Press, 2008.

Holland, R.F. *European Decolonization 1918–1981: An Introductory Survey*. Basingstoke: Macmillan, 1985.

Israel, Milton. "Indian Nationalist Voices: Autobiography and the Process of Return". *Political Memoirs: Essays on the Politics of Memory*. Ed. George Egerton. London: Frank Cass, 1994.

Jayal, Niraja Gopal. *Citizenship and its Discontents: An Indian History*. Cambridge, MA and London: Harvard University Press, 2013.

Joshi, Sanjay. *Fractured Modernity: Making of a Colonial Middle Class in Colonial North India*. New Delhi: Oxford University Press, 2001.

Kakar, Sudhir. *The Indians: Portrait of a People*. 2007. New Delhi: Penguin, 2009.

BIBLIOGRAPHY

Kapila, Shruti. "Self, Spencer and *Swaraj*: Nationalist Thought and Critiques of Liberalism, 1890-1920". *Modern Intellectual History* 4.1 (2007): 109-127.

———. "The Enchantment of Science in India". *Isis: A Journal of the History of Science Society* 101.1 (2010): 120-132.

Karatani, Rieko. *Defining British Citizenship: Empire, Commonwealth and Modern Britain*. London and Portland, OR: Frank Cass, 2003.

Kaviraj, Sudipta. *The Unhappy Consciousness: Bankimchandra Chattopadhyay and the Formation of Nationalist Discourse in India*. Delhi: Oxford University Press, 1995.

———. *The Invention of Private Life: Literature and Ideas*. Ranikhet: Permanent Black, 2014.

Koditschek, Theodore. *Liberalism, Imperialism, and the Historical Imagination: Nineteenth-Century Visions of a Greater Britain*. Cambridge: Cambridge University Press, 2011.

Kopf, David. *British Orientalism and the Bengali Renaissance: The Dynamics of Indian Modernization 1773-1835*. Berkley, CA: University of California Press, 1969.

Kumar, Krishan. *The Making of English National Identity*. Cambridge: Cambridge University Press, 2003.

Kymlicka, Will. *Multicultural Citizenship: A Liberal Theory of Minority Rights*. Oxford: Clarendon Press, 1995.

Lahiri, Shompa. *Indians in Britain: Anglo-Indian Encounters, Race and Identity 1880-1930*. London and Portland, OR: Frank Cass, 2000.

Lazarus, Neil. "Introducing Postcolonial Studies". *The Cambridge Companion to Postcolonial Literary Studies*. Ed. Neil Lazarus. Cambridge: Cambridge University Press, 2004. 1-16.

Lokugé, Chandani. "Introduction". *India Calling: The Memories of Cornelia Sorabji, India's First Woman Barrister*. By Cornelia Sorabji. Ed. Chandani Lokugé. New Delhi: Oxford University Press, 2001.

Macaulay, Thomas Babington. "Minute by the Hon'ble T. B. Macaulay, dated the 2nd February 1835". http://www.columbia.edu/itc/mealac/pritchett/00generallinks/macaulay/txt_minute_education_1835.html Accessed 11 May 2020.

Mahomet, Sake Dean. *The Travels of Dean Mahomet*. 2 vols. Cork: Connor, 1794.

Maine, Henry Sumner. *Ancient Law: Its Connection with the Early History of Society and its Relation to Modern Ideas*, n.d.

Majeed, Javed. *Autobiography, Travel and Postcolonial Identity: Gandhi, Nehru and Iqbal*. New York: Palgrave, 2007.

Mantena, Karuna. *Alibis of Empire: Henry Maine and the Ends of Liberal Imperialism*. Princeton and Oxford: Princeton University Press, 2010.

Markovits, Claude. *Merchants, Traders, Entrepreneurs: Indian Business in the Colonial Era*. Basingstoke: Palgrave Macmillan, 2008.

Matikkala, Mira. *Empire and Imperial Ambition: Liberty, Englishness and Anti-Imperialism in Late-Victorian Britain*. London and New York: I.B Taurus, 2011.

Meer, Ameena. "Salman Rushdie". *Conversations with Salman Rushdie*. Ed. Michael R. Reder. Jackson: University Press of Mississippi, 2000. 110-122.

Mehrotra, Arvind Krishna. *The Oxford India Anthology of Twelve Modern Poets*. Delhi: Oxford University Press, 1992.

———. "Editor's Preface". *A History of Indian Literature in English*. Ed. Arvind Krishna Mehrotra. New York: Columbia University Press, 2003. xix–xxii.

Mehta, Jaya. ""Some Imaginary 'Real' Thing": Racial Purity, the Mutiny, and the Nation in Tagore's *Gora* and Kipling's *Kim*". *Rabindranath Tagore: Universality and Tradition*. Ed. Patrick Colm Hogan and Lalita Pandit. Madison: Fairleigh Dickinson University Press and London: Associated University Presses, 2003. 199–212.

Mehta, Uday Singh. *Liberalism and Empire: A Study in Nineteenth-Century British Liberal Thought*. Chicago and London: University of Chicago Press, 1999.

Merton, Robert K. *Social Theory and Social Structure*. 1949. New York: The Free Press, 1968.

Mishra, Pankaj. "The Last Englishman". *Prospect*, 20 Nov. 1997. Accessed 15 Dec. 2019.

Michael, Joseph. "Advertisement for *And Gazelles Leaping*." *Times Literary Supplement* 19 Feb. 1949: 116. *Times Literary Supplement Historical Archive*. Web 16 Mar. 2012.

Mishra, Sudesh. "The Two Chaudhuris: Historical Witness and Pseudo-Historian". *The Journal of Commonwealth Literature* 23.1 (1988): 7–15. Accessed 5 Jan. 2020.

Mitford, Mary. *Our Village*. London and New York: Macmillan, 1893.

Modood, Tariq. *Multiculturalism: A Civic Idea*. 2nd ed. Cambridge: Polity, 2013.

Mohanram, Radhika. *Imperial White: Race, Diaspora and the British Empire*. Minneapolis, MN: University of Minnesota Press, 2007.

Mookerjee, Girija K. *The Indian Image of Nineteenth-Century Europe*. Bombay and London: Asia, 1967.

Moore, Thomas. "The Harp That Once through Tara's Hall". *Irish Melodies*. London: Longmans, Green, and Co, 1866.

Moraes, Dom. *Gone Away: An Indian Journal*. London: Heinemann, 1960.

———. *My Son's Father: An Autobiography*. London: Secker and Warburg, 1968.

———. *Bombay*. Amsterdam: Time-Life Books, 1979.

———. *Never at Home*. New Delhi and London: Penguin, 1994.

———. "Exile". In *Cinnamon Shade: New and Selected Poems*. Manchester: Carcanet, 2001a.

———. "Letter to My Mother". In *Cinnamon Shade: New and Selected Poems*. Manchester: Carcanet, 2001b.

Moraes, Dom, and Sarayu Srivatsa. *Out of God's Oven: Travels in a Fractured Land*. New Delhi: Viking, 2002.

———. *The Long Strider: How Thomas Coryate Walked from England to India in the Year 1613*, New Delhi: Penguin, 2003.

Mukherjee, Durba, and Sayan Chattopadhyay. "'Walking the Indian Streets': Analysing Ved Mehta's Memoirs of Return." *Life Writing*. Doi: 10.1080/14484528.2020.1855089 Accessed 25 Dec. 2020.

Mukherjee, Meenakshi. "The Anxiety of Indianness: Our Novels in English". *Economic and Political Weekly* 28.48 (1993): 2607–2611.

———. "Introduction". Trans. Sujit Mukherjee. *Gora*. Ed. Rabindranath Tagore. New Delhi: Sahitya Akademi, 1997.

Mukherjee, Sumita. *Nationalism, Education and Migrant Identities: The England-Returned*. New York: Routledge, 2010.

BIBLIOGRAPHY

Mukherji, Sajni Kripalani. "The Hindu College: Henry Derozio and Michael Madhusudan Dutt". *A History of Indian Literature in English*. Ed. Arvind Krishna Mehrotra. New York: Columbia University Press, 2003. 41–52.

Murshid, Ghulam. *Lured by Hope: A Biography of Michael Madhusudan Dutt*. Trans. Gopa Majumdar. New Delhi: Oxford University Press, 2003.

———. *The Heart of a Rebel Poet: Letters of Michael Madhusudan Dutt*. Trans. Gopa Majumdar. New Delhi: Oxford University Press, 2004.

Naik, M. K. *A History of Indian English Literature*. New Delhi: Sahitya Akademi, 1982.

Naipaul, V. S. *An Area of Darkness*. London: A. Deutsch, 1964.

———. "Jasmine". *The Overcrowded Barracoon*. London: Andre Deutsch, 1972. 23–29.

Nandy, Ashis. "Sati: A Nineteenth Century Tale of Women, Violence and Protest". *Rammohun Roy and the Process of Modernization in India*. Ed. V. C. Joshi. New Delhi: Vikas, 1975. 168–194.

———. *The Illegitimacy of Nationalism: Rabindranath Tagore and the Politics of Self*. In Return from Exile. Delhi: Oxford University Press, 1998. 1–94.

———. *An Ambiguous Journey to the City: The Village and Other Odd Ruins of the Self in Indian Imagination*. New Delhi: Oxford, 2001.

———. *The Intimate Enemy: Loss and Recovery of Self Under Colonialism*. 2nd ed. Oxford: Oxford University Press, 2009.

Nandy, Pritish, ed. *Strangertime: An Anthology of Indian Poetry in English*. New Delhi: Hind Pocket Books, 1977.

Narasimhaiah, C. D. *Raja Rao*. New Delhi and London: Heinemann, 1973.

Narayan, R. K. *Swami and Friends*. London: Hamilton, 1935. Print

Nayar, Pramod K. "Colonial Proxemics: The Embassy of Sir Thomas Roe to India". *Studies in Travel Writing* 6.1 (2002): 29–53. Accessed 21 May 2020.

Nehru, Jawaharlal. *Toward Freedom: The Autobiography of Jawaharlal Nehru*. New York: John Day, 1941.

———. *The Discovery of India*. 1946. New Delhi: Oxford University Press, 1989.

Nixon, Rob. *London Calling: V. S. Naipaul, Postcolonial Mandarin*. New York and Oxford: Oxford University Press, 1992.

Orwell, George. "The English People". *Essays*. New York, London and Toronto: Alfred K. Knopf, 2002. 608–647. Print

Pandey, Surya Nath. "Angularities of a Prodigal Son: A Post-colonial Approach to Dom Moraes's Poetry". *Writing in a Post-Colonial Space*. Ed. Surya Nath Pandey. New Delhi: Atlantic, 1999. 65–76.

Parthasarathy, R., ed. *Ten Twentieth-century Indian Poets*. Delhi and New York: Oxford University Press, 1976.

Pels, Peter and Oscar Salemink. Introduction: Locating Colonial Subjects of Anthropology. *Colonial Subjects: Essays on the Practical History of Anthropology*. Eds. Peter Pels and Oscar Salemink. Ann Arbor: University of Michigan Press, 1999.

Porter, Bernard. *The Absent-Minded Imperialists: Empire, Society, and Culture in Britain*. Oxford: Oxford University Press, 2004.

———. *The Lion's Share: A History of British Imperialism 1850 to the Present*. 1975. London and New York: Routledge, 2012.

BIBLIOGRAPHY

Ramaswamy, Sumathi. "En/gendering Language: The Poetics of Tamil Identity". *Comparative Studies in Society and History* 35.4 (1993): 683–725. Accessed 15 Dec. 2019.

Ranasinha, Ruvani. *South Asian Writers in Twentieth-Century Britain: Culture in Translation*. Oxford: Clarendon Press, 2007.

Rao, P. V. Narasimha. *Ayodhya: 6 December 1992*. New Delhi: Viking, 2006.

Rastogi, Pallavi. ""The World Around and the World Afar All Seemed Compassed": Cosmopolitan Ethnicity and the Victorian Metropolis". *Women's Studies: An Inter-Disciplinary Journal* 32.6 (2003): 735–739.

———. "Timeless England Will Remain Hanging in the Air: Metropolitan/Cosmopolitanism in Nirad Chandra Chaudhuri's *A Passage to England*". *Prose Studies: History, Theory, Criticism* 28.3 (2006): 318–336. Accessed 5 Jan 2019.

Raychaudhuri, Tapan. "Europe in India's Xenology". *Past and Present* 137 (Nov. 1992): 156–182. Accessed 17 Aug. 2019.

———. *Europe Reconsidered: Perceptions of the West in Nineteenth-Century Bengal*. 2nd ed. New Delhi: Oxford University Press, 2002.

Rege, Josna E. *Colonial Karma: Self, Action, and Nation in the Indian English Novel*. New York: Palgrave, 2004.

Roy, Rammohun. "Letter from Rammohun Roy to Lord Amherst, governor-general in council, dated 11 December 1823". *The Great Indian Education Debate: Documents Relating to the Orientalist-Anglicist Controversy, 1781–1843*. Richmond: Curzon Press, 1999.

Runnymede Trust. *The Future of Multi-ethnic Britain*. London: Profile Books, 2000.

Rushdie, Salman. *The Satanic Verses*. London: Vintage, 1988.

———. "Imaginary Homelands". *Imaginary Homelands: Essays and Criticism 1981–1991*. London: Granta in Association with Penguin, 1991a.

———. "In Good Faith". *Imaginary Homelands: Essays and Criticism 1981–1991*. London: Granta in association with Penguin, 1991b. 393–414.

———. "Introduction". *Mirrorwork: 50 Years of Indian Writing 1947–1997*. Eds. Salman Rushdie and Elizabeth West. New York: Henry Holt, 1997. vii–xx.

———. *Joseph Anton: A Memoir*. London: Jonathan Cape, 2012.

Rushdie, Salman and Elizabeth West. *Mirrorwork: 50 Years of Indian Writing 1947–1997*. New York: Henry Holt, 1997. vii–xx.

Sarkar, Sumit. *Modern India: 1885–1947*. Chennai: Macmillan, 1983a.

———. *'Popular' Movements and 'Middle Class' Leadership in Late Colonial India: Perspectives and Problems of a 'History from Below'*. Calcutta: Bagchi for Centre for Studies in Social Science, 1983b.

———. "The Complexities of Young Bengal". *A Critique of Colonial India*. Calcutta: Papyrus, 1985a.

———. "The Radicalism of Intellectuals: A Case Study of Nineteenth Century Bengal". *A Critique of Colonial India*. Calcutta: Papyrus, 1985b.

———. "Renaissance and Kaliyuga: Time, Myth and History in Colonial Bengal". *Writing Social History*. Delhi: Oxford University Press, 1997.

———. *The Swadeshi Movement in Bengal: 1903–1908*. 1973. Ranikhet: Permanent Black, 2010.

Sarkar, Tanika. "Nationalist Iconography: Image of Women in 19th Century Bengali Literature". *Economic and Political Weekly* 22.47 (1987): 2011–2015. Accessed 18 Jun. 2019.

Seal, Anil. *The Emergence of Indian Nationalism: Competition and Collaboration in the Later Nineteenth Century*. Cambridge: Cambridge University Press, 1968.

Sen, Samita. "Motherhood and Mothercraft: Gender and Nationalism in Bengal". *Gender and History* 5.2 (1993): 231–243. 8 Dec. 2013.

Silverman, Kaja. *The Threshold of the Visible World*. New York and London: Routledge, 1996.

Sinha, Mrinalini. "The Age of Consent Act: The ideal of masculinity and colonial ideology in nineteenth-century Bengal". *Shaping Bengali World, Public and Private*. Ed. Tony K. Stewart. East Lancing: Michigan State University, 1989. 99–111.

Sorabji, Cornelia. *Sun Babies: Studies in the Child-Life of India*. London: John Murray, 1904.

———. *Between the Twilights: Being Studies of Indian Women by One of Themselves*. London and New York: Harper and Brothers, 1908.

———. *Therefore: An Impression of Sorabji Kharsedji Langrana and his Wife Franscina*. London: Oxford University Press, 1924.

———. *India Recalled*. London: Nisbet, 1936.

———. *India Calling: The Memories of Cornelia Sorabji, India's First Woman Barrister*. Ed. Chandani Lokugé. New Delhi: Oxford University Press, 2001.

———. *An Indian Portia: Selected Writings of Cornelia Sorabji, 1866–1954*. Ed. Kusoom Vadgama. Groombridge: Blacker Limited, 2011.

Sorabji, Richard. *Opening Doors: The Untold Story of Cornelia Sorabji: Reformer, Lawyer and Champion of Women's Right in India*. London and New York: L. B. Tauris, 2010.

Spivak, Gayatri Chakravorty. *An Aesthetic Education in the Era of Globalization*. Cambridge, MA and London: Harvard University Press, 2012.

Sri, Aurobindo. *Autobiographical Notes and Other Writings of Historical Interest*. Pondicherry: Sri Aurobindo Ashram, 2006.

Srivatsa, Sarayu. "Out of the Oven". *The Hindu* 6 Jul. 2003.

Suleri, Sara. *The Rhetoric of English India*. Chicago and London: University of Chicago Press, 1992.

Tagore, Rabindranath. "Bharatbarsher Itihash. *Rabindra-Rachanabali*. Vol. 4. Kolkata: Viswabharati, Bengali year 1347a. 377–387.

———. "Brahman". *Rabindra-Rachanabali*. Vol. 4. Kolkata: Viswabharati, Bengali year 1347b. 387–402.

———. *Gora. Rabindra-Rachanabali*. Vol. 6. Kolkata: Viswabharati, Bengali year 1347c. 109–572.

———. "Nababarsha". *Rabindra-Rachanabali*. Vol. 4. Kolkata: Viswabharati, Bengali year 1347d. 367–377.

———. "Rammohun Roy". *Rabindra-Rachanabali*. Vol. 4. Kolkata: Viswabharati, Bengali year 1347e. 511–523.

———. "Swadeshi Samaj". *Rabindra-Rachanabali*. Vol. 3. Kolkata: Viswabharati, Bengali year 1347f. 526–552.

———. "Vidyasagarcharit". *Rabindra-Rachanabali*. Vol. 4. Kolkata: Viswabharati, Bengali year 1347g. 477–501.

———. "Acharer Atyachar". *Rabindra-Rachanabali*. Vol. 12. Kolkata: Viswabharati, Bengali year 1349a. 205–210.

BIBLIOGRAPHY

———. "Coat ba Chapkan". *Rabindra-Rachanabali*. Vol. 12. Kolkata: Viswabharati, Bengali year 1349b. 223–229.

———. "Prachya o Pratichya". *Rabindra-Rachanabali*. Vol. 12. Kolkata: Viswabharati, Bengali year 1349c. 236–250.

———. *My Reminiscences*. New York: Macmillan, 1917. Print

———. *The Religion of Man: Being the Hibbert Lectures for 1930*. New York: Macmillan, 1930.

Thapar, Romila. "The Theory of Aryan Race and India: History and Politics". *Social Scientist* 24.1/3 (1996): 3–29. Accessed 15 Oct. 2019.

Tharu, Susie and K. Lalitha. "Literature of the Reform and Nationalist Movements: Background". *Women Writing in India: 600 B.C. to the Early Twentieth Century*. Eds. Susie Tharu and K. Lalitha. London: Pandora, 1991.

Thieme, John. "Passages to England". *Liminal Postmodernisms: the Postmodern, the (Post-) Colonial and the (Post-) Feminist*. Eds. Theo D'haen and Hans Bertens. Amsterdam: Rodopi, 1994. 55–78.

Trautmann, Thomas R. *Aryans and British India*. Berkley, CA: University of California Press, 1997.

Varadarajan, Siddharth, ed. *Gujarat: The Making of a Tragedy*. New Delhi: Penguin, 2002.

Varma, Pavan K. *The Great Indian Middle Class*. 1998. New Delhi: Penguin, 2007.

Viswanathan, Gauri. *Masks of Conquest: Literary Study and British Rule in India*. 1989. London: Faber and Faber, 1990.

Watson, John Forbes and John William Kaye, eds. *The People of India: A Series of Photographic Illustrations, with Descriptive Letterpress, of the Races and Tribes of Hindustan, and Reproduced by Order of the Secretary of the State for India in Council*. 8 vols. London: India Museum, 1868–1875.

Webb, W. L. "Salman Rushdie: *Satanic Verses*". *Conversations with Salman Rushdie*. Ed. Michael R. Reder. Jackson: University Press of Mississippi, 2000. 87–100.

White, Nicholas J. *Decolonisation: The British Experience since 1945*. London and New York: Routledge, 2014.

———. "Setting Intertextuality and the Resurrection of the Postcolonial Author". *Journal of Postcolonial Writing* 41.2 (2005): 144–155.

Wicomb, Zoë. "Zoë Wicomb in Conversation with Hein Williemse". *Research in African Literatures* 33.1 (2002): 144–152.

INDEX

Act of Union of 1707 81
Age of Consent Act 38
Alexander, Graham 34
Altrincham (Lord) 90
Amherst (Lord) 7
anthropology 40, 42
Appadurai, Arjun 41
Aryan xxxv, xxxvii, 67–72, 101, 144
Aryan migration *see* Aryan
Atlee, Clement 77, 87
Auden, W.H. 105, 120
autobiography: national 51–52, 54–55, 63; political 51; symbolic 115; as travelogue 114–115, 118
Ayodhya 22, 117–119, 124, 125

Babri Masjid 22, 124, 125
Bagchi, Jasodhara 22, 23
Bakhtin, Mikhail 15
Barry, Brian 96
Basak, Gourdas xx, xxiv, xxv, xxvi, 135
Bauböck, Rainer 96
Bengal x, xix, xxii, xxiv, xxv, xxvii, xxxii, xxxv, 1–3, 5, 7, 8, 14, 24, 57, 68; East Bengal 52, 55, 56, 59, 60, 66, 69, 72, 73, 78, 100, 103, 112
Bengali middle class *see* middle class
Bengali woman 3, 46
Bethune, John Drinkwater xxv–xxvi, xxxiii, xxxiv
Bhabha, Homi xix
bhadralok 19
Bhattacharya, Shankarlal 128
body xi, xii, xxxiv, xxxviii, xxxix, 72, 82, 106–110, 112, 113, 132, 135, 137; of Gora 19–21, 23, 24; of Moraes 106, 109–111, 119–121, 127

Boer war 64
Bombay xxxviii, 34, 103, 104, 115, 116, 119, 127, 128, 135, 136, 138, 143; Presidency 29, 31, 32
Bourdieu, Pierre 107
Boym, Svetlana 124, 125
Brahmo 7, 8, 10, 16, 20
Brennan, Timothy 145
Britain xiii, xiv, xxi, xxxviii, 28, 61, 77–80, 85–95, 97–99, 144, 145
British empire (British Raj) ix, xiii, xv, xix, xxviii, xxxi, xxxii, xxxvi, xxxviii, 18, 38, 45, 48, 49, 52, 54, 55, 61, 64, 65, 74, 76–92, 94, 99, 132, 134
British Nationality Act of 1948 90–91
British Nationality Act of 1981 91
Britishness *see* Englishness
Brooke, Rupert 65, 66
Buchanan, Francis 40
Burton, Antoinette 27, 32, 36

Calcutta xxii, 2, 6, 17–19, 21, 33, 54, 59–63, 71, 72, 121, 131
Caldwell, Robert 68
Canning (Lord) 40
Cantle, Ted 97
Chakrabarty, Dipesh x–xi, xxviii, 109
Chattopadhyay, Bankimchandra xxii, xxviii–xxx, xxxi, xxxii, xxxv, 2–5, 7–10, 130, 137
Chaudhurani, Saraladevi 47
Chaudhuri, Amit xviii, xxii–xxiv
Chaudhuri, Dhruva 76–77
Chaudhuri, Nirad C. xii, xvi, xviii, xx, xxxiii, xxxv, xxxvi–xxxviii, 1, 2, 51–52, 55–56, 79, 82–84, 90, 91, 95, 100–101, 103, 112, 130, 132,

158

INDEX

135, 137; and Aryans 69–72; and Banagram 57–63, 65–67, 71; and Calcutta 54, 59–63, 71, 72; criticism of British imperialism 87–89; criticism of multicultural Britain 95–100; and the ideals of imperialism 84–87; and imagined England 60, 63–67; and Kishorganj 52, 56–64, 66, 71–73; mourning for post-Second World War England 76–79; and national history 52–54; and Oxford 73, 89, 100, 112, 113
Chaudhuri, Rosinka xix, xxii, xxiv
Chaudhuri, Supriya 23
Christianity: Christians xxvii, 22; Christian missionary 16, 30, 34; religion xiii, xxi, xxiv, 30, 31, 36, 38, 104
citizenship xxxviii, 48, 57, 58, 61, 62, 78–79, 81–88, 100, 145
city 18, 21, 54–60, 62, 65, 104, 116, 118, 127, 128, 142
civilising mission ix, xxvi, xxxviii, 36–38, 77, 87
clock time 57, 58, 62, 71
Colebrooke, H.T. xxviii, 5
Colley, Linda 81
Colls, Robert xii, 79, 82
Commission on the Future of Multi-Ethnic Britain 93
Commonwealth Immigrants Act of 1962 91
Commonwealth Immigrants Act of 1968 91
Congress 24, 47
Constable, John 66–67, 72
Cornwallis (Lord) xxviii
Coryate, Thomas 122–128, 134
Court of Wards 39, 42, 45

deracination 4, 9
Derozio, Henry xxviii, 4–5
Derrida, Jacques 18, 21
Desai, Kiran 131, 133–134, 137, 142
Duff Cooper Prize 72
Dufferin, Hariot (Lady) 39
Dutt, Michael Madhusudan xx–xxvii, xxxiii, xxxiv, 109, 135, 137, 143

England xii, xiii, xiv, xx, xxi, xxv, xxxiv, xxxv, xxxvii, xxxviii, 1, 4, 7–11, 27, 28, 30–34, 36, 37, 40, 42, 54, 55, 60, 62–67, 69, 72–74, 76–79, 87, 89, 99, 100, 103, 104, 109, 110, 112–116, 120, 122, 123, 126–130, 133, 135–139
English *see* Englishness
Englishness ix, xii, xiii, xvi, xviii, xxiv, xxxvii, xxxviii, xxxix, 1, 6, 8, 15, 18, 30–32, 72, 79, 82, 89, 94–95, 101, 132, 136
ethnography *see* anthropology
Europeanness *see* Englishness
exile xxiii, xxiv, xxvi, 14, 54–56, 60, 62, 63, 67, 103, 116, 119, 123, 126, 128, 129, 139

Fabian, Johannes 42
Fanon, Frantz 107–108
Franscina 30, 32–33, 35
First World War xxxi, 45
Fisher, Michael xxi
Foucault, Michel 107

Galbraith, John Kenneth ix
Gandhi, Mohandas Karamchand xvii, xxxi–xxxiii, xxxvi, xxxvii, 24–25, 46, 48, 51, 54, 55, 103, 114, 130
Ghose, Aurobindo 103
Ghose, Manmohan 103, 104
Ghosh, Amitav 131–133, 142
Gooptu, Suparna 47
Government of India Bill of 1919 48
Government of India Bill of 1935 48
Greenblatt, Stephen xiv, xvi
Guha, Ranajit xxviii, 24
Gujarat riots 117, 119
Hardy, Thomas 98
Hawthornden Prize xviii
hexis 107
Hindu xv, xxi, xxvii, xxix, xxx, xxxi, xxxii, xxxv, xxxvi, xxxvii, 1, 3–5, 7–9, 13, 14, 16, 17, 19, 21, 22, 27, 30–32, 35, 36, 67–73, 100, 103, 124–126, 130, 137, 143
Hindu College xv, xx, 2, 4
Hobhouse, Mary (Lady) 32, 36–37
Holden, Philip 51, 54
home xxiii, xxxvi, xxxviii, 9, 10, 21, 27–30, 32, 34, 38, 40, 42, 47, 54–56, 58–60, 62–67, 70–73, 82, 91, 103, 108, 110, 116, 118, 124–128, 143, 145; homecoming xxiv, xxv, 54–56, 63, 67, 72, 111, 124, 143;

INDEX

homegrown 99, 130; homeland xxxvii, 28, 68–72, 109, 112, 113, 116, 120, 123–126, 128, 129; homeless 23, 60, 63; homely 66; homesickness xxvi; hometown 138, 139; unhomely 62

Ilbert Bill 83
Ilkley Literature Festival 98–100
Immigration Act of 1971 91
Indian National Congress *see* Congress
Indianness xvii, xviii, xix, xxiii, xxiv, xxv, xxvi, xxvii, xxxi, xxxii, xxxv, xxxvi, xxxvii, xxxix, 4, 6, 7, 11–21, 23–25, 27, 28, 32–34, 40, 74, 101, 110, 112, 121, 136, 137
indigeneity xix, xxi, xxii, xxiv, xxvi, xxvii, xxviii, xxx, 1, 3, 4, 10, 14, 18, 22–24, 71, 91, 143
indigenism *see* indigeneity
indigenous *see* indigeneity
Iqbal, Muhammad 114
Israel, Milton 51
Iyengar, K.R.S. xvii, xix

Jayal, Niraja Gopal 82, 83
Jehangir (Mughal emperor) 122, 125, 126
Jenkins, Roy 92–93
Jones, William xxviii, 5, 67
Jonson, Ben 122, 127

Kaviraj, Sudipta xvi
Kharsedji, Sorabji 29–30
Kipling, Rudyard 29, 88, 98, 101
Kumar, Krishan 79–80
Kymlica, Will 93

Lacan, Jacques 106
Layall, Alfred C. 37
liberalism 4, 80, 82, 84, 88, 92, 93, 96, 97, 101
literature of return 104, 106, 113, 114
London xii, xxi, xxxix, 1, 6, 27, 29, 32–34, 48, 49, 54, 65, 79, 80, 82, 88, 90, 109, 112, 116, 117, 119, 120, 135, 136, 138, 140
Lytton (Lord) 83

Macaulay, T.B. xiv–xv, xxviii, 37, 38, 80, 92
Mackenzie, Colin 40

Mahomet, Sake Dean 1
Maine, Henry James Sumner 61, 62, 66
Majeed, Javed 114
Malgudi xvii, 56
Max Müller, Friedrich xxxvii, 35, 67–69, 72
Mehrotra, Arvind Krishna xix, xxii
Mehta, Uday Singh 80, 88
memsahib 3
metropolitan audience xxvi, xxxiii–xxxiv, 27, 32, 35, 43, 65, 98, 136
metropolitan readership *see* metropolitan audience
middle class ix–xii, xiii, xiv, xv–xvi, xvii, xix, xx, xxii–xxiii, xxiv, xxvi, xxvii, xxviii, xxxi, xxxii, xxxiii, xxxv, xxxviii, xxxix, 1–8, 10, 12, 13, 15, 16, 19–21, 24, 25, 56, 67, 76, 86, 88, 103, 117, 130, 131, 135, 139
Mirror Stage 106
Mitford, Mary 65, 67
Mittra, Peary Chand 4
modern self x–xii
modernity x, xi, 37, 61, 109
Modood, Tariq 94
Mohanram, Radhika xxxiv, 81, 82
Monier-Williams, Monier 35
Moraes, Dom xvi, xviii, xx, xxiv, xxxviii–xxxix, 1, 103–110, 113, 130, 132–135, 137, 138; death 128–129; *Gone Away* 114–116, "Letter to My Mother" 110–111; *The Long Strider* 122–128; *My Son's Father* 116; *Out of God's Oven* 117–121
Morley-Minto Reform 83
Mukherjee, Bharati 112
multiculturalism xxxviii, 76, 78, 79, 89–100
Muslim xxix, xxxvii, 21, 22, 31, 32, 125, 126

Naidu, Sarojini 47, 48
Naik, M. K. xviii, xix, xxii
Nandy, Ashis xiii–xiv, xxx, 6, 17, 55
Narasimhaiah, C. D. xvii
Naipaul, V.S. 104, 115
Narayan, R.K. 56
nationalism xix, xxii, xxvii, xxviii, xxxi, xxxii, xxxiii, xxxv, xxxvi, xxxvii, 1, 4–6, 11, 16, 20, 24, 25, 44–49, 51, 52, 94, 103, 104, 124, 132

INDEX

Nehru, Jawaharlal ix, xv, 51, 54, 103, 104, 114, 115, 130
Nixon, Rob 115
nostalgia 55, 66, 70, 72, 124–126, 128, 132
Notting Hill riots 91

Odcombe 122, 123, 126, 128
oriental 34, 97, 98; orientalist xxviii, xxxvii, 5, 35, 67, 69, 134
Orwell, George 81
Oxford xxxvi, 6, 32, 35–39, 41, 73, 89, 100, 103, 104, 112, 113

Parekh report 93, 94
Parsee 29–32
Poona 29, 32
Powell, Enoch 91
proprioceptivity 107–108, 127
purdahnashin xxxvi, 27, 28, 32, 35, 36, 38–48
Queen Victoria's Proclamation of 1858 80, 83

racism xxxiv, xxxviii, 76, 91, 94, 95, 97, 133; anti-racism laws 92
Raj *see* British empire
Raychaudhuri, Tapan xiii, 2, 69
Reddi, Muthumeenakshi 47
Reddy, C.R. xvii
reference group xii, xxxix, 24, 131
Regulating Act of 1773 80
Renaissance x, xiv, xxviii, 5
Revolt of 1857 22, 37, 40
Roe, Thomas 122
Round Table Conference of 1931 48
Roy, Rammohun 7, 9, 14, 15, 51, 86, 144
Rushdie, Salman xvi, xxxix, 98–99, 112, 113, 131, 134; *The Satanic Verses* 135–146

Sarkar, Sumit ix–x, 57
Second World War xxxviii, 73, 76, 77, 99, 132
Seeley, John 79
Shakespeare, William 64, 65, 127

Silverman, Kaja 106–108
sonnet xxiii, xxiv, xxv, xxvi, 5
Sorabji, Cornelia xvi, xviii, xx, xxxiii, xxxiv, xxxvi, xxxvii, xxxviii, 1, 25, 27–28, 48–49, 51, 74, 100, 101, 104, 113, 114, 130, 132, 137; as "Indian woman" in England 32–35; isolation in India 28–32; othering the *purdahnashins* 40–44; *purdahnashins* as a vocation 35–39; women in the nationalist movement 44–48
Sorabji, Richard 27
Spender, Stephen 110
Srivatsa, Sarayu 116–121, 123, 125, 127
Suleri, Sara 40
Swadeshi movement xxxii, xxxv, 6, 24, 46, 103

Tagore, Debendranath 7
Tagore, Dwarkanath 6, 7
Tagore, Rabindranath xxxii, xxxv, 1, 5–12, 27, 88, 144; *Gora* 15–25; locus of Indianness 12–15
Tarkachuramani, Sashadhar 8
Thapar, Romila 68
Thomas, Dylan 105, 120

Victoria (Queen) 64, 80, 83
Vidyasagar, Iswarchandra xxii, 14, 15
village xvii, xxxii, 21, 25, 47, 54–60, 62, 63, 65–67, 71, 72, 119, 122, 123, 128
Viswanathan, Gauri xv
Vivekananda, Swami 8

Webster, John 65
Western education (English education) ix, x, xiv, xv, xxviii, 1–4, 8, 9, 11, 18, 36, 55, 57, 60, 108, 136
Wicomb, Zoë 112–113
Wordsworth, William 65

Young Bengal 4

zenana 38–49
Zoroastrian 29, 31

Printed in the United States
by Baker & Taylor Publisher Services